Effective Second Language Writing

Edited by Susan Kasten

Maria Dantas-Whitney, Sarah Rilling, and Lilia Savova, Series Editors

TESOL Classroom Practice Series

Teachers of English to Speakers of Other Languages, Inc.

Typeset in ITC Galliard and Vag Rounded
by Capitol Communication Systems, Inc., Crofton, Maryland USA
Printed by United Graphics, Inc., Mattoon, Illinois USA
Indexed by Pueblo Indexing and Publishing Services, Pueblo West, Colorado

Teachers of English to Speakers of Other Languages, Inc.
1925 Ballenger Avenue, Suite 550
Alexandria, Virginia 22314 USA
Tel 703-836-0774 • Fax 703-836-6447 • E-mail tesol@tesol.org •
http://www.tesol.org/

Publishing Manager: Carol Edwards
Copy Editor: Jean House
Additional Reader: Terrey Hatcher
Cover Design: Capitol Communication Systems, Inc.

ISBN 9781931185639
Library of Congress Control No. 2009938085

Table of Contents

Utilizing Technology in the Writing Curriculum

Re-visioning, Revising, and Editing ESL Compositions

Dedication

To English as a second language writing teachers and their students everywhere. May all of your subjects and verbs come to an agreement.

To the talented contributors to this volume. Your level of professionalism and passion for teaching are inspirational.

To Dan, who fully supported this endeavor with encouragement, advice, and the gift of perspective.

Series Editors' Preface

D1609646

The TESOL Classroom Practice Series showcases state-of-the-art curricula, materials, tasks, and activities reflecting emerging trends in language education and in the roles of teachers, learners, and the English language itself. The series seeks to build localized theories of language learning and teaching based on students' and teachers' unique experiences in and out of the classroom.

This series captures the dynamics of 21st-century English for speakers of other languages (ESOL) classrooms. It reflects major shifts in authority from teacher-centered practices to collaborative learner- and learning-centered environments. The series acknowledges the growing numbers of English speakers globally, celebrates locally relevant curricula and materials, and emphasizes the importance of multilingual and multicultural competencies—a primary goal in teaching English as an international language. Furthermore, the series takes into account contemporary technological developments that provide new opportunities for information exchange and social and transactional communications.

Each volume in the series focuses on a particular communicative skill, learning environment, or instructional goal. Chapters within each volume represent practices in English for general, academic, vocational, and specific purposes. Readers will find examples of carefully researched and tested practices designed for different student populations (from young learners to adults, from beginning to advanced) in diverse settings (from pre-K–12 to college and postgraduate, from local to global, from formal to informal). A variety of methodological choices are also represented, including individual and collaborative tasks and curricular as well as extracurricular projects. Most important, these volumes invite readers into the conversation that considers and so constructs ESOL classroom practices as complex entities. We are indebted to the authors, their colleagues, and their students for being a part of this conversation.

The classroom practices discussed in *Effective Second Language Writing* reflect various trends and methodologies; however, the underlying theme in this volume of the Classroom Practice Series is the need for clear and meaningful communication between English as a second language (ESL) writers and their readers. While approaches differ, two core beliefs are constant: ESL students have something important to say, and ESL writing teachers can help them say it. Effective instruction starts with meaningful writing tasks, integrates a variety of skills and technologies, builds competencies, requires critical thinking, and employs appropriate resources. This volume of ideas and insights will enable ESL teachers to help their writing students find purposeful voices that resonate across countries, customs, disciplines, and cultures.

Maria Dantas-Whitney, Western Oregon University
Sarah Rilling, Kent State University
Lilia Savova, Indiana University of Pennsylvania

CHAPTER 1

No Matter Where We've Been, Here We Are!

Susan Kasten

A discussion of writing trends could begin with an exploration of the cave dwellers' attempts to document their existence. Were those early pictographs a product of a bottom-up methodology? Were they influenced by regional linguistics? Were they peer edited? No one knows. Perhaps few care. One thing we do know about the beginning of writing was that it had a purpose. People used it to communicate. By its very nature, writing has always been an investigation and representation of the human experience. By writing, we discover not only *what* but also *how* we think.

Concerns of English as a second language (ESL) writing teachers may not seem directly connected to pictographs. However, the issues of clarity, coherence, and control have always been integral to communication. Writers, whether holding a flint or a laptop, face daunting challenges when they begin to compose. As F. Scott Fitzgerald noted, "All good writing is swimming under water and holding your breath" (Winokur, 1986, p. 105). Unfortunately, it turns out that writing is much more complicated than not breathing under water. It involves intellect and curiosity, logic and language, structure and soul.

Questions about the complex tasks facing ESL writers and their teachers abound. What is essential for ESL writing students to know? What do ESL teachers need to understand about writing instruction and assessment? What influence, if any, does a first language (L1) have on a second language (L2), and what difference does language choice play in writing? Can technology aid language production? Are writing skills learned sequentially? Can writing be taught? What is good about a good composition? On career surveys, why don't people ever indicate that they want to become ESL writing teachers? These questions, among a host of others, challenge every conscientious writing instructor.

L2 writing has taken its place as a distinct academic discipline. Since 1992, it has had its own scholarly periodical, *Journal of Second Language Writing*. Even so, the history of ESL writing has not been without controversy. In the mid-20th century, error correction substituted for writing instruction because writing was viewed largely as practice in producing targeted language patterns. The stimulus for student writing came from genuine texts, usually literature. Writing was seen not as a skill, but rather as an extended linguistic exercise in composing error-free prose. Silva and Matsuda (2001) confirmed the attitude that writing instruction had no independent place in ESL curricula when they asserted that prior to the 1960s, L2 "writing was regarded as but a secondary representation of language" (p. xiv).

However, a schism occurred when some teachers and theorists sought to de-emphasize surface writing elements, such as grammar, structure, spelling, and punctuation, in favor of teaching writing exclusively as a process. While the process and product camps held equally firm convictions about the validity of their respective approaches, various other theories about teaching ESL writing emerged. Along with the new theories came new questions concerning writing topics, academic discourse expectations, contrastive rhetoric, and effective teacher response. The emergence of multiple pedagogies left teachers with confusing assumptions and opposing philosophies, neither of which led to clearly defined instructional practices (Raimes, 1991). In 1993, Silva lamented that there was still "no coherent comprehensive theory of L2 writing" (1993a, p. 668). Azar (2007) argued in the opening plenary of the 2007 annual Teachers of English to Speakers of Other Languages (TESOL) convention that ESL had entered a postmethods era. How can ESL instructors find their way through the bewildering labyrinth of conflicting theories about language, especially when some educators not only teach multiple sections of unskilled student writers but also oversee lunchrooms, serve on committees, supervise study halls, manage car pools, patrol restrooms, plan the prom, present at conferences, and publish?

The role of writing in teaching English to speakers of other languages is far from clear. For one thing, as Blanton (2002) reports, ESL writing has struggled to find a home. It has been the foster child in English, linguistics, remedial, and developmental studies. It has been sandwiched between swing dance instruction and income tax seminars in nonacademic extension programs. It has been taught in church basements, locker rooms, and coat closets. Should ESL writing belong to composition studies, applied linguistics, foreign language study, bilingual education, or interdisciplinary studies (Matsuda, Canagarajah, Harklau, Hyland, & Warschauer, 2003)? To confuse matters more, Raimes (1991) concluded that shifts in writing pedagogy have produced at least four different academic approaches, each with its own orientation. Traditional rhetoric focuses on form, yet the main concern for the expressionists is the writer. Academic rhetoric centers on content, but the central focus of social constructivism is the reader. In theory, these diverse methods segregate instructional purpose, but in reality, they overlap, which confirms Silva's (1990) remark that the endless carousel of methodologies makes both ESL writing students and their teachers dizzy. He concluded that the mixing of various theories has resulted in a toxic stew that could potentially poison any agreement on the central issues of the discipline.

As confusing and contradictory as the short history of ESL writing may be, ESL instructors do not get an excused absence from the fray. Teachers are responsible for designing a classroom curriculum that is based on sound theory and research. Instructors should not surrender that core duty to antiquated criteria, nor should they capitulate to profit-minded publishers. Students deserve course content that is driven by principled decisions based on professional experience, observation, and research. Today, instant accessibility of information leaves no shortage of available literature on ESL writing. Within seconds, a Google search responds with more than a quarter of a million entries for "ESL writing." Google Scholar instantly offers approximately 3.5 million documents on "ESL methodology." Moreover, resource-sharing agreements have turned regional libraries into international research centers. The Online Computer Library Center and Research Libraries Information Center have made digital materials available literally at teachers' fingertips. It is obvious that comprehensive information about ESL writing is easy to access. However, even the best search engine cannot reveal whether teachers, by and large, actually make use of the available data to design their ESL curricula.

This volume of the TESOL Classroom Practice Series began with an invitation for teacher–researchers to share their insights regarding the effectiveness of current pedagogical theories in the ESL writing classroom. The call intentionally allowed for diverse issues, such as placement criteria, course design, writing tasks, and assessment. It also invited the examination of cultural, social, political, psychological, and rhetorical issues and expectations that are intertwined in the writing process. Included in the amalgamation of possible topics for the book was the influence of each student's L1, gender, personality type, cultural background, educational experience, and personal goals. The thoughtful, cogent chapters gathered in this volume serve to demonstrate how current theory and research affect the way teachers design curricula, choose writing tasks, assess student performance, and conduct their own academic inquiries.

The first section of the book, Designing Writing Tasks, focuses on choices the writers make with rhetorical structures and syntax and the teacher's need to devise writing projects that encourage students to generate, arrange, and communicate ideas effectively. Nigel A. Caplan discusses ESL writing methodology in "Beyond the Five-Paragraph Essay: A Content-First Approach," the first chapter in the section. He argues that teaching traditional rhetorical patterns or strictly adhering to the process approach provides ESL students with writing tools that are academically insubstantial. His research led him to propose sustained-content language teaching, an approach that balances students' academic freedom of expression with accountability for their ideas, logic, and assumptions. Linda Forrester's chapter, "Modern Heroes: From Content to Composition via Critical and Creative Thinking," promotes comprehensive, content-based ESL integrative learning, in which thinking is fundamental to writing and, thus, connected to context. Her chapter explores using a central theme in order to encourage a matrix of thought and language. Next, Shawna Shapiro's chapter, "Writing to Embody: Engaging Students in Written Role Play," deals with content by introducing language play in ESL classes as a way to liberate students and their teachers from viewing writing as an isolated skill. Her research reveals that ludic discourse helps learners gain greater fluency and innovation in their L2 by encouraging them to read, interpret, and relate information in both speech and writing. In Chapter 5, "Using Second Language Learning as Content in a University ESL Writing Course," Mark A. James explores authentic and purposeful writing assignments. He chose content that exposed students to text-centered writing, critical thinking, and reflective response. Because the students were L2 learners themselves, they could easily connect their own cultural and linguistic experiences to the academic content. The next chapter, "Meaningful Writing Opportunities in the Community College: The Cultural and Linguistic Autobiography Writing Project," by Gloria Park, demonstrates a need to connect writing assignments to the multilingual, multinational, and multicultural experiences of ESL students. To ensure that ESL classes are student centered, her curriculum draws from students' immigrant perspectives. The sequenced autobiography project allows writers to explore their new situations without ignoring their roots. Thus, students' dual identities are validated, making the connection between life at home and life at school easier. In the last chapter of this section, "Media Participation as an End Point for Authentic Writing and Autonomous Learning," Stephen Soresi's research links the need for authentic materials in the receptive skills of reading and listening to the need for authentic end points in the productive skills of writing and speaking. Traditionally, the end point for students' writing was an unknown, invisible reader. Soresi's chapter outlines an approach that clarifies the readers' identity and the writer's purpose.

In the second section of the book, Focusing on Academic and Professional Writing Skills, Amina M. B. Megheirbi discusses a meaningful academic task in "Multitext Synthesizing in Research Writing." She states that, despite its importance to university-bound students, synthesis writing has received little, if any, attention from the academic community. Even in some strenuously academic ESL writing classes, students continue to narrate their own experiences and ideas, so expecting them to synthesize and restate information from different sources without adequate instruction is unrealistic. A series of miniprojects leads students through investigating a research question, critically reading and linking authentic texts, and producing coherent writing. Miao Yang's "A Process–Genre Approach to Teaching Writing to Medical Science Graduate Students" originated from her students' dissatisfaction with both the process and product approaches to writing. Yang's research resulted in a genre-based approach to writing abstracts, an authentic end point for doctors publishing in academic journals. Teaching students to communicate clearly and appropriately in their professional and academic communities combines the process and genre approaches by adding explicit linguistic information about specific types of writing. The next chapter, "'It May Be Possible' to Teach the Use of Hedging in EFL University Writing," by Jingjing Qin and Erkan Karabacak, addresses the need for instruction in the essential skill of shading and nuancing language. This chapter suggests that when students are exposed to authentic content, taught in a reasoned sequence, and held accountable for presenting opposing points of view, they gain a heightened sensitivity to hedging. In Chapter 11, "Service Learning and Writing With a Purpose," Denise Vaughn describes how to engage ESL students in their social communities. By working for approved nonprofit agencies, students have ample opportunity to use their oral and aural skills in practical and meaningful situations, while at the same time learning about career expectations. Additionally, they are required in their writing to analyze, evaluate, and reflect on their service-learning projects. Likewise, Jennifer Haan and Karyn Mallett's chapter, "From the Classroom to the Boardroom: Grammar and Style Across Genres in ESL Professional Writing," includes the community-based service-learning project, which pairs ESL students with clients to create promotional materials for actual businesses. To prepare ESL students to join the workforce, the course addresses style and usage suitable for professional writing, including practice in writing proposals, memos, progress reports, promotional documents, usability guides, and PowerPoint presentations. The varied assignments develop an awareness of the purpose, audience, and content of business communication.

The third section of the book, Enhancing Critical Writing Skills, highlights the skills necessary for critical writing. Peter McDonald's chapter, "Discourse Analysis: Bridging the Gap Between Linguistic Theory and Classroom Practice in Writing Classes," considers textual awareness and cohesion. This approach teaches students to examine authentic texts using both top-down and bottom-up methods, which provide essential information for detailed analysis of rhetorical patterns. Clarity, coherence, and cohesion are also at the heart of Holli Schauber's "A Case for Writer-Generated Annotation." This chapter explains how ESL writers can examine the meaning and purpose of each sentence in relation to its context. By doing so, students recognize global relationships between words in sentences, sentences in paragraphs, and paragraphs in compositions.

No 21st-century discussion of classroom practice can ignore technology, so the fourth section of the book, Utilizing Technology in the Writing Curriculum, centers on effective applications of electronic tools. Christopher A. Baldwin's chapter, "Wiki Writing Web: Development of a Web Site to Improve Writing Motivation in Exam Courses," encourages the use of technology in peer review and correction, resulting in multileveled collaboration and an increased motivation to produce clear, global communication. In addition, he examines the roles of feedback, error correction, and washback in an L2 writing classroom. "A Chain Story Blog," by Najla Malaibari, combines creative writing with online supplemental tools, such as images, audio files, and Web site links. This chapter introduces an activity in which students prepare and produce stories in a nonthreatening environment where critical analysis, reflection, and feedback are supported and directed by their peers, their teacher, and the entire Internet community. An added benefit is that publishing the students' work promotes a sense of pride and gives writing a purpose beyond the classroom. The final chapter in this section explains how to use the Internet to access real and natural usage in English. Vander Viana's "Authentic English Through the Computer: Corpora in the ESOL Writing Classroom," illustrates the advantages of using online corpora tools. Since ESL writers do not have native-speaker intuition or infallible resources to help them choose which words and phrases are commonly or rarely used, corpus-based exercises aid the exploration of vernacular and academic English. Students need to know what combinations of words are meaningful, not merely what word combinations are possible. Viana contends that full mastery of the language centers on choosing precise wording for lucid communication.

Finally, the last section of the book, Re-visioning, Revising, and Editing ESL Compositions, discusses methods for examining and re-examining compositions. Soo Hyon Kim's chapter, "Revising the Revision Process With Google Docs: A Classroom-Based Study of Second Language Writing," was a result of integrating a computer-mediated revision approach with an ESL writing curriculum. Kim tracked writing progress as students experienced different kinds of feedback. The study examined the students' choice of revision tools and the substance of their changes in order to discover which feedback produced the most substantial and positive results. Donald Weasenforth, Margaret Redus, and Nancy Ham Megarity's chapter, "Great Expectations: Whose Job Is This Anyway?" also deals with editing issues in the ESL writing classroom. Their goal was to encourage student autonomy in proofreading and editing skills by providing sequenced training, effective strategies, and reliable tools. After reviewing writing course syllabi, they discovered that proofreading skills were not specifically mentioned and that editing practice primarily consisted of detecting surface errors. In order to place the responsibility for the final writing product into the hands of their students, they designed a method for teaching writers how to assess their own work.

The classroom practices discussed in this volume reflect various trends and methodologies; however, the underlying theme is the need for clear and meaningful communication between ESL writers and their readers. While approaches differ, two core beliefs are constant: ESL students have something important to say, and ESL writing teachers must help them say it. Effective instruction starts with meaningful writing tasks, integrates a variety of skills and technologies, builds competencies, requires critical thinking, and employs appropriate resources. May this volume of ideas and insights enable ESL teachers to help their writing students find purposeful voices that resonate across countries, customs, disciplines, and cultures.

Susan Kasten has taught in Japan, England, and five states in the United States. Most recently, she has served as a teacher and the curriculum coordinator of writing at the University of North Texas's Intensive English Language Institute. Her interest in curriculum has resulted in coauthoring and editing a series of writing and spelling workbooks.

Designing Writing Tasks

CHAPTER 2

Beyond the Five-Paragraph Essay: A Content-First Approach

Nigel A. Caplan

Academic writing presents particular difficulties to second language (L2) writers. Their texts are typically less grammatical, less complex, and less organized than native speakers' writing (e.g., Hinkel, 2004; Pally, 2000b). For teachers working with academically oriented L2 learners, the challenge is not necessarily to make them good writers, but to make them at least good enough to begin their college courses.[1]

One response to this challenge has been to teach a highly structured writing format derived from current–traditional rhetoric: the five-paragraph essay. Regardless of the actual number of paragraphs, the five-paragraph essay is taken here to mean a rigid organizational device with one introductory paragraph culminating in a thesis statement, (usually) three body paragraphs headed by topic sentences, and a concluding paragraph. The thesis statement itself, written as a preliminary step, is a précis that typically guides the organizational pattern. The writer's task, therefore, is to force three ideas into an hourglass shape.

The attraction of this writing formula is clear: It is easy to teach, learn, and grade. The five-paragraph essay battles incoherence and usually produces structured writing. However, this approach essentially suppresses critical thought and "shut[s] down thinking" (Rorschach, 2004, p. 19) through its exclusive focus on "surface features" at the expense of "deep features" such as content, analysis, development, and cohesion: the "intellectual task" of writing (Elbow, 1991, p. 149). Research has shown that it is the *deep* features that L2 writers do not

---

[1] Parts of this introduction are from "Beyond the Writing Textbook," by N. A. Caplan, A. S. McCullough, and L. R. Stokes, 2006, *State of the Art: Selected Proceedings of the 2005 MITESOL Conference*, pp. 92–101. Copyright 2006 by Michigan Teachers of English to Speakers of Other Languages. Reprinted with permission.

have and do not acquire from their English as a second language (ESL) classes (Pally, 2000a). Furthermore, these are the very features that they will need in their academic courses (Hale et al., 1996).

To succeed academically, all writers must have something to say about their topic and be able to analyze it critically: Content comes first. To that end, this chapter presents an alternative to the five-paragraph essay: a content-first approach that teaches analytic, academic writing. This is not to banish the thesis statement and other aspects of current–traditional writing instruction, but rather to model the scope and sequence of instruction on Elbow's (1991) observation:

> I suspect students can learn the surface features of academic style better if they have first made good progress with the underlying intellectual practices. When students are really succeeding in doing a meaty academic task, then the surface stylistic features are more likely to be integral and organic rather than merely an empty game or mimicry. (p. 150)

CONTEXT

The materials described in this chapter were developed for an upper intermediate writing class in the Intensive English Program at Michigan State University, in the United States. Many students in this course were anticipating full admission to the university, mostly as undergraduates, and they were all international, rather than immigrant, students. To better prepare them for academic classes, the traditional reading–writing class was replaced in 2003 by the content-based writing course described here and a separate reading class.

The writing class was immediately designated as a Sustained Content Language Teaching (SCLT) course, that is, one that combines its focus on a single "carrier topic" with language instruction (Murphy & Stoller, 2001, p. 3), which means that students "study content that is complex enough and enduring enough that argumentation and rhetorical conventions can be identified, practiced, and questioned" (Pally, 2000b, p. 9). Unlike episodic, or theme-based, content, the author and his colleagues designed their own materials around a literary text (fiction or nonfiction), thus supplying the academic content area. A typical L2 writing textbook focusing on the five-paragraph essay was also initially assigned.

The first term's results were inauspicious. Students continued to produce five-paragraph essays that lacked critical engagement with the course content. In short, they lacked both the analytical skills and the language with which to perform the analysis. In response, the course focus shifted to a content-first orientation, in which organizational and linguistic tools are introduced through the study of content to give students successful academic writing strategies.

CURRICULUM, TASKS, AND MATERIALS

Structuring the Course

In her introduction to a collection of essays on SCLT, Pally (2000b) identifies a major obstacle to a content-first approach: selecting a content area that is accessible to the students and familiar to the instructor. To overcome this difficulty, a literary text that is suitable for the students' language level is chosen. The texts for the course have included *The Outsiders* (Hinton, 1967), *The Game of Silence* (Erdrich, 2005), and *All My Sons* (Miller, 1947), leading to an exploration of teenage sociology, indigenous cultures, and the American dream, respectively. The material must be complex enough to elicit the critical thinking students need to practice, but not daunting. The major advantage of a sustained approach is that, unlike current–traditional rhetoric, it closely imitates college-level academic writing by engaging students in "advanced cognitive and information-processing tasks" (Hinkel, 2004, p. 13). SCLT immerses students in the content area, building knowledge and schema, thus facilitating high-level cognitive skills, while still maintaining a rigorous focus on language teaching (Murphy & Stoller, 2001, p. 3).

Each course follows a similar pattern. Students access the content through personal writing, examine the text analytically, compare it to other texts and movies, and finally research related topics for a culminating paper. The sequence of writing tasks introduces students to critical writing by leading them through a literary text and an academic content area. As such, it mirrors the four "stances" found in an analysis of meaning-making processes of first language (L1) readers (Langer, 1990, p. 238).

At first, readers "step in to an envisionment," or the world of the text (Langer, 1990, p. 238) by writing about their personal experiences with a central theme in the book. For example, *The Outsiders* (Hinton, 1967) dramatizes the conflict between two teenage gangs and the complex relationships within and between them. In order to "step in" to this topic, students write about their own experiences of friendship, cliques, and peer pressure. Although this kind of personal writing is not found in academic courses (Hale et al., 1996), it activates prior knowledge and builds students' confidence so that they can relate to the content area. Furthermore, this task builds a basic vocabulary necessary to analyze the text.

Readers in Langer's (1990) second stance are described as "being in and moving through" (p. 241) the text. To achieve this, students read the novel in "literature circle" groups (Daniels, 2002). Discussion roles encourage students to interpret the text by asking questions, discussing passages, highlighting lexical choices, and making connections beyond the text. Discussion is a crucial part of this stage, a pedagogical choice supported by the National Council of Teachers of English guidelines: "Writers . . . need opportunities to talk about what they are writing about, to rehearse the language of their upcoming texts and run ideas by trusted colleagues before taking the risk of committing words to paper"

(National Council of Teachers of English [NCTE], 2004, Section 8). The first formal writing task is an expository essay in which students develop and support an argument in response to the text. In *The Outsiders*, the most sympathetic character from the higher class gang, the "Socs," tells the hero, a member of the opposing "Greasers," that "things are rough all over" (Hinton, 1967, p. 35). The essay asks students to discuss the extent to which they agree with this statement. Since students have been immersed in the text through reading and speaking, this assignment once more starts with content, not form.

Having finished the book, readers can "step back," Langer's (1990) third stance. In this stage, readers draw on other experiences to understand the text or use the text to "rethink their prior knowledge" (p. 244). In the next assignment, students step back from the text to watch one or more related movies on teen-age sociology. In writing, students can compare the types of families, friendships, and gangs in the novel and their movie, or they can use the movie to illuminate an aspect of the novel, such as its portrayal of grief (there are three deaths in *The Outsiders*, all linked in some way to the hero). In some terms, classes watch the movie adaptation of the novel (Aubry & Coppola, 1983) and write about whether or not it successfully communicates Hinton's characters and ideas. The students are familiar enough with the content to write from a position of expertise and develop cogent arguments.

Finally, readers "step out" (Langer, 1990, p. 245) from the text and reflect on the reading and learning experience. In practice, this means a library research paper examining a problem facing today's teenagers, such as gangs, drugs, alcohol, depression, suicide, or bullying. Hale et al. (1996) found that research papers in any number of disciplines are commonly assigned to undergraduate students, and these assignments give students the independence to explore their own topic while building essential research and composition skills for their future studies.

Teaching Content First

A content-first orientation to writing involves tolerating a degree of disorganization in the early stages and re-evaluating traditional textbook guidelines, such as the equivalence between idea and paragraph. In other words, although a paragraph must have unity and deal with only one major idea, not all ideas can be expressed in one paragraph. Rather than planning three ideas, and therefore three paragraphs, before starting an essay, content-first writers begin with a focus: the germ of an idea, which will be developed through the process of writing about it. Thus, "writing is a tool for thinking" (NCTE, 2004, section 4). For instance, students write a discovery draft (Murray, 2004), which is a very rough, private attempt at formulating their essay's argument. After that, students refocus their ideas and choose a main line of thought before composing the first draft.

It is axiomatic that "writing can be taught" (NCTE, 2004, Section 1) and, therefore, it is also possible to teach analytical writing. Simply writing "analyze!" in the margin has little effect; analysis must be modeled. Many textbooks include models of student writing, but these examples are usually completed drafts. However, it can be very helpful to model the process of developing good content (Koch, 2007). For example, students often fail to integrate or analyze quotations. In class, the teacher can model a good interpretation of a quotation (or, better, multiple interpretations) and then have students analyze several other key sentences from the book. By practicing one deep feature of writing at a time, students can improve their writing skills. As Koch argues, writing instruction needs to shift from the "what" (thesis statements, topic sentences) to the "how" of writing, which includes how to think and write in a critical mode.

This approach to writing necessitates multiple revisions. Peer review can make the teacher's workload manageable and improve writers' critical-thinking skills. The key to peer review is to ask questions that focus on literary content first. For instance, instead of asking if the essay has a clear thesis, peers are asked to restate the main idea of the essay in their own words. This is more useful since it requires an extended response and because it shows whether the writer's focus is clear. Instead of asking peers to count the supporting sentences, they are asked what else they would like the writer to explain. This elicits requests for more quotations, clarification, justification, examples, and interpretation. Therefore, it is essential that writers think critically about their peers' comments and decide which advice to take (Williams & Evans, 2000).

Once the teacher reads the drafts, a content-first orientation can be maintained through feedback. If students have never been held accountable for their ideas because they have been focusing on mode rather than meaning, they may expect feedback limited to organization and language. Responding to argument, development, and analysis forces students to focus on content. Although feedback and grading are largely a matter of individual style, asking content questions produces good revisions: Why do you think this is true? How does the literary text support your argument? How does the quotation support your main idea? Why does the character/narrator/author say this? Questions beginning with *why* or *how* elicit critical, thoughtful answers and better revisions.

Teaching Organization

Well-written academic texts are organized through multiple forms of cohesion (Hinkel, 2004). Cohesion allows the ideas to flow logically and maintains unity at the discourse level. A five-paragraph essay, however, with its prescriptively mandated components "can create a coherent essay that is not necessarily cohesive" (Hinkel, p. 280). Most L2 writing textbooks teach cohesion, but they usually limit their discussion to adverbial connectors (e.g., *first, second, third, in addition, however, in conclusion*). However, research has shown that native speakers use these words and phrases in writing less often than nonnative speakers, whose use of connectors can obfuscate rather than clarify (Hinkel, p. 292). These results suggest that L2 writers need to learn other, less formulaic strategies to produce texts that conform to the conventions of academic writing.

Experience with this sustained content course has shown that cohesion can be taught most effectively as a revision tool once students have written a draft and begun to analyze their ideas. Consequently, rhetorical devices are properly used to develop content. Through instruction and peer review, students learn to outline their drafts *post-hoc* and not as a prewriting stage. For example, peers are asked to draw maps and diagrams of their classmates' essays as part of their review. In this way, writers' attention can be drawn to the discourse level. Writing models also help students notice the gap between their writing and their target: good, cohesive, academic texts (e.g., Hinkel, 2004). Students can then be directed to apply Hinkel's techniques, such as repeating key words, using synonyms, substituting subject and demonstrative pronouns, and using general nouns (*fact, results, approach, method, characteristic, conditions,* etc.) to their current draft.

It is also valuable to think beyond formal outlines by exploring alternative plans for writing. Murray (2004) recommends starting with readers' questions, trees or geometric shapes, and a loose system of organizing ideas into the beginning, middle, and end of the essay. Writers can also use an outline as a map and draw a trail from the starting point (the focus of the essay) to the end (the central idea or discovery). Although most textbooks acknowledge that writing is a recursive process, they do not show how and when to modify an outline. Waiting until after writing has begun to write an outline can be a dynamic step, demonstrating how writing and thinking influence each other.

And then there is the thesis statement, which is often promoted as the gold standard of academic writing. A thesis statement can be useful, even necessary. However, in the planning stage, it almost invariably fossilizes students' thinking and commits them to a point of view that may be unsustainable. It is, of course, reasonable to revise a thesis statement, but this rarely happens in practice. When the writing process—with a definite article—is reduced to "a rigid formulation" (Matsuda, 2003, p. 78), it becomes incompatible with the recursive nature of good writing. By contrast, once an essay has already undergone multiple revisions, then drafting a thesis statement enables the writer to determine if the essay maintains a clear focus, and if not, it suggests further revisions. Once more, the rhetorical device serves the content first.

Focusing on Lexicogrammar

Although the guiding philosophy of this chapter is that all writing must start with analytical content, lexicogrammar—that is, vocabulary, grammar, and the intersection between the two (Biber, Johansson, Leech, Conrad, & Finegan, 1999)—must be a major focus because "without clear, reasonably accurate, and coherent text, there can be no academic writing in a second language" (Hinkel, 2004, p. x). Arguably, a vacuous essay in flawless English is worth no more than a cogent analysis obscured by grammar errors and poor word choice. Nonetheless, corpus analyses of common features of written academic discourse promote the direct teaching of high-frequency grammatical structures and lexical items. The lexicogrammar of academic writing must be taught because it is very different from spoken English and somewhat different from other written registers (Carter & McCarthy, 2006), meaning that it is unlikely to be acquired through interaction or incidental learning.

Thanks to corpus research, it is now possible to define the grammar and vocabulary necessary for academic writing. Coxhead (2000) has identified a basic lexicon of 570 word families that occur frequently across multiple disciplines; L2 writers who use words from this academic word list (AWL) will produce texts that are more target-like. Textbooks such as Zwier's *Building Academic Vocabulary* (2002) and Huntley's *Essential Academic Vocabulary: Mastering the Academic Word List* (2006) provide examples of how to teach academic vocabulary in depth at the advanced levels, although there are fewer materials for lower levels. Web sites (e.g., Cobb, 2007) allow teachers and students to examine a text and analyze the distribution of academic vocabulary compared to general vocabulary, using lists such as West's (1953). These resources can help counter a potential drawback of SCLT, that content-specific vocabulary may be taught at the expense of the AWL (Donley & Reppen, 2001), leaving students underequipped to read and write in other academic disciplines. Mindful of this pitfall, teachers can make academic vocabulary review salient and frequent.

In practical terms, for each formal essay students in this SCLT writing course are directly taught a selection of relevant AWL words, and they practice producing the words in discussion and writing in the context of the topic. For example, when writing about the two gangs in *The Outsiders*, students may find these items useful: *alike, include, likewise, disparity, gap, exclude, marginalize, differ*. Students need substantial input for each word (see Nation, 2001; Zwier, 2002) to learn parts of speech, word family members, definition, example sentences, restrictions, domain, and collocations. For this reason, the number of words introduced for each assignment is limited. Students appreciate having the lexical tools to help them express their ideas more clearly and academically (see Donley & Reppen, 2001, for other corpus-based teaching techniques appropriate to courses based on nonfiction and academic texts).

In the same fashion, there are grammatical structures which occur frequently across academic disciplines but less so in other discourses, including passive voice, nominalization, demonstrative pronouns, modals of certainty, impersonal constructions, noun clauses, subordination, linking verbs, adverbial clauses, and certain (mostly real) conditional structures (Biber et al., 1999; Carter & McCarthy, 2006; Hinkel, 2004). These corpus findings have simplified the scope of grammar teaching in academic writing. For instance, among modal verbs in the Longman corpus, *can, could, may, will,* and *would* are the most common in academic discourse, while *must* and *should* are also used to mark strong obligation. This pattern is very different from conversation or other forms of writing.

Other modals, such as *had better, have to, shall, ought to,* and *used to* need not be taught since they occur with low frequency in academic prose (Biber et al.). This is a deliberately reductive approach to grammar instruction, but it is an efficient one, targeting only the lexicogrammar that will most improve students' writing.

Academic writers' tendency to use certain grammar structures is a result of the content of expository writing. Noun clauses allow writers to quote, paraphrase, and analyze their sources ("the author shows that," "the article claims that," "the research suggests that"). Passive constructions are economical when the agent is unknown or uninteresting, and they can also introduce analysis ("it can be said that," "this is shown to be," "X is contrasted to Y"). Modal verbs of certainty allow writers to hedge (Hinkel, 2004), which is an essential academic skill. These structures are not simply "window dressing"; they help students "appreciate the range of choices they have" and enable them to move beyond "simple, vague, underdeveloped, unsophisticated sentences" (Koch, 2007). Good thinking requires good grammar to become good writing.

An important component of this SCLT writing course is its integrated grammar curriculum, developed through experience and a review of the relevant literature. Grammar instruction begins with verb tenses (only the most common forms in academic writing: present simple, past simple, and present perfect) and moves through conjunctions and conjunctive adverbs, modals of possibility, and the passive, and then onto dependent clauses: adjective, noun, adverb, and conditional. If time allows, the course ends with count–noncount nouns and articles. For each point, students learn the form, meaning, and use in academic writing, and they practice the grammar through focused literary content. This is by no means a fixed sequence, nor is it comprehensive: Most students are expected to take another ESL writing course before they enroll in 1st-year composition. The grammar component of the class expands the writer's toolbox and moves the product closer to the target. Pleasingly, the structures taught begin to appear in students' essays—not always correctly at first—as they realize that analytical thinking and the grammar used to express it develop simultaneously.

REFLECTIONS

The content-first SCLT writing course has been popular with students and teachers. Students have appreciated the mixture of freedom (to explore a topic) and structure (regular input on development, organization, and lexicogrammar). Although most instructors in the course have enjoyed working with the content, the difficulty of finding content-first textbooks results in substantial preparation time. Little has changed since Murphy and Stoller (2001) noted the lack of appropriate SCLT material. This is a bigger problem for novice teachers because experienced teachers can often draw on their own resources to craft their course. Possible solutions are to develop in-house course packs, to write a textbook based on the course (Pally, 2000a), or to compile sourcebooks (Powell & Ponder, 2001).

Assessing writing is always a challenge. One of the most salient criticisms of process writing is that it often weights the students' processes as much as their written products; this is in opposition to most high-stakes writing assessment, which focuses exclusively on product (see, e.g., Hinkel, 2004). Although the content-first approach is founded on principles of process writing, this pedagogy of L1 writing must be applied selectively to ESL contexts. Students' grades must balance process (their development as writers) with product (their readiness for the next level). Portfolio assessment partially resolves this dilemma. In this SCLT course, the students revise their major essays throughout the term, but all grades are temporary until students submit their portfolio of final drafts. Each student's portfolio is evaluated for the progress it evidences, but more importantly, it is assessed for the quality of the final drafts. Students who show the ability to think critically, write cohesive essays, and use academic vocabulary and grammar with reasonable mastery proceed to the next level (usually a credit-bearing ESL writing class). Thus, portfolio assessment allows students to apply their newly developed skills to their earlier writing in order to showcase their capabilities.

Each group of students is different, so the course is, therefore, different every term. It remains a challenge to select sustained content that will engage all (or most) of the students, to write materials that exploit the content area while teaching language and composition skills, and to find ways of inviting students to think and write deeply about ideas. Whatever the difficulties, this content-first course has shown that there is a world of writing beyond the five-paragraph essay, and it is one worth exploring.

ACKNOWLEDGMENTS

Parts of the introduction appeared in *The Selected Proceedings of the 2005 Michigan Teachers of English to Speakers of Other Languages (MITESOL) Conference*, edited by Christen Pearson, Nigel Caplan, and Carol Wilson-Duffy. The author is grateful to his coauthors, Andrew McCullough and Ruelaine Stokes; to MITESOL for reprinting permission; and to students from the course for their contributions.

Nigel A. Caplan is an ESL specialist at the University of North Carolina at Chapel Hill, in the United States. At the time of writing this chapter, he was an instructor at the Michigan State University English Language Center, also in the United States. He has presented workshops on writing at regional and international Teachers of English to Speakers of Other Languages conferences and published papers and textbooks.

CHAPTER 3

Modern Heroes: From Content to Composition via Critical and Creative Thinking

Linda Forrester

Learning to produce college-level academic writing in a second language is a challenging process. How can English as a second language (ESL) instructors best assist students in writing well in English? Should the primary focus be on grammar, sentence structure, syntax, poetic devices, vocabulary, creative expression, or textual analysis? All of these elements can be combined in a comprehensive, content-based ESL writing course designed around a unified theme. At the heart of current instructional theory is the idea of *integrative learning*. This involves bringing together ideas, materials, and activities from various sources and disciplines in order to create a learning experience that has the potential for further evolution. The benefits of integrative learning in the ESL classroom are widely recognized.

LaGuardia Community College (LCC), one of the 23 institutions that comprise the City University of New York (CUNY), is home to a multinational, multilingual student body. Currently there are students from more than 160 countries, with approximately two-thirds of LCC students born outside the United States (Fertoli, 2007). In order to serve its diverse students, LCC has been at the forefront of the innovative *learning communities* movement since the 1970s. Second language (L2) writing is often taught in paired or clustered classes, so ESL is partnered with content courses. The rationale, very simply, is that understanding academic materials and acquiring facility in second language (L2) writing are mutually supportive and inseparable. As van Slyck notes, "learning communities create social as well as intellectual networks, which increase student retention and success. Equally important . . . learning communities at their best engage students in a way that develops higher-order thinking skills—analysis, synthesis, reflection, evaluation—in a truly interdisciplinary context" (2006, p. 167). Obviously, a strong thematic focus helps students develop language, content knowledge, and an awareness of the thought process.

ESL instructors often encourage their students to "think in English" as they write. It isn't that English is better than any student's first language (L1). Thinking in English has merit because the cyclic process of thinking in another language, mentally translating into English, writing, and then thinking again is time consuming. Moreover, translating from L1 doesn't reinforce syntactic structures or develop style and phrasing in English. However, this admonition "to think in English" rings hollow if students are presented with a noncontextual writing topic. They need prior knowledge of and communicative practice with the subject matter, thus making a strong curricular theme fundamental to the writing process. Through thematic reading, discussion, and vocabulary acquisition, students are able to build a conceptual base in English when developing ideas. A colleague remarked, "They don't learn to write in a vacuum!" This, of course, is entirely true. In order to think in a second language, students require not only linguistic facility and fluency but also something to think about.

Willingham (2007) suggests, "The processes of thinking are intertwined with the content of thought (that is, domain knowledge)" (p. 8) and he goes on to note that "Prior knowledge and beliefs . . . influence how one interprets data" (p. 17). He explains that contextual background knowledge enables readers not only to understand the literary text but also to make valid predictions: "The cognitive system gambles that incoming information will be related to what you've just been thinking about. Thus, it significantly narrows the scope of possible interpretations of words, sentences, and ideas" (p. 11). How crucial these ideas are, particularly when reading, reasoning, and writing in a second language. The schema theory of learning through the apprehension of interrelated skeins of context enables L2 writers to gather, process, and use new information expressively.

As thinking cannot be divorced from content, it is equally inseparable from language. Students well understand the old adage from Funk and Lewis (1942) that "Words are the tools of thinking" (p. 4). This is not to say that the interplay of words is all that occupies our minds. There are many modes of nonverbal mental activity. In *Thinking in Pictures,* Grandin (1995) describes her experience as a *visual* rather than a *verbal* thinker. Autism has caused images to precede words in her mind. Surely visual thinking is used by artists throughout the world, and musicians must be able to think aurally. Nevertheless, for most of us, most of the time, language and thought are intimately intertwined. Are words a byproduct of thought, or do they induce thought? Perhaps they do both—although this mystery is beyond the purview of this chapter. Suffice it to say that for L2 learners, the connection between thought and language is concrete.

A thematic approach to L2 acquisition, particularly in writing classes, engages learners and fosters intellectual curiosity. While working with theme-based, interdisciplinary materials, students delve deeply into the English language, triggering challenging questions about the content.

CONTEXT

The advanced level ESL course at LCC is writing-intensive, designed to prepare students to compete in non-ESL college classes. After passing the course, students prepare to take the ACT College Entrance Exam, after which they enter Freshman Composition. The advanced ESL writing class is, therefore, quite rigorous. The class cited here was a group of 23 students, representing eight different first languages, from 10 countries, with a wide range of educational backgrounds and life experiences. The use of a common theme became an indispensable means of creating a unified focus.

The theme for this 6-week, intensive course was modern heroes. It was a natural choice. Each January, LCC offers an extensive commemoration and celebration of Martin Luther King, Jr.'s birthday. King is considered a hero throughout the world and is familiar to most ESL students. The hero theme was reinforced during the first week of the term by two dramatic New York City events that captivated the city. A man named Wesley Autrey threw himself in front of an oncoming subway train to rescue a younger man who had fallen onto the tracks during an epileptic seizure. Autrey pinned him down while the train rolled over them. Both were left unharmed (Buckley, 2007). This extraordinary event left millions asking, "Would I have done that?"

Two days later, as Autrey was being fêted as the "Subway Superman," two men in the Bronx, Pedro Nevarez and Julio Gonzalez, saved the life of a baby who had fallen from a fire escape. Gonzalez heard people screaming and looked four stories up to see the child dangling. He grabbed his friend and rushed to the site just in time. The baby fell, feet first, into Nevarez, knocking him over, and then bounced into the protective arms of Gonzalez, knocking him down, too. The baby was safe, and heroism was on a roll in New York (Massey, 2007). The mere thought that human beings were capable of such deeds of valor was heartening and captured the imagination of the class.

In the weeks that followed, the class discussed and read articles about these heroes and others, participated in the Martin Luther King, Jr., programs, recited and reflected on King's "I Have A Dream" speech (1963), sang along with Mariah Carey's song "Hero" (Carey & Afanasieff, 1993), and saw a film, *Maria Full of Grace* (Mezey & Marston, 2004), about a young Colombian woman who worked as a "mule," transporting cocaine to New York in her body. Students then attended a lecture by the film's associate producer. They read a valiant poem and learned a heroic quantity of related vocabulary. They wrote extensively in their daily journal entries and biweekly essays. The momentum around the hero theme grew, and so did the results.

Gianelli (1997) states, "By organizing material thematically for the students, we create a powerful integrated learning environment where students have little problem assimilating new information. Language learning is also facilitated because theme-related language and vocabulary are used and reused in new contexts, all of which are meaningfully related" (p. 144).

As the term progressed, the students were not only assimilating theme-centered concepts and vocabulary. They were also retaining them, exploring them individually, and employing them correctly in subsequent writing assignments. When references to earlier discussions appeared in their essays, the synthesis of thought and language became evident.

CURRICULUM, TASKS, MATERIALS

To discuss the progress of student writing in light of the hero theme, it is necessary to delineate some of the readings, materials, and activities that entered into the integrative mix. Although these elements must be differentiated in order to be described, it should be remembered that they never took place in isolation. Reading was followed by discussion, which then found expression in writing. Therefore, the following description of the process is not strictly in chronological order.

Reading Narratives

First, there was Autrey's act of heroism. The class read the article, "A Man Down, a Train Arriving, and a Stranger Makes a Choice" (Buckley, 2007). Dramatically written, the article provides a resource for important discussion topics as well as a review of conditional forms and examples of illustrative language ("heart pounding," "brakes screeched," "cries of wonder") and alliteration ("bumps and bruises," "suffered a seizure," "collapsed and convulsing"). Language and writing style were highlighted as the students focused on the event and their reactions to it.

Students also read Gentleman's (2006) article, "In India, a Maid Becomes an Unlikely Literary Star," which details a maid's struggle to overcome great adversities and go on to write a successful memoir, *A Life Less Ordinary* (Halder, 2005). While the Gentleman article was less directly tied to the hero theme, the class agreed that the protagonist, Baby Halder, who was abandoned and abused, suffered dire poverty, and experienced the drudgery of domestic service, was indeed heroic. This article was used to examine prereading and comprehension techniques. Students studied the headline; identified the author, the date, and the news source; looked at pictures and captions; and asked themselves content questions before skimming the first and last paragraphs. There was a brief discussion about what had been ascertained thus far. Then small groups were assigned to read two or three paragraphs of the story, after which they summarized the main points before writing three questions about their section. Then, the groups, in turn, read their segments to the class as the other students followed the text. They stated the main ideas and asked questions, which their classmates answered without looking at the text. This activity was effective, for Baby Halder, the Indian maid turned author, appeared in both discussion and writing throughout the term.

Reading a Poem

One cold, snowy morning in January, students read a short poem (Eisenberg, 2000), a favorite of mine, taken from CUNY's online writing lab:

> From the frozen sky
> In glorious splendor
> Snowflakes fell to earth
> Dazzling in white
> Dressed to perfection
> Although they were dying
> —Norah Eisenberg

The class read it together several times and discussed the unfamiliar words—*splendor, dazzling*, and *perfection*—and then they wrote about the poem's content in their journals. They expressed their ideas about the juxtaposition of life and death and the necessity of living fully and purposefully. As they shared their journals, the excitement about the poem became contagious. One student said it was like a sick person dressing up for a farewell party. This reminded another student of a poignant movie he'd seen about AIDS. There was no need to interpret this poem for these international students. They felt it and internalized it, and they agreed that the snowflakes were heroic.

The students enthusiastically asked for more poetry. Each student brought in a short poem (with copies for all), taught the vocabulary, and explained the essence. One shy young man brought in a lyric poem he had composed. The others admired it, which generated a greater self-confidence in the budding poet. The exercise added a layer of richness that was felt by all, personalizing the theme of heroism.

Reading a Speech

In preparation for the college-wide commemoration of King's birthday, the class read and discussed an excerpt from his famous speech, "I Have a Dream" (1963). The students had a three-fold assignment: They studied the text independently, rehearsed and recorded it, and then wrote a short reflection and reaction to the speech. In class, each individual played the recording (or read the text aloud), and then read his or her reflection. The readings were remarkably nuanced and varied; the individual accenting of words indicated the perceptions of the reader, and the written reflections demonstrated the universality of King's message.

One student wrote

> When I was reading the Martin Luther King speech . . . I felt a strange feeling in my heart, like something wanted to say to me: "Wake up!" I felt love from my heart for

all suffering people. When I was reading his sermon, I felt . . . his willing power to rescue suffering people. I realized that he wanted a place where there would be only happiness; men and women would be helpful to each other.

Another stated

"I Have a Dream" means . . . that all people should be treated the same. Color and skin don't matter at all. All human beings are created by God. Everybody has the same organs inside our bodies. All human blood is red. So why did whites discriminate against blacks? Why did blacks sit in the back? I think he brought hope for us to live in this country. Otherwise, they would also discriminate against us. Because of his long segregation, we have gotten social equality and justice.

The writings indicate the extraordinary degree to which today's immigrant and international students are able to comprehend and identify with the struggle of the U.S. civil rights movement in the 1960s. "If he had not fought for civil rights at that time, we could not have come to America and studied together in our class," stated one individual. She was able to see a direct bridge between King's visionary work and the opportunities now available to her friends, family, and fellow students. Because the subject was personal, the writing that emerged was strong and revelatory.

Viewing Documentaries

The class saw two films as part of the King Celebration on January 9, 2007. First, they viewed *Citizen King* (Bagwell, 2004), a documentary about the early civil rights movement, the Ku Klux Klan, Brown vs. the Board of Education, and the murder of Emmett Till. Students considered the issue of segregation and discussed race relations in their countries of origin. Then they joined the greater college community for *Eyes on the Prize: Part I (1954–56), Awakening* (Williams, 1987), a classic documentary containing clips of King's activities and speeches during the last 5 years of his life, culminating with his final, prophetic speech the night before he was assassinated. Many in the audience wept.

Students were asked to take notes during the film in order to write down, as closely as possible, the exact words of at least one speaker. The following ideas came from class members. About King: "He took all the fear out of you" and "In his death there is hope for redemption." And King's own words: "I can't make little mistakes anymore—only big mistakes," "All labor has dignity," "All people in the world have the right to three meals a day for their bodies, education and culture for their minds, and dignity, equality and freedom for their spirits," "Injustice anywhere is a threat to justice everywhere." This last quotation, taken from "Letter from a Birmingham Jail" (King, 1963), was particularly resonant with the class because the ideas in this text led to fertile discussion and journal writing on the question: "Am I my brother's keeper?" Students reached the conclusion that heroism does not usually take place in isolation; it entails a connection and sense of responsibility to the community. One student mentioned to me, months after the term concluded, that she felt that the focus on King had helped her to reassess her selfish and self-absorbed attitude. She was a good writer at the beginning of the term, and a broadened outlook made her a more powerful one.

Studying Vocabulary, Collocations, Word Trees, and Grammar

As the term progressed and the students read about, discussed, and watched videos about heroes and heroic events, they naturally absorbed content-based words and phrases into their working vocabulary. This process was assisted by frequent vocabulary minilessons, where the class practiced theme-related vocabulary in discrete units. For example, all forms of the word *hero* were explored, including the nouns *hero, heroes, heroine, heroism,* and *antihero*; the adjective *heroic*; and the adverb *heroically*. Then students composed sentences using these words. Also, they considered related synonyms and antonyms—*bravery, valor, courage, fear, coward, cowardice, valiant, courageous, afraid, fearful, cowardly, scared, frightened*—and their usage.

Often, what impedes fluent L2 writing is not only a lack of vocabulary but also an inability to use correct word forms. The vocabulary base must be broadened, but the words themselves must be practiced and the parts of speech understood. Students recorded words, idioms, and collocations related to the hero theme and then created diagrams, or "word trees," to show vocabulary relationships. New phrases emerged, such as *stand up for, sacrifice (oneself) for others,* and *put aside fear*. When revising essays, the students were encouraged to incorporate these new words and phrases into their writing and to underline them. This reinforcement helped the students to retain and expand their vocabulary.

Throughout the term, units of grammar and syntax were taught contextually. Authentic texts were used to highlight targeted concepts. When characters and situations from course content were employed in examples, tricky forms, such as the hypothetical conditional and reported speech, became more accessible. Working with these examples made students' linguistic investigations and practice meaningful, and they found that a better understanding of the structure of the English language was within their grasp.

Listening to a Song

These lyrics from Mariah Carey's song "Hero" inspired the class: "There's a hero if you look inside your heart—you don't have to be afraid of who you are" (Carey & Afanasieff, 1993). The class listened to a recording of the song several times and then sang the lyrics along with the recording. The song encourages all people, perhaps especially those who are sometimes dispirited while pursuing a college education in a second language. When their self-confidence is low, Carey's song reminds them that they need only to tap into this inner source of strength. According to Hyde (2007), "a work of art is a gift" (p. xvi). The students found this song to be a beneficent work of art.

Watching a Movie

And then there was a question about Maria. Was she, as a movie protagonist, a heroine? The film *Maria Full of Grace* (Mezey & Marston, 2004) offered students a glimpse into a brutal underworld, where the idea of heroism is ambiguous. Frustrated with her dead-end job and her demanding family in Colombia, and finding herself newly pregnant, Maria accepts a job as a "mule" or "human suitcase" to conceal illegal drugs inside her body and transport them into the United States. In many ways, Maria is brave and strong. However, the question remains: Is she heroic? The answer was less obvious, which made for an interesting persuasive essay topic, with writers weighing in on both sides.

The film's associate producer, Orlando Tobón, who played himself in the film and assisted in its creation, spoke to a LCC audience. As an important personage in the Colombian immigrant community, he tells a classic U.S. immigrant success story: arriving alone as a teenager with $16 in his pocket, working innumerable jobs, earning a college degree, and eventually opening a travel agency. Locally, his fame springs from his generosity and love for the community. Several Colombian students in the class knew of him, so the group was eager to meet and speak with him. They were not disappointed, leaving the lecture with autographed copies of his book, *Jackson Heights Chronicles: When Crossing the Border Isn't Enough* (2006), and a sense that they, too, could play a positive role in the community. Students found that Maria may be less than heroic, but Orlando Tobón, travel agent, film producer, community activist, and problem solver, is indubitably a hero and a model for immigrant and foreign students of all nationalities.

Writing About Heroes

Throughout the term, the class received instruction concerning essay organization, thematic development, figurative language, editing, and revising. They practiced free writing and brainstorming. In composition, the first half of the term concentrated on narrative writing, while the second half explored persuasive and comparative formats. The culminating narrative essay required students to write about a time when they had been heroes. Or, as an alternative, they could write about an episode when someone had behaved heroically on their behalf. Student writers were asked to include sensory details, and they were encouraged to analyze what they had learned from the experience.

The themes of students' essays covered a broad range. A young mother withstood intense pain to deliver her first child without anesthesia. A boy rescued a classmate from a gang of bullies. One student saved her sister from a murderous ex-husband, another gave CPR to a woman on a subway train, and a third stood up for the rights of her coworkers against an authoritarian manager. There was a story of a heroic fireman, a heroic teacher, a heroic husband, and a heroic dog. If some stories were embellished, it hardly mattered. In fact, it could be argued that learning to produce an imaginative rendering of events is also a valuable part of the narrative expression. These essays were passionate. By the time they were writ-ten, theme-centered vocabulary and syntax had been assimilated and practiced, so the writing was coherent and fluent. After revising the essays, students read them to their spellbound classmates. As a result, the group also became cohesive, and the level of mutual respect rose markedly. The essays were compiled into a book-let, *Twenty Tales of Heroes*, which served as a souvenir for the class.

REFLECTIONS

What we think about matters. It matters in the choices we make and in the way we live our lives. It also matters in how well we educate ourselves and others. This idea is the foundation of a content-centered approach to L2 acquisition, particularly in regard to the development of expressive L2 writing. Working with a strong theme such as modern heroes inspires students and sets the bar of achievement high. It allows for the integration of a broad range of diverse, yet interrelated, materials, which, when mixed together, form an unpredictable syn-thesis. Under the textually diverse umbrella of the hero theme, ideas converged. Sometimes all elements clashed in jarring resistance, and other times they blended smoothly. Under this thematic umbrella, students shared insights and perceptions gleaned from both culture and experience.

The teaching of L2 writing to an international group of students is a complex process. In "Individualism, Academic Writing and ESL Writers," Ramanthan and Atkinson (2006) point out fundamental differences in perception between Asian and Western cultures on such issues as *writer's voice* and *individualist expression*. Does writing about personal experiences come naturally or does it seem artificial and self-obsessed? Did a particular student grow up thinking of herself as part of a group or as the "Lone Ranger"? Was another student encouraged to infuse writing with memorized proverbs and maxims, only to find them frowned upon in the United States? Does peer-critiquing make some students squirm? Teach-ers need to know their students in order to have "a complex, multi-dimensional understanding of individuals-in-context" (Ramanthan & Atkinson, p. 179):

> The twenty or so years of socialization and education into particular ways of knowing and being in the world that international undergraduates bring with them to 'West-ern' Anglophone universities should not be considered insignificant or ruled out of court, any more than it should be mistaken for the full measure of the person.

An awareness of students' backgrounds, as well as their present circumstances, is essential to good pedagogy. When choosing a course theme for a diverse, mul-ticultural class, it is wise to make that theme as inclusive as possible, focusing on that which unites rather than that which separates.

Modern heroes was a theme that cut across cultural boundaries. The Western concept of the hero, born of classical mythology, may invoke the image of a rugged individualist. Yet there are heroes in every culture, some who are valued for their self-sacrifice rather than their ingenuity and individuality. Also, there are many avenues of heroism. For instance, a heroic dog, famous in Korea, died to save his blind master from a fire, and a heroic mother in Bangladesh welcomed two homeless families into her small house after a raging flood had destroyed their homes. The idea of heroism implies courage in the face of adversity and the ability to take quick, often unpremeditated, action. However, many heroes are revered for their humility as well as their valor. Autrey repeatedly told crowds of cheering New Yorkers that he was no hero; he had simply done the right thing. No one doubted his sincerity.

The qualities of courage, decisiveness, integrity, and modesty are highly valued by ESL students, and a consideration of them in class met few objections. As it happened, all of the heroes cited in this course were members of racial or ethnic minorities. They were good guides because their unique perspectives and valiant deeds offered a compass to international students who often found the process of navigating their way into mainstream U.S. society perplexing.

This ESL writing class proved to be creative, dynamic, and largely student-centered. There was an improvisational freedom in this method for me, but there were also risks. Perhaps the very intensity of the hero theme made certain emotional reactions inevitable. One student, for example, despite my persistent emphasis on the idea of *unity,* used the "I Have a Dream" reflection to vent his long-held, bitter resentment against a nation whose people, he felt, had treated his own dismissively. Three students from the "oppressor" country had to weather his invective (which he had the grace to say was not meant for them personally) until the discussion was redirected. On another occasion, a student wrote of her regret for an occasion on which she had *not* behaved heroically. The writing brought unsettling memories, yet writing about these remnants of times past was cathartic.

Becoming educated inevitably results in change, which is sometimes painful. The hero theme, however, proved overwhelmingly positive in its effect on this group of students precisely because, by donning the mantel of heroism, they were better able to face change, look their fears in the eye, and come to a deeper understanding of their own potential.

The hero theme had an impact on all the students, and all made demonstrable progress in writing. Even students who did not pass the final examination acknowledged that they had learned from the class and suggested that the end of the term was not the end of their learning experience. Powerful ideas have a way of working in us long after they are introduced. In the case of these students, the ideas considered through a study of heroes and heroic behavior proved beneficial. What's more, students acquired a verbal framework in their L2 for use in thought, speech, and written expression, on a theme that is timeless and applicable in all situations. This foundation will support them well in their academic careers and the journeys that lie ahead.

―――――――――

Linda Forrester teaches ESL in the Education and Language Acquisition Department at LaGuardia Community College, City University of New York, in the United States. She teaches all levels and skills, specializing in L2 writing. She holds a bachelor's degree in music from Indiana University of Pennsylvania and a master's degree in teaching English to speakers of other languages from Adelphi University, both in the United States.

CHAPTER 4

Writing to Embody: Engaging Students in Written Role Play

Shawna Shapiro

One of the most unexpected lessons a writing teacher might learn from her students is this: Typing paper that has been soaked in tea, dried, crumpled up, and then torn around the edges, passes quite nicely for old parchment. A seventh-grade student named Satoko taught her classmates this trick after they had expressed admiration for the visual authenticity of her Oregon Trail journal, a written role-play assignment in which students pretended to be pioneers writing about their experiences and emotions as they headed west. Although students sometimes have to be reminded that their actual writing is more important than the paper on which it is written, the fact that students focus on this sort of detail indicates true *engagement* in the writing process—a key objective in using written role play with students.

Having students write from someone else's point of view forces them to integrate both creativity and critical thinking. This integration is difficult to achieve because many writing activities (indeed, entire curricula) tend to emphasize one of these two aims over the other. As a result, teachers often alternate the more fun activities with those that are cognitively challenging. When students write from another person's perspective, however—especially the perspective of someone they have read from or learned about—they reach higher levels of understanding while still getting to play in their work of language learning. This chapter describes the rationale for written role play at secondary and postsecondary levels and offers samples and reflections to encourage practitioners to experiment with these activities in their own classes.

CONTEXT

In most academic writing classes, particularly those at advanced adult levels, creativity tends to be ignored in the wake of content, organization, and clarity. It is not that writing teachers actively dislike creative writing—on the contrary, many of us write poetry, prose, or personal reflections on our own time. I, for one, fondly remember the fiction writing course I took as an undergraduate English major and have always wished to give my students a similarly positive experience with writing. A major concern, though, is how to integrate the pleasure of writing with the academic rigor that students need and expect in an advanced writing class. This integration was made a bit easier for me when teaching a middle school block course in which language arts and U.S. history were integrated.

In this teaching situation, assignments could be designed to encourage imagination and language play. In one group assignment, students developed a newspaper based on fictional or real events during the U.S. Revolutionary War (1775–1781). Each group's final project included feature articles, editorials, advice columns, advertisements, and a number of other student-generated odds and ends. Students enjoyed delegating particular pieces of the project to various group members, based on their strengths and interests. Other favorite assignments involved less time commitment. After researching a particular U.S. state, for example, each student made a brochure advertising that state to potential tourists. Each panel of the assignment was devoted to a different aspect of that state (e.g., geography, economy, main attractions). This activity worked well with a spoken component in which students persuaded their classmates to visit that state. A final activity that worked well in these middle school classes was fictional letter writing or journaling.

Introducing Ludic Writing

Linguists often refer to these more playful language tasks as *ludic* in nature (Cook, 2000). Ludic activities, Cook explains, help students to achieve greater levels of fluency, as they allow them both to learn and to manipulate the rules of language. Ludic language is particularly important in writing classes because many students have had writing instruction that presents forms as rigid and confining. By writing in an alternative genre or persona, students build rhetorical flexibility and simultaneously develop a deeper understanding of course content.

Written role play, as a subset of ludic language, works well for a number of reasons: First, it is a convenient means to integrate two content areas, such as language arts and social studies. In addition, it works well with a pre-existing curriculum because it does not require a complete redesign of objectives, only an expansion of the means by which those objectives are practiced and assessed. More than anything else, however, I use written role play because students seem to enjoy the chance to experiment in their writing. Several students who might have balked at a multiparagraph essay assignment would painlessly complete the same amount of writing in an alternative format, especially if allowed to exercise a bit of creative license. This is not to say that the more typical genres of writing were avoided; rather, alternative writing tasks led to more controlled, high-stakes writing assignments in middle school classes.

When I began teaching writing to both native and nonnative speakers at the university level, however, I hesitated to use these sorts of assignments. Would these tasks be appropriate for students at the university level? Would students see them as childish? Would they be seen as diversions from the "real" writing that students were expected to practice? In addition, the course curriculum was already intensive. Was there even sufficient time for written role play? As I continued to follow the regular course sequence, however, I began to reconsider my hesitancy. I could feel that the creativity in my students' writing was missing. The monotony of academic summaries, reading response, and research papers was weighing heavily on the writers, not to mention their reader.

How could space be made for written role play at a university level? Eventually I recalled that I had experienced it myself, in oral form, in a graduate-level educational philosophy course. The culminating activity for the course was a performed (yet unrehearsed) "conversation" in which each student impersonated one of the many authors we had read throughout the course. In the class session prior to the actual performance, we had reviewed the central points in each author's work. We had then been assigned an author to represent in the next class. Like many other students in the course, I was a bit cynical about this exercise: Couldn't we simply write a paper summarizing the reading or contrasting it with another scholar's work? Was it even possible to represent the thoughts of a writer whose work we had only begun to understand? Sensing our anxiety about both the dramatic and the academic challenges of this activity, the professor explained that the aim of the activity was generative, not evaluative: We would be graded on our effort and engagement, not on the literal accuracy of our statements or the extent of our acting talents.

After we entered the classroom two days later, we sat in a circle around the table. We displayed our authorial identity with a nametag. The professor served as moderator, asking questions when the energy of the interaction began to lull. Our performance was in no way idyllic, due in part to our class's lack of familiarity with this sort of activity. Many of us were hesitant, afraid that we might somehow misrepresent our author's ideas. Still, I was impressed by several aspects of this experience: First, the professor had insisted that we share ideas in the first person, rather than as a third-person summary. I originally thought this was an unnecessary detail and was somewhat annoyed by her persistent reminders to use *I*. However, I must admit being amazed by the change in tone that occurred when a student's comment that "She would probably respond that . . ." was rephrased as "I think that . . ." The ideas came to life, despite our lingering tentativeness in representing them. In fact, I felt that our hesitancy was probably more authentic than we realized; after all, any unrehearsed conversation is likely filled with pauses, fillers, and moments of awkward silence.

Second, although we had not been asked to alter our tone or register as we embodied each author's voice, several of us did so almost organically. We found ourselves using a more formal register and specialized vocabulary, speaking with greater syntactic complexity. Although one might have assumed that this playacting could easily lapse into parody, it actually had the opposite effect of encouraging a greater depth to our conversation because we abandoned our own voices in an attempt to engage the thoughts of another person. Despite my original skepticism about the pedagogical value of this activity, I found myself thinking in new ways, beginning during my preparation for the activity. As I considered the questions and responses that my constructed "I" might offer to his or her "colleagues," I saw connections and contradictions I had previously overlooked. I realized how many of the themes raised in our readings overlapped and intersected. Only later did I realize that this sort of academic role play is well supported by several veins of research.

Connecting With Research Findings: Language Play and Academic Literacy

As recent work in the field of language play has shown, creativity and experimentation are central to the language acquisition process for both children and adults (Carter, 2004; Cook, 2000). In order to truly make the language our own, language users need to be given the space and permission to construct meaning in our own ways, including through what some scholars call *ludic discourse*, which "involves the use of language for the purpose of amusing and entertaining oneself or others" (Tarone, 2005, p. 490). This playful use of language has only recently become a topic of research and instruction (Broner & Tarone, 2000; Murphey, 1998). One of the primary purposes of this sort of play is to help learners progress toward greater fluency and innovation in their language use, as a counterbalance to the prevalent concern for accuracy, particularly among adolescents and adult learners (Tarone, 2000). In essence, language play increases language learners' sense of ownership.

Although most of the discussion of language play tends to focus on speaking, scholars and practitioners in academic literacy have begun to find connections in their work, as well. Casanave (2002), for example, uses a metaphor of writing games to depict the various situations and conventions that multilingual students encounter as they develop as writers. Similarly, Canagarajah's (2002) discussions of *critical academic literacy* highlight the challenges that students face as they develop multiple identities both inside and outside the classroom. As instructors, he argues, we can create spaces for our students to explore and express these various selves through reading and writing activities. This sort of pedagogy facilitates the development of *multiliteracies* as an alternative to the more constricted view of academic literacy that tends to be more prevalent in reading and writing classrooms. Johns (1999) has found that this sort of approach—which she describes as "socioliterate" (p. 159)—is particularly important for nonnative-speaker permanent residents or immigrant students, whose long-term residency in the United States often leads to high fluency in some registers but not in others. This rhetorical flexibility in writing is also important, as Belcher (2006) points out, to students' ability to anticipate and respond to the communicative tasks in their "imagined futures" (p. 133). When we present students with new purposes and personas for writing, we help them develop the ability to adapt their language skills to multiple situations. Research suggests that written role play can contribute to the development of active reading skills as well. In his overview of "reading–writing relations," Grabe (2001) describes reading and writing skills as both codependent and mutually supportive. In other words, better reading leads to better writing, and vice versa. Because academic English as a second language (ESL) courses in the United States tend to focus on a single skill (i.e., listening, speaking, reading, or writing), this interaction between skills is sometimes over-looked. The most effective literacy practices, Grabe (2001) argues, work against this trend by using integrated-skills tasks and extensive dialogue about those tasks. Newell, Garriga, and Peterson (2001) expand on these principles, arguing that students must learn how to "shape their own interpretations" (p. 165) in academic writing, rather than simply restate an author's main ideas. This process of moving from comprehension to interpretation is inherent to a student's ability to complete advanced academic work. Written role play is one of the most effective ways for students to begin that process because it allows them to try on the role of author in a creative and liberating way.

CURRICULUM, TASKS, MATERIALS

Having considered my background in role play through my own educational experience, I decided to try it with my university-level academic writing class. Perhaps a similar activity, in written form, would help students engage more deeply with the course readings. At minimum, it would provide a welcome divergence from the norm. To begin, students were asked to compose a "conversation" between the two scholarly authors that they had been reading. My goals for the assignment were that the students would (a) demonstrate reading comprehension, (b) participate in a deeper engagement with the readings, and (c) incorporate greater creativity and risk-taking in their writing. To help my students achieve these goals, I first needed to find readings that were engaging but also challenging, so the complexities could be explored in writing. The readings needed to have been written by authors who had points of agreement and disagreement. Finally, students needed some sort of structure, prompt, or situation that would lead them into the assignment so that they could put the authors into conversation.

In my particular class, the theme of the readings was bias. The students first read an excerpt from Berger's *Ways of Seeing* (1990), which discusses the complex relationship between art and its audience, showing that "the way we see things is affected by what we know and what we believe" (p. 106). A few weeks later, the students read an excerpt from Gross's *Rhetoric of Science* (1990), which introduces the concept of Aristotelian rhetoric and argues that this "art of persuasion" is at work even in a seemingly objective field such as natural science. The students needed to see how both readings related to the larger class theme of bias, and to begin considering how those readings might be used as a conceptual lens to look at an artifact of their choosing later in the course sequence.

The assignment prompt was as follows: *In a two-page paper, put Berger and Gross into conversation about a specific topic or concept. Use each author to ask questions of the other and to extend or challenge the other's ideas. Consider the genre possibilities for this assignment: an e-mail exchange, a dramatic dialogue, a series of letters, etc. The outcome of this written role-play assignment was anything but certain. Would the students' creative juices flow? Which genre would they choose? And more than anything, would they take this piece of writing as seriously as they did their academic essays?* At first, the students responded with an anxiety mirroring my own when I had been faced with a similar task in my graduate course. Their most prevalent question was not, however, "Why are we doing this?" but rather, "How?" "What do the two have in common?" they asked. "That's what you're supposed to figure out," was my mischievous response. To help them generate some ideas, the class completed a short brainstorm list. Then they held a short debate based on one of the issues listed. Half of the class represented Berger and the other half Gross. The intensity of the debate was impressive: The students were clearly energized by this type of persuasive speaking activity. Afterward, when asked about their readiness to begin writing, the class was both relaxed and enthusiastic. Although a few students lamented not having samples of the assignment to use as a model, most seemed to look forward to experimenting on their own.

On the assignment's due date, I collected the essays eagerly but with limited expectation, since the task was a stretch for students, both cognitively and linguistically. Upon initial reading, I found the variety of responses students offered to the assignment as surprising as it was pleasing. In these assignments, Berger and Gross encountered one another at a museum, a cafe, or a pub. They interacted via oral conversation, e-mail, letters, and (in one case) instant messaging. Frequently, the two authors responded to each other's work with both admiration and a critical eye, quoting themselves or each other occasionally for emphasis. I enjoyed reading these pieces and the ludic language they displayed. Almost all of the many incarnations of this exchange had elements of style or content that could be considered playful. Many of the students used the assignment as an opportunity to offer imitations, often bordering on parody, of academic register.

One student, a long-term U.S. resident, whose work tended to be above average in content but often lacking in academic style, actually attempted to play with academic register. As a reader, I enjoyed the conversational, yet authoritative, tone to the letters he produced. As a teacher, I also appreciated having a window into his understanding of the readings. I could see points in his letters that signified a deep level of comprehension and others that indicated aspects of the readings with which he was still grappling. Another writer—a female international student who had been in the United States for a shorter amount of time—presented the exchange as a dramatic dialogue in which the two authors debated on a point-by-point basis. In this way, the writer clearly represented the relationships between the two authors' ideas. Other students chose to center the dialogue around a particular issue or object, such as a piece of art or literature. One memorable example involved the analysis of a diet and exercise program, commenting on the rhetorical repertoire of words and images used for marketing for such products, with each author weighing in as a consultant (visit http://www.shawnashapiro.com/ to view samples of student work).

REFLECTIONS

While written role play has its benefits, it raises particular complications as well. The very nature of written role play is a bit messy: It is both creative and academic, and this makes it difficult for students to pin down. For example, some students struggled with issues of register, producing exchanges that were stilted or inconsistent in tone. One student in particular presented the dialogue between the authors as an e-mail exchange from one buddy to another. Although he did engage the authors in an exchange of ideas, this student did so with a combination of registers that was difficult to follow. On one hand, the exchange was somewhat informal, using humorous e-mail addresses, a casual subject line ("Better than Lit?") and several colloquial expressions (e.g., "What's that all about? ☺"). Yet these elements were interspersed with a more formal tone and word choice. The contrast between these two registers was awkward. At the same time, however, this hybrid style showed the student's sincere attempt to embody the authors in written form, as well as to fuse his voice with theirs. This sort of complexity can be intriguing for a teacher, as it allows for more interesting conversations with the class about concepts such as voice and intertextuality.

What almost all students experience in completing this sort of assignment is a process of risk-taking. At first, they are afraid, just as I was in my graduate course, that they will misrepresent the authors or that they might sound pretentious. They are worried that the two authors might have little to say to one another. Nevertheless, because the activity is different from the norm and because it encourages writing in a more playful way, students seem to understand that accuracy on this assignment is secondary to engagement.

For those teachers who wish to incorporate written role play in their classes, the following guidelines serve as a starting point:

- Choose readings that are engaging and somewhat accessible but which reflect points of disagreement among authors.

- Make clear the objectives of the assignment, perhaps showing students a rubric for how it will be assessed.

- Use speaking activities (debate, small-group work, dialogues, etc.) as "prewriting," so students have a line of thought started before they work independently on the assignment.

- Consider discussing as a class the elements of academic register, so students can begin to imitate this style in their writing. Similarly, if allowing students to write in a more informal genre, discuss those features as well.

For most ESL students, the notion of writing as a performance is nothing new. They have been asked to play the role of academic writer many times and have had to perform this role on a variety of stages, including standardized tests, college application essays, and research papers. Rarely, however, are they allowed to approach a written performance from an alternate identity—to use writing as a chance to try on another persona. Yet if language is inherently playful, dialogic, and multivocal, as linguists tell us it is, then writing as someone else might just be one of the most authentic writing opportunities students will ever experience.

Shawna Shapiro is a doctoral candidate in English language and rhetoric specializing in academic literacy at the University of Washington, in the United States. She has taught English, ESL, social studies, and Spanish at all levels. She also facilitates teacher training courses and workshops at several sites in her community.

CHAPTER 5

Using Second Language Learning as Content in a University ESL Writing Course

Mark A. James

This chapter describes an innovative approach to content-based instruction (CBI) in a freshman English as a second language (ESL) writing course at a university in the United States, using *second language learning* as the course content. To implement the approach, the students read scholarly articles about topics, such as the needs of ESL students at English-medium universities, and then they wrote essays about this content. The students produced academic essays that illustrated various benefits of this course design.

This chapter describes this curriculum innovation in detail so that other ESL writing teachers can determine its relevance for their own programs. Included are an explanation of why this CBI approach was adopted, details about both the teaching environment and the innovation itself, and examples of students' writing to illustrate learning outcomes. The chapter concludes with reflections on this curriculum innovation.

CONTEXT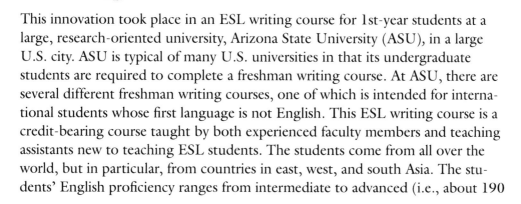

This innovation took place in an ESL writing course for 1st-year students at a large, research-oriented university, Arizona State University (ASU), in a large U.S. city. ASU is typical of many U.S. universities in that its undergraduate students are required to complete a freshman writing course. At ASU, there are several different freshman writing courses, one of which is intended for international students whose first language is not English. This ESL writing course is a credit-bearing course taught by both experienced faculty members and teaching assistants new to teaching ESL students. The students come from all over the world, but in particular, from countries in east, west, and south Asia. The students' English proficiency ranges from intermediate to advanced (i.e., about 190 to 207 on the computer-based Test of English as a Foreign Language). Most of the students are in their 1st year of university studies, and they represent a broad range of major areas of study, including business, education, engineering, liberal arts, and sciences.

The general goal of the ESL writing course, as stated in the *Writing Programs Teachers' Guide* handbook, which is given to all writing instructors at ASU, is "to introduce students to the importance of writing in the work of the university and to develop their critical reading, thinking and writing skills so that they can successfully participate in that work" (Arizona State University Writing Programs, 2009, para. 1). In other words, the general goal of this course is for students to develop skills that they can *transfer* (James, 2006; Perkins & Salomon, 1994) to other academic courses.

One potential barrier to meeting this goal is differences that exist between the ESL writing course and students' other academic courses. Typical assignments in the ESL writing course require students to write about personal experiences rather than to write about a specific text (e.g., a chapter in a textbook, or a research article). This contrasts with the *text-responsible* writing that students often have to do in other academic courses (Leki & Carson, 1997): "Writing classes require students to demonstrate knowledge of a source text much less frequently than other academic courses do" (p. 39). Researchers have suggested that transfer of learning outcomes from a writing course can suffer when tasks differ (Leki & Carson, 1994) or when students do not see connections between courses (Beaufort, 1998; Dias, Freedman, Medway, & Pare, 1999; Dyke Ford, 2004).

One way an ESL writing course might bridge this gap is by using CBI, an approach that is growing in popularity across academic contexts (Crandall & Kaufman, 2002; Kaufman & Crandall, 2005). CBI involves "the integration of particular content with language-teaching aims" (Brinton, Snow, & Wesche, 2003, p. 2). For example, in an ESL writing course, traditional language teaching aims might include the introduction of various writing strategies (e.g., description, definition, comparison and contrast), as well as grammar instruction and vocabulary building. If the course adopts a CBI approach, these language goals will be targeted by having students read, discuss, and then write about a particular content area. The content in a CBI writing course for engineering students, for instance, might include a series of thematic articles about inventions, alternative fuels, or waste management (James, 2006). A CBI approach can facilitate the use of text-responsible writing assignments and, thereby, help make the ESL writing course similar to students' other academic courses.

Compared to more traditional ESL writing instruction, CBI requires an additional important instructional decision be made: Teachers must choose suitable content. Ideally, the content chosen will be relevant and interesting to the students so that they will be motivated. Just as importantly, the content should be familiar to the teacher so that the students will view the teacher as a specialist who is comfortable with the content. When students in an ESL writing course represent a diverse collection of majors, most of which do not overlap with the teacher's own academic background, choosing suitable content can be challenging. (See Figure 1 for guidelines for choosing suitable content.)

One choice of content that may be suitable in such an ESL writing instruction context is *second language learning*, which is relevant to the students in the course because they are second language (L2) learners. This content is also familiar to many ESL writing teachers because of their training in teaching English to speakers of other languages, education, or linguistics. Casanave (2003) described the use of similar content (i.e., applied linguistics content) in an English for academic purposes course for graduate students. In contrast, this chapter focuses on an undergraduate setting, examining the usefulness of L2 learning content in one section of a required ESL writing course.

CURRICULUM, TASKS, MATERIALS

Curriculum Structure

This curriculum innovation included both structural and procedural parts. The two main structural parts were (a) a package of authentic readings with subject matter related to L2 learning and (b) writing assignments that were text-responsible.

Reading Materials

The authentic readings included six items related to the following four narrow topics (i.e., one for each of the four writing assignments):

- general characteristics of English education in other countries

- academic needs of ESL university students in the United States

- effective strategies for ESL writers

- computer-assisted language learning (CALL)

Is the content

- relevant to students' backgrounds (e.g., learning English as a second language), current situations (e.g., studying at a university), and interests (e.g., in technology)?
- accessible to students linguistically and conceptually (e.g., not too technical, not too long)?
- similar to the kind of content students will face in target contexts (e.g., academic)?
- familiar enough to the teacher that the students can view the teacher as a specialist who is comfortable with the content?

Figure 1. Tips for Selecting Content

These four topics were related to L2 learning and were meant to be relevant to the students' backgrounds as learners of English and to their current situations as ESL students at a university in the United States, as well as to their interests in computers and technology.

The six items in the reading package included articles and book chapters that were related to these topics and that were linguistically and conceptually accessible to the students. These items were substantive in the sense that they provided information and ideas that were new to many of the students, but they were not too long or too technical. The items included two short book chapters that describe English education in the Philippines (Espinosa, 1998) and Thailand (Pibulchol, 1998), one academic journal article that describes an empirical study of ESL students' academic language needs (Zhu & Flaitz, 2005), one academic journal article that describes an empirical study of strategies used by ESL writers (Wolfersberger, 2003), and two shorter articles that describe CALL (Chao, 2004; Kawabata, 2006).

Writing Assignments

The four major writing assignments, which were designed to require students to draw on the information from the authentic readings, comprised the second structural part of the curriculum innovation. Besides being text-responsible, these assignments also had to address the learning outcomes targeted in the course textbook so that the students would have opportunities to demonstrate these learning outcomes. The main part of the course textbook is divided into seven chapters based on seven different purposes for writing: (a) to describe personal experience, (b) to describe observations, (c) to inform, (d) to solve problems, (e) to evaluate, (f) to persuade, and (g) to respond. Therefore, the four writing prompts were designed to address one or two of these purposes and to reflect all seven purposes collectively:

- **Assignment 1:** Describe the English education system in your country. Compare this to the English education system in the United States and to the systems we have read about (i.e., Thailand and/or the Philippines).

- **Assignment 2:** Describe an academic problem that is faced by international students at this university. Relate this to published research on students' academic needs. Propose a practical solution to this problem.

- **Assignment 3:** Describe the strategies you use to write in English. Relate this to published research on writing strategies. Evaluate suggestions about using writing strategies.

- **Assignment 4:** Describe the pros and cons of CALL, based on an analysis of published discussions. Discuss the possibility of using CALL for ESL writing education at this university.

Each of the assignments also included suggestions that referred students to the relevant chapters or articles from the reading package and textbook, requirements (e.g., length), and grading criteria (i.e., content, organization, vocabulary, language use, and mechanics).

Curricular Procedures

To address the four major writing assignments during the 15-week term, the basic framework of the course consisted of four similar cycles, each lasting seven or eight class sessions.

1. At the beginning of each cycle, students were given instructions for the major writing assignment.

2. Throughout the cycle, material from the course textbook was discussed and practiced. This material included (a) various writing strategies, such as describing by providing details or explaining by using definitions and (b) basic structural features, such as paragraph development, sentence structure, grammar, and vocabulary.

3. In the middle of the cycle, students brought their rough drafts of the assignment to class to share with peers and receive feedback from peers, as well as to submit for teacher feedback.

4. At the end of the cycle, students handed in their final draft of the assignment to be graded.

Beyond this basic framework, the procedure had to be different from the other sections of the course because time had to be made in each cycle to discuss the reading content. This was done at the beginning of each of the four cycles. For example, when the first assignment was introduced, the students discussed the characteristics of English education systems in their home countries. Then, for homework, the students read the two short book chapters on English education in Thailand and the Philippines. In the following class, there was a discussion of these chapters, which allowed the students to share the similarities and differences between English education in the countries they had read about as compared to English education in their home countries. Similarly, when the second assignment was introduced, the students worked in small groups to complete the task outlined in Figure 2.

The class discussed the groups' responses, and then for homework they read an article describing a research study on ESL students' academic language needs. In the subsequent class, there was a discussion of the similarities and differences between the research plan the student groups had proposed and the research design described in the article.

Another procedural part of this curriculum innovation involved using unannounced reading quizzes throughout the term to encourage the students to read

---

Discussion Task

Develop a plan for a research study to answer this question: What are the academic language needs of international students at American universities? (For example, what data would you gather? How would you gather these data?) Briefly describe the results that you anticipate.

Figure 2. Small-Group Task for Second Assignment

the package of authentic texts. The reading quizzes were easy for students who had done the required reading, but they were difficult for students who had not. For example, the quiz that followed the article describing an empirical study of strategy use among ESL writers had six multiple-choice questions, including the following:

This study used _____ to gather data.

(a) classroom observations   (b) multiple-choice tests
(c) think-alouds   (d) questionnaires

Only those students who had done the required reading would know the answers.

A final procedural part of this curriculum innovation was that for any short, in-class writing activities the students did, instead of random subject matter, the students wrote about something relevant to the subject matter of the upcoming assignment. For example, for one in-class writing task during the fourth cycle in the course, the students were given the following prompt: Write a paragraph describing a benefit of CALL.

Outcomes of the Innovation

This curriculum innovation has had a positive impact on learning outcomes. The four assignments allowed students to demonstrate most, if not all, of the learning outcomes that were targeted across sections of the ESL writing course, including techniques for (a) developing content by using description, exemplification, and definition; (b) organizing with an appropriate thesis statement, topic sentences, and unified, coherent paragraphs; and (c) using suitable and accurate language. However, the assignments also allowed students to demonstrate learning outcomes that may be less typical of ESL writing courses. To illustrate, several excerpts from students' final drafts of assignments are presented in this section. (In these excerpts, names have been changed to preserve confidentiality, but nothing else has been modified.)

The first excerpt, which was a paragraph from the middle of the second main assignment, was written by Timothy, a computer systems engineering major. In his four-page paper, Timothy described several academic language needs faced by international students; the following paragraph focuses on one of those needs.

Excerpt 1

Verbal communication skill is the most important and fundamental for International Students at ASU. Therefore, my writing contradicts the published research, in which Zhu and Flaitz (2005, p. 11) concluded that "good writing skills are perceived to be the international student's most critical area of need". To overcome this problem, they can go to writing center and ask for advice how to improve their writing. However, it is important for them to be able to address their problem as clear as possible so they can let the instructor to understand their problem. Therefore, verbal communication is treated as their first aid. Thus, it is obvious that English verbal communication skill is very important and yet difficult for International Students at ASU.

This excerpt illustrates one of the main features of the curriculum innovation: Rather than writing based only on personal experience, this writing was text-responsible. In this excerpt, the use of the citation and quote is an indication that Timothy had done the required background reading. However, a closer look at Timothy's use of this source is interesting. First, he focused on the conclusion made by the researchers, which shows his understanding of the hierarchy of information. Second, he pointed out that his own idea about the importance of verbal communication skills contradicted his source's. Given that the research article came from a peer-reviewed scholarly journal, Timothy's disagreement with this source is notable because students often accept ideas presented in published texts as "fact." This is an example of higher order thinking, a primary goal of most academic courses.

The second excerpt, which was a paragraph from the middle of the third main assignment, was written by Ariel, a speech and hearing science major. In her four-page paper, Ariel described several writing strategies that she used in her university work. This paragraph focuses on one of those strategies:

Excerpt 2

While drafting, I am constantly revising and rehearsing my work to keep me on the right track of my ideas. It is easy to lose track of one's ideas when writing in L2. I am constantly thinking in both languages and translating as I go along writing my paper, going back a couple of sentences to ensure than I keep on the same idea or than I am transitioning into a new idea smoothly. Rehearsing is a helpful strategy since it gives you an overall look at the material and ideas you are writing about. It also allows you to correct previous and interconnected ideas. As shown in Wolferberger's (2003) study this is a strategy used for students in their composing process. Rehearsing and revising allows one to create more ideas and to bring new text for the draft. Going back and rereading one's work does not mean correcting grammar and structure. Its main purpose is to develop more ideas and to make sure you are on the right track with the content. Correcting will come later in editing and seeking assistance.

Excerpt 2 illustrates another feature of the curriculum innovation: Connections are made between students' personal experience and the content. In this excerpt, Ariel described her own drafting process and then linked it to the required reading on strategy use. Throughout the course, the students had been told that one way to communicate their understanding of an idea to their readers is to link the concept to personal experience. The link that Ariel made demonstrates her understanding of *rehearsing*, a concept that had been presented in the article that the class read. This link also stimulated Ariel to reflect on her own L2 learning experience. Besides describing her drafting process, Ariel evaluated it by referring to it as "helpful" and by explaining that it "allows" several important composing behaviors. In this way, the subject matter of the assignment gave this student a lens for critical examination of her own L2 learning experience. In other words, instead of only practicing various L2 writing strategies as a student might do in a traditional ESL writing course, she was able to look behind the scenes at actual research on L2 writing strategy use, which gave her an interesting perspective from which to examine her own use of L2 writing strategies.

The third, and final, excerpt was a paragraph from the middle of the third main assignment. This excerpt was written by Yasuko, a secondary education major. In her four-page paper, Yasuko discussed the use of CALL, and this paragraph focuses on one of the advantages:

Excerpt 3

Second, CALL permits great interaction by communication. Kawabata (2006) mentions the authentic language text. Through the internet, everybody can discover thousands of fresh and worldwide information sources. So students can reach authentic reading materials 24 hours a day and wherever they are. And the internet gives students the chance of communicative and authentic language uses with speakers of the target language by e-mails, web boards, or chat-rooms. As for chatting, the growth of audio- and audio-visual chatting enables the real-time conversation. Furthermore, CALL enables immediate feedback between teachers and students by e-mail in the outside of a classroom. The communicative interaction must promote language learning significantly.

Excerpt 3 illustrates one more feature of the curriculum innovation: Exposure to and use of language from an academic discourse community broadens students' ability to understand and use essential academic vocabulary from different disciplines. The excerpt includes terms (e.g., *authentic, communicative*) that had been used in the required reading and that are key terms in the L2 learning discourse community. Unless Yasuko is going to study or work in this particular community in the future, she will not likely need to use these terms in quite the same way again. However, Yasuko's use of these terms demonstrates a general strategy: When she did the required reading on CALL, she identified several key terms and then incorporated those terms into her own writing for the assignment. Being able to identify and then correctly use key terms in a given area is a strategy that can be transferred across disciplines.

These examples of students' writing reflect the positive impact that this curriculum innovation had on learning outcomes. Another perspective worth considering, though, is the students' attitudes toward the curriculum innovation. Throughout the term, the students displayed favorable attitudes toward the course and the innovation. In fact, most students participated in discussions of the required readings and made an effort to do well on the writing assignments and quizzes. However, on the formal course evaluation completed by students at the end of the term, this section of the ESL writing course was rated below the average for the course. Some of their comments are relevant to the curriculum innovation. When asked to identify the least helpful elements of the course, some comments had to do with the CBI nature of the course and the L2 learning content (these quotations from student evaluations are unmodified):

- I don't know, but I think the CALL will be the least.

- Reading assignments were least helpful.

- Internet articles (some were hard to find).

- (least) quizzes = even I read the reading, it doesn't reflect on the quizzes most of the time.

The evaluation form also allowed the students to make general comments about the course. Two of these student comments reflected the CBI nature of the course:

- I love writing stories, so I wasn't really happy that we didn't get to write stories like 'a day I will never forget' and stuff like that.

- The essay (assignment) toppics should be more challenging and leave space for creativity!

Given the positive impact this curriculum innovation had had on learning outcomes, the students' ratings of and comments about the course were somewhat disappointing. Nevertheless, they provide a perspective that has to be considered.

REFLECTIONS

The concern that motivated this curriculum innovation was with differences between this ESL writing course and other academic courses in terms of the kind of writing students were doing. The introduction of a CBI approach involving L2 learning content was effective because it provided a rationale for students to experience text-responsible writing. Through this writing, the students practiced and demonstrated various writing and critical thinking skills, and they reflected on their experiences as ESL writers.

Besides these learning outcomes, several more general conclusions can be drawn about this use of L2 learning content. First, L2 learning content is relevant to students in an ESL writing course. Although the students in this course came from diverse backgrounds and academic disciplines, they had one important characteristic in common: They all had plenty of experience learning and using English as a second language. As a result, all of them were able to relate, on at least some level, to the content they were discussing, reading, and writing about for the major assignments. This is not always the case with content that is used in CBI. Also, in their assignments, the students were able to write about abstract ideas and link them to concrete, personal experiences. In this way, the use of L2 learning content brings together the benefits of personal writing and CBI.

Second, in an ESL writing course, L2 learning content is accessible to students. For example, in the article that described a research study of the needs of ESL students at English-medium universities (Zhu & Flaitz, 2005), the students read about research techniques and abstract notions such as *cultural competence* and *classroom norms*. Having the students deal with technical, challenging content was beneficial because it paralleled their experiences in their courses in other disciplines. However, the L2 learning content was particularly effective in this sense: Because it was personally relevant to the students, it was relatively accessible.

Using L2 content in an ESL writing course has one more benefit: the teacher's familiarity with the content. In this particular course, because I had previously received teacher training and studied L2 education, being the "content expert" during class discussions or when working one-on-one with the students was a comfortable role. This meant that the students were guided not only in their use of various writing skills and strategies but also in their understanding and use of the content they were reading and writing about. When students summarized information from readings to use in their assignments, they could get help focusing on important ideas from an L2 learning specialist in ways that would not have been possible had the subject matter been related to other disciplines, such as chemistry or history. Since the course assignments required text-responsible writing, holding students accountable for the various texts was relatively easy because I was familiar with the content. Calling the students' attention to key technical vocabulary and monitoring their use of this language was second nature to me. One final benefit was that the students themselves could view the instructor as a content specialist, as they do in their other academic courses.

However, the importance of treating all students in multiple sections of ESL writing courses comparably must be considered. In this particular course, although the students practiced and developed writing skills that would be useful in their other courses, they were not completely positive about the instructional approach. The fact that this innovation was made in only one section of a multi-section course may have been problematic. While students in this section were doing required readings and text-responsible writing assignments, students in the other sections of the same course were doing nontext-responsible assignments, so students could view this section of the course as being more difficult or requiring more work than other sections. One way to avoid this perception might have been to try the curriculum innovation in one section of the course for only part of the term. Another way might have been to try the curriculum innovation in all sections of the course simultaneously. A third way might have been to try the innovation in one section of the course and to make sure that other sections of the course required similar kinds of work from the students. The key would be to make sure students feel that different sections of the same course are comparable.

A CBI approach with L2 learning content can be used quite effectively for ESL writing instruction. This chapter focused on the context of a freshman ESL writing course at a university in the United States. Whether this particular instructional model can be adopted in other ESL writing instruction contexts in the same manner remains a question. The potential benefits of this approach, as have been described in this chapter, make it a worthwhile consideration.

Mark A. James is an assistant professor of applied linguistics at Arizona State University, in the United States. He has also taught ESL and applied linguistics courses at universities and language schools in Canada, Puerto Rico, and Japan. He is interested in curriculum, teaching, and learning issues in L2 education.

CHAPTER 6

Meaningful Writing Opportunities in the Community College: The Cultural and Linguistic Autobiography Writing Project

Gloria Park

Beginning in 2002, the Cultural and Linguistic Autobiography Writing Project (CLA) became a component of the preacademic adult English as a second language (ESL) writing curriculum at Montgomery College. The rationale for designing and implementing this project was borne out of the necessity to create more meaningful writing topics in academic writing courses for university-bound students enrolled in a community college preacademic ESL program. Even with the best intentions of teachers wanting to promote a student-centered learning atmosphere in ESL classrooms, the students are often asked to produce writing tasks that have minimal, if any, connection to their multilingual and multicultural immigrant experiences. This disconnectedness discourages students from gaining interest in writing in the English language, thus creating further challenges when trying to improve writing skills. In a 16-week-long, project-based writing course, one pedagogical initiative promoting student-centered writing tasks involves having adult ESL students write about who they are and what they have experienced throughout their journeys in the United States or in other English-speaking countries (i.e., language and culture learning process) (See Brisk, 1998; Meyers, 2000; Ovando, Combs, & Collier, 2006; Park, 2007; Park & Suarez, 2007; Wu, 1994).

As a second language student, my own lived experiences were based on passive instruction and traditional, teacher-centered activities (Park, 2008) and, more often than not, involved teacher-generated writing topics that had nothing to do with my own dual identities as a second language learner and a visible minority woman. To bring the personal closer to the academic experiences, the CLA writing project became a major part of the reading and writing curriculum for intermediate and high-intermediate students at a large metropolitan community college offering a preacademic ESL program. In this chapter, the project will be described, followed by a description of materials.

CONTEXT

Montgomery College is a 2-year community college that caters to the educational and professional needs of Washington, DC, area residents. It houses the Workforce Development and Continuing Education (WD & CE) program, where the preacademic English language program is located. This program has expanded to four sites for students who reside and work in those locations. In addition to those sites, there are also special contract programs serving companies employing numerous immigrant workers and international expatriates.

The six components of the program goals have been created through dialogic exchanges among some of the instructors teaching in the preacademic ESL program at this community college and the program's director. Overall, the program provides a supportive environment in which learners, at their particular levels, engage in multiple learning activities whose goals center on the following six components:

- Develop speaking and writing skills to communicate effectively in everyday, social, academic, and professional situations.

- Develop listening and reading skills to understand and use information from a wide variety of oral, written, and technological sources.

- Become aware of their own individual learning styles and develop strategies to monitor and direct language learning as they pursue their personal, academic, and professional aspirations.

- Use life experiences and knowledge as they work cooperatively with others from diverse backgrounds to achieve learning goals.

- Develop the language skills and cultural knowledge needed to enter and participate successfully in U.S. academic and professional settings.

- Gain greater understanding of and sensitivity for other cultures in the classroom and within contemporary U.S. society as they negotiate their cultural identity.

These learning components, although specifically articulated for our community college adult ESL program, are an essential part of assisting ESL students from all academic and professional backgrounds to reach their highest English language proficiency level and to overcome any cultural and racial barriers in negotiating their identities in U.S. academic and social contexts.

Ovando, Combs, and Collier (2006) state that helping students access different learning goals and identity options within and beyond classroom contexts should be an ongoing assessment tool used by all teachers, especially ESL teachers. Furthermore, other scholars have demonstrated how individuals from linguistically, culturally, and racially diverse backgrounds are often targets for discrimination and marginalization (Kubota, 2004; Kubota & Lin, 2006; Nieto, 1999, 2002; Park, 2006). To minimize these marginalizing practices and at the same time improve ESL students' linguistic proficiency levels, there should be an urgent call to tap into the ways in which writing topics can encourage students to write about their lived experiences. This practice would help students gain greater understanding of and sensitivity to other cultures represented within and beyond academic communities. One conceptual response to this call is to have students engage in personal narrative writings that provide meaningful ways to connect their academic learning with their personal journeys, which could help adult ESL students validate their experiences in the United States (i.e., Pavlenko, 2003). In this way, adult ESL students not only engage in meaningful genre production, but they also work on developing our program goals.

CURRICULUM, TASKS, MATERIALS

The Cultural and Linguistic Autobiography (CLA) Writing Project

The specifics of this project were borne of crafting my own autobiography and negotiating my linguistic, cultural, and racial identities as a second language learner and a visible minority woman (Park, 2004; Park & Suarez, 2007). The goal in instituting this project in academic writing courses is to provide students with a comfortable and learner-friendly environment conducive to using a new language, exploring each other's cultures, and providing a place for humanness in the learning sphere (i.e., Freire, 1998; Price & Osborne, 2000). This, in turn, helps validate students' linguistic, cultural, racial, and gendered identities so that they can make connections between their home lives and their lives in school and work. Since the summer of 2002, in multiple sections of an academic writing course, this project has been implemented in accordance with the writing needs and goals of the students.

Birth of the CLA Writing Project in 2002

The introduction of this project to adult ESL students began with its conceptual framework. First, the concept of autobiography (Florio-Ruane, 2001; Pavlenko, 2003) was introduced, and I shared with my adult ESL students that I had also completed an autobiography with my professor. In that, my understanding of myself and my experiences as a second language learner and an ESL teacher helped me to understand my students better. I was given a variety of questions to respond to in crafting my own autobiography. However, the adult ESL students' autobiographies needed to have specific language learning and culture learning questions that they may not have had opportunities to write about in other academic settings. To this end, questions were designed and separated into four parts: (a) Part I: Write about yourself and your family, (b) Part II: Write about your language learning experience, (c) Part III: Write about your culture learning experience, and (d) Part IV: Epilogue. The following sample questions were given to the learners:

- Write about yourself, your work, and your hobbies.

- Write about your childhood memories.

- Describe your early schooling experiences.

- Write about your feelings when you first decided to or had to come to the United States.

- Write about some difficulties or challenges you had in this new country (other than the language learning difficulties).

- Write about an interesting experience you had with a native speaker of English. What happened? Was it a pleasant or embarrassing experience? How did you feel, and how do you feel now?

- Write about your initial English language learning experience in this country.

- Write about an experience you've had with a language other than English. How did you learn it? Who did you use it with?

- Write a description of a letter to a friend or relative in your home country who is planning to immigrate to this country. What advice do you have for this person?

- Describe your experience. What have you gained? What have you learned about yourself while completing this autobiography writing project?

The writing prompts were dispersed throughout the chapters, and each class utilized the writing process approach in completing the autobiographical narratives. For beginning writers, I gave feedback on the initial draft; then the students revised and submitted a final second draft. For those students whose narratives needed more work, the process was repeated until their stories clearly communicated what the students wanted to express. With advanced writers, there were a few peer editing and commenting sessions in addition to teacher feedback. Toward the end of each course, the class compiled all of the CLA writings into a bound book of narratives, and each student was provided with a copy of the book.

REFLECTIONS

In the preliminary stage of introducing the CLA writing projects in the adult ESL writing courses, I was apprehensive. Such a project involves emotions connected to reliving one's memories. However, as a nonnative-English-speaking teacher, I quickly overcame the feeling of apprehension since in many ways, constructing my own autobiography was therapeutic for me. I am reminded that my journey is not that different from what my adult ESL students may be facing in the United States. When I began to share my own history with my students, I often saw them indicating that they, too, had stories to tell. Ever since that awakening, I have had success in engaging students in producing personal, lengthy, and detailed narratives. At times, writing in English is very challenging for them, but continuous mentoring and guidance throughout the writing process has been successful.

Many students are ready and willing to share their stories of triumphs and challenges; however, immigrant students' stories are not often heard or read. Providing opportunities for students to write about their lived experiences is a powerful pedagogical tool that not only empowers their ever-changing identities, but also guides them in continuously improving their English proficiency. Although this writing project was designed and implemented in adult ESL courses housed in a community college, it can be adapted for all grade, language, and content levels. By tweaking the writing prompts or including a variety of readings, the students can begin to write their way toward better understanding themselves as learners.

Gloria Park currently teaches at Indiana University of Pennsylvania, in the United States. She has also taught teaching English to speakers of other languages at the University of Maryland, College Park, and ESL at Montgomery College, both in the United States. Her areas of research and teaching interests are experiential writing pedagogy and equity issues in second language and teacher education.

CHAPTER 7

Media Participation as an End Point for Authentic Writing and Autonomous Learning

Stephen Soresi

The benefits of authenticity in second language (L2) education have been well documented (Breen, 1985, Peacock, 1997). These discussions often involve authentic L2 materials, or "text authenticity," used for *receptive* skills, such as reading or listening (Day, 2004; Morrison, 1989; Sanderson, 1999); however, this chapter shows how a *productive* skill, writing, can also benefit by employing an authentic end point.

This chapter details a practice for engendering writing skills using both an internal end point (i.e., peer review) and an authentic external end point for written work (i.e., media participation through letters to the editor, reader's forums, and essay contests). Which of those formats worked best in practice and which corresponding in-class writing tasks were the most effective will be addressed in this chapter.

CONTEXT

The practices and suggestions here are based on my experimentation with media participation over 3 years with nearly 300 Japanese university students. These students, representing a wide range of language abilities, submitted essays to different media outlets. Prior to submission, all students received regular in-class feedback on their drafts from three internal end points: (a) Individual peer review comments and a rubric score, (b) general teacher comments (i.e., not specific proofreading of each work), and (c) an in-class vote for the best essay of the day. Based on this review process, students revised and edited their essays weekly.

Most made autonomous efforts to learn from, keep up with, and compete with their peers.

The teacher commented on some common discourse-level errors instead of each sentence's error. Within this context, such microlinguistic feedback can send the writer a potentially damaging message that sentence syntax is more important than macrolinguistic, or discourse level, concerns, such as cohesion, development, and clarity. Those factors were encouraged through peer review by using a unique rating scale that rewards macrolinguistic writing skills.

Two aspects of the writing abilities of Japanese young adults are widely known in English language teaching circles. First, Japanese university students are considered false beginners with 6 or more years of English language education, but minimal demonstrable language skills, especially in writing or speaking (Grundy, 1994). Even those with high marks in English courses may lack writing skills because most students and teachers study English to prepare for high school and university entrance exams, which employ multiple choice, fill-in-the-blank, or other psychometric testing methods. Because those tests do not directly measure writing or speaking, those language skills are undervalued in favor of strategic learning for tests based on extremely detailed aspects of certain language forms (Brown, 2000).

Second, when most Japanese students compose a persuasive essay for submission to print media, one common problem is excessively long descriptions of background information preceding their main point. For example, in an essay questioning the prime minister's policies, some students might start with "Mr. XYZ is the Prime Minister of Japan." Or "Mr. ABC became Prime Minister this summer."

In my experience, Japanese learners at the university level do not seem to write according to a singular rhetorical preference. Rather, their various writing issues could be collectively related to a lack of writing experience. Specifically, students are not accustomed to expressing themselves in English in written or spoken form; thus, nearly all students' writing exhibits cross-lingual issues.

CURRICULUM, TASKS, MATERIALS

Classroom Practices

Offering participation in the mass media alone did not solve a major issue of low homework completion rates. Many Japanese university students expect their lessons to be based on completion of a textbook, submission of a final essay, or passing a final exam (McVeigh, 2002). Many do not expect to think, write, rethink, and rewrite meaningful compositions. Thus, certain classroom practices were necessary to help ensure that all students would participate in the writing process. The following information describes the practices that increased the homework completion rate and ensured that students' writing would be process-oriented.

Especially for weaker and less motivated students, an assignment based on a sentence count was a good place to start (e.g., "Write seven sentences about the homework topic. If you are able, please vary sentence patterns by using simple, compound, and compound–complex sentences."). Once everyone had participated in the initial assignment, then the number of required sentences was increased for subsequent rewrites.

The use of a sentence count was also more compatible with the aims and process this writing class followed. For example, when rewriting, students had to enhance their essays by incorporating new sentences and expanding existing ones to offer specific examples, supplemental explanations, comparisons, or contrasts. Such advice for rewrites naturally added sentences, contributing to the comprehensibility of their essay while constructively focusing their attention on effective communication.

Just before submitting their essays to media outlets, students checked their word counts, but requiring a specific word count can create problems. The most serious were that students strung out sentences unnecessarily and avoided short sentences. In this way, requiring a word count without paying adequate attention to the content of each sentence could indirectly hinder comprehensibility.

Using an increasing sentence count for several rounds of rewrites also served as a countermeasure to an increasingly serious issue: translation software use. Free online software can produce a quick, but awkward, translation of text from L1 to L2. The temptation for students to use the software is made even stronger when the writing assignment is product-oriented rather than process-oriented.

Classroom Management

Each class's peer review system started by circulating the completed homework essays. Those with completed assignments sat in the front rows, exchanged essays, and engaged in peer review. Those without homework could not join the peer review, so they sat in the back of the classroom and worked independently to complete their homework. This positioning alone objectively admonished those who were not prepared for class. In the group-conscious Japanese society, this practice improved homework completion rates. Teachers with students from different cultures may find that more openly punitive measures work better.

Classroom Peer Review With the CDEFG Scale

Peer review was based on the clarity, development, entertainment value, fresh perspective, and grammar (CDEFG) scale, which enforces discourse-level factors. Allowing approximately 5 minutes for 150- to 300-word essays, teachers should begin the peer review with a clarity check as round 1. Students pass their essay to a classmate who rates only its clarity on a scale of 1 to 10 written under the "C" on the CDEFG scale (see Table 1), with 1 ranking low and 10 ranking high. After this, the essays are passed to the next person for round 2, in which students rate

Table 1. A Sample of a Peer-Completed CDEFG Rubric Scale

Rating Round	C Clarity	D Development	E Entertainment Value	F Fresh Perspective	G Grammar
Round 1	8	—	—	—	—
Round 2	7	8	6	—	—
Round 3	7	7	6	9	—
Round 4	8	9	7	8	9
Round 5	7	8	6	8	9

Note. The CDEFG scale is handwritten following the drafts of students' short essays, which are then circulated to peers for ratings. Peers score only for "C" (clarity) in round 1, so the other traits are left blank, represented by "—" in the table. For round 2, peers score only "CDE," and "FG" are blank. For round 3, peers rate "CDEF" and leave "G" blank. For rounds 4 and 5, all traits are scored.

clarity, development, and entertainment value, or "CDE." Basically, students ask themselves, "Is this essay clear, well-developed, and entertaining?" For the next round, students expand the scale to include "F," fresh perspective, to determine whether the essay offers an original point of view. Finally, in rounds 4 and 5, the students also consider "G," grammatical accuracy, so each trait gets a score (see Table 1 for a completed CDEFG rubric).

Round 1: Clarity ("C") assessment: Is every sentence clear? Does every sentence communicate its meaning?

Round 2: Repeat the "C" assessment.
Development ("D") assessment: Is the essay well developed with logical examples and details?
Entertainment ("E") assessment: Is the essay entertaining or engaging? Does it keep the reader interested?

Round 3: Repeat the "CDE" assessments.
Fresh perspective ("F") assessment: Does the essay have a fresh perspective and an original point of view?

Round 4: Repeat "CDEF" assessments.
Grammar ("G") assessment: Does the author use good grammatical structures to express ideas?

Round 5: "CDEFG" assessments are made a final time.

Based on feedback from the CDEFG scale and the teacher's overall advice, students rewrite their essays, and the in-class peer review process is repeated several times. The students self-edit a final time before sending a final copy by e-mail to both the newspaper and the instructor.

Some optional classroom practices for the peer review include

- Writing peer comments: To supplement their CDEFG scoring, peers write comments on each essay. One caveat was that the seriousness, frankness, and effectiveness of comments varied widely.

- Voting for the best essay: After circulating and evaluating five fellow students' essays, each student votes for the best one. This can be considered an authentic internal end point for their writing if students vote sincerely and those receiving votes value the outcome.

- Checking the clarity of each sentence: Students place either a star or a question mark at the end of each sentence to indicate whether it is clear or not.

- Checking cohesion between each sentence: Students evaluate the cohesion between each sentence by putting either a dash for clear cohesion or a triangle when they are not sure of the cohesion. This option works best for essays shorter than 20 sentences.

- Evaluating the essay "face": Students evaluate only the title and first five lines of an essay. The CDEFG scale can be used.

- Editing: Students make suggestions about grammar, syntax, spelling, etc., whenever they notice an error.

Classroom Curriculum Caveats

One consideration when adopting this approach to teaching writing is that group dynamics affect peer evaluation, as students may be anxious about offending others and insecure about their own language ability and authority. As a countermeasure, the rating system outlined here allows peer feedback to be indirect, while still addressing the content, clarity, development, and coherence of the essay.

Another consideration is to determine what kind of media is best for student participation. A letter to the editor may be the first thing that comes to mind, and for some Japanese universities' English language programs, such a submission is a course requirement. However, in practice, letters to the editor did not work as well as another newspaper format, the monthly readers' forum on special topics, which asks readers to write about a specific topic and submit 150- to 300-word essays. The newspaper then selects 20 to 30 short essays for publication. The letter to the editor format proved more problematic in practice than the readers' forum for the following reasons:

- Readers' forum essays require expressing an opinion about a predetermined issue. For a letter to the editor, many students were not able to formulate a salient main point beyond their personal feelings, despite repeated rounds of revisions and exposure to examples of assertive or persuasive essays. Therefore, their discussions of "bad news," such as crime, followed a similar pattern as discussions of "good news," such as space exploration, in which their main points never evolved beyond personal reactions, such as "I was surprised." In short, their letters to the editor resembled a conversational diary entry. On the other hand, the readers' forum forced them to deal with topics, such as "Do you oppose or support the death penalty?" which elicited their opinions more effectively. However, by the time students started developing clear assertions in their letters to the editor, the rewrite process had begun to drag, causing overall fatigue with the task.

- Uniform topics promoted deeper thinking about a single topic. For this learning context, fixed topics were much more effective in practice than allowing students to write about any topic. With a letter to the editor, students took on different topics, making it difficult for the teacher to give appropriate and compelling advice to the class as a whole.

- For the peer review process, diverse topics did not work as well as uniform topics. First, during peer reading, a common topic meant that every essay that students read was directly relevant to their own effort. More importantly, a uniform topic helped students quickly comprehend, then learn and borrow from each others' essays.

- Media publishing practices favored classroom participation in the readers' forum. One problem with using the letter to the editor as an end point involves the timing and certainty about whether students' essays were published by the newspaper or not. Letters to the editor in the local English language dailies in Japan are often published without informing the writer. The readers' forum, on the other hand, was published on a set date, so most participants bought the paper that day and clearly knew which students did or did not have their essays published, which made for a more satisfactory closure to the process. Overall learning impact can be affected by this and other factors (see Table 2).

Classroom Participation in a Media-Sponsored Essay Contest

A third type of written media participation experimented with is a newspaper-sponsored essay contest, which provides an authentic end point for students' compositions and motivates them to craft a longer essay about social issues. Some problems, however, include the fact that in the end, very few people win the contest, so rarely do students' essays appear in the newspaper. Furthermore, the contest schedule left too much time between students' submissions and the announcement of the results, causing loss of interest.

Submitting essays to local newspapers meant that students had to deal with topics that may not be intrinsically interesting to them, such as the ban on beef imports, the prime minister's fiscal policies, or whaling prohibition. Other topics that were familiar to them were sacrificed for the prestige of dealing with and

Table 2. Comparison of the Three Media Formats Used as Writing End Points

Factors & Features	Essay Contest	Letter to the Editor	Monthly Reader's Forum
Extra Reward	Prestige and Money	Prestige	Prestige
Topic	Choice from three	Open	One set topic
Number of Revisions	10–12	3–7	2–4
Publication	Set date	No set date	Set date
Time until published	5 weeks	Varies	1 week
Maximum Length	800 words	300 words	300 words
Major Caveat	Long process causes fatigue	Open-topic choice causes problems	Political topic is disliked by some students
Peer Review Considerations	Much content convergence among students	Having diverse topics limits learning from others' essays	Same topic enables learning among classmates

publishing essays on more serious themes. Of course, simply conveying the topic to them was not enough. They needed background information on most issues, or they needed to have the topics modified to more manageable questions. For example, instead of the newspaper's topic ("Do you expect the new Cabinet to stay the course?") students answered a related topic ("Which Cabinet member are you interested in, and what do you want him or her to do?")

Many students found all news topics difficult or uninteresting. If this were the case, they were encouraged to write exactly why that topic was difficult or boring so that they could build their main point as an assertion or suggestion from there.

When students tried to explain their views of current events, clarity suffered. Some students attempted direct translations of comments that they saw in the newspaper or on television. Others tried to use what they considered "advanced" vocabulary or terminology without offering any supplemental explanation. This occurred despite instructions to students to make their points with simple and clear language, rather than specialized political terminology (see Table 3 for topic examples).

REFLECTIONS

Media participation is not a perfectly authentic task, nor can it be a magic motivational factor inducing instant learner autonomy. Media participation and the peer review system prior to submission were designed to "create the atmosphere and conditions in which (learners) will feel encouraged to develop the autonomy they already have" (Benson, 2003, p. 305). Knowing their essays would be reviewed

Table 3. News and Current Events Topics Covered

Media Format	Topic
The Daily Yomiuri's monthly readers' forum on news topics	Do you support or oppose lifting the ban on importing U.S. and Canadian beef?
	Evaluate the outgoing prime minister's policies.
	Should a whaling moratorium continue or be terminated?
	Do you support or oppose the death penalty?
	How can we help reduce poverty?
	Does the chirping of spring birds and autumn insects sound like music?
	Do you expect the new Cabinet to stay the course?
Letters to the editor (Headlines were proofread and enhanced by the newspaper's editors.)	Government should offer training for pet owners.
	Parenting is a simple, but demanding, duty.
	Patriotic education should not be connected to militarism.
	Learn about people with disabilities through service dogs.
	Workplaces should adopt realistic views on smoking.
	Does a good education determine your earning potential?
The Asahi Herald sponsored essay contest	Should Japan encourage international student exchanges?
	What is it that makes the Japanese culture appealing and how can this country's culture be conveyed to the world?
	How to best utilize information technology in college
	What I hope to be in 20 years
	What I propose or am doing about global warming
	How can media, including newspapers, affect daily life?

and voted on by peers and understanding that eventually their essays would be submitted to newspapers, students invested extra effort to sharpen their writing skills and to learn from their classmates' compositions.

While a few participants' submissions were accepted for publication in local news media outlets in Japan, many were not. Such "failure" did not seem to decrease motivation. On the contrary, many students doubled their efforts to compose solid, short essays, mostly for the thrill and prestige of having a piece of writing published in the paper. Also, many realized that media participation was achievable thanks to their few successfully published classmates.

Written work was sent to media outlets "as is." No student was expected to produce error-free essays, which obviously left much of their original phrasing or word choices intact. From a research perspective, the lasting benefits of syntax and grammar correction have been thoroughly debated (Ferris, 2004), but it was interesting in this case to also see how students' English was treated by local news media. In fact, certain nonnative speaker word choices and use of loan words were left intact and published by local media. The linguistic gate-keeping function of a teacher who asserts monocentric native speaker norms may differ from gate-keeping standards of local news media. This may be one way that English evolves into a pluracentric language (Kachru, 2005). In other words, certain nonnative speaker L2 forms may make some teachers cringe, but they develop and function legitimately in certain speech communities, such as Japanese participating in local English language media.

ACKNOWLEDGMENTS

I appreciate Professors Yuko Takeshita's and Tak Suzuki's valuable input, as well as Seo Sanae's support.

Stephen Soresi teaches in Yokohama, Japan, at Toyo Eiwa University's Department of Social Sciences. He has a doctorate from the Aoyama Gakuin University's Graduate School for International Communication.

Focusing on Academic and Professional Writing Skills

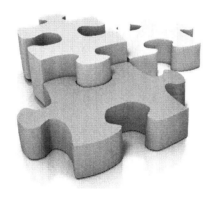

CHAPTER 8

Multitext Synthesizing in Research Writing

Amina M. B. Megheirbi

As students pursue their academic studies in institutions of higher education, they are expected to perform tasks that involve processing written, and sometimes aural, input to construct a meaningful written or oral output. According to Jordan (1997), the integration or synthesizing of information from multiple sources "has received little attention" in academic writing courses (p. 171). In fact, many English as a second language (ESL) writing courses focus on the expression of the students' own ideas and experiences. This chapter focuses on teaching ESL students essential language skills incorporating source materials into their own academic writing.

Assuming that students can construct meaningful output based on intertext conceptual linkage without adequate practice is an overestimation of their capabilities. In a study conducted by Campbell (1990), students, both native and nonnative English speakers, were unable to integrate source information correctly into their own academic writing. Instead, they copied directly from their sources without adequate documentation. She recommends sequenced training and instruction to help students develop the skill of integrating texts from different sources to support their personal ideas.

CONTEXT

I conducted an investigation of academic research papers in English written by a group of university students from Garyounis University in Benghazi, Libya. In the final year of study, each student submits a research paper on a topic related to his or her major to fulfill graduation requirements. Twenty-five samples of these research papers, submitted between the years 2003 and 2005, were collected and examined. This study revealed that these students lacked the skills needed for linking information from multiple sources in order to produce coherent and cohesive academic writing. When dealing with multiple sources, students were unable to relate one text conceptually to another, to direct the flow of writing by using their own voice, or to integrate and synthesize information from multiple sources into their own writing.

These findings are similar to the findings of a previous needs assessment of ESL science students at the United Arab Emirates University in 1992. As a result, special writing tasks (miniprojects) were designed and implemented in the English for Science course to help students practice synthesizing source information (Megheirbi et al., 2003–2004). In these minitasks, students were presented with a research topic, an outline, and three to four short readings that contained information about the topic. Guided by the outline, they used the readings to write a short essay on the research topic.

CURRICULUM, TASKS, MATERIALS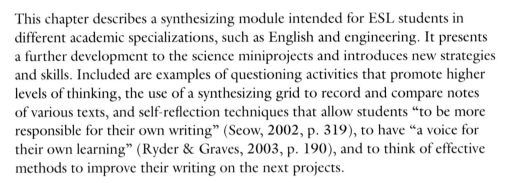

This chapter describes a synthesizing module intended for ESL students in different academic specializations, such as English and engineering. It presents a further development to the science miniprojects and introduces new strategies and skills. Included are examples of questioning activities that promote higher levels of thinking, the use of a synthesizing grid to record and compare notes of various texts, and self-reflection techniques that allow students "to be more responsible for their own writing" (Seow, 2002, p. 319), to have "a voice for their own learning" (Ryder & Graves, 2003, p. 190), and to think of effective methods to improve their writing on the next projects.

Synthesizing Module Overview

The main components of this module are miniprojects that are based on both a process and product approach to writing, integrating reading tasks with written outcomes. Students are encouraged to participate in collaborative learning that focuses their attention on conceptual relationships of various texts. The activities are also designed to encourage critical thinking (Scriven & Paul, 2001) by investigating a variety of subject-specific research topics.

Even though the synthesizing process looks linear, the stages of synthesizing are, in fact, recursive. For example, as students take notes they may return to the outline to expand or modify their ideas, and as they revise they may need to write another draft (see Figure 1).

The topics chosen for the miniprojects are related to students' content areas. Students will be more confident if they are exploring "topics more central to their academic and intellectual lives" (Leki & Carson, 1994, p. 93). These topics are intended to motivate them so that they "have an investment in examining [their writing], improving it, and eventually revising it for readers" (Raimes, 2002a, p. 309).

After topics are chosen, both practical and philosophical research questions are generated to examine the issues. Practical questions usually generate a problem–

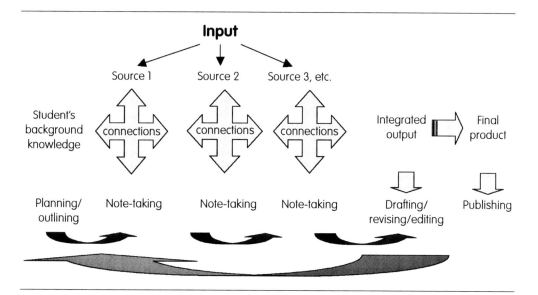

Figure 1. The Process of Synthesizing

solution approach, such as investigating problematic English sounds for Arabic learners. The philosophical questions involve discussing a topic and forming a point of view, such as political correctness in English or a cross-cultural examination of political correctness in translated texts.

After consulting with the core subject instructors, the writing teacher chooses relevant readings. Although the idea is to provide students with concise, manageable texts, it is essential that these texts contain enough information for the students to form and answer research questions.

During the initial stages, work on the research question and outline are guided, but not controlled, by the teacher. These activities, therefore, progress from explicit instructions to supportive instructions following a model that encourages a slow release of responsibility (Pearson & Gallagher, 1983). Students are, first, given adequate instructional support. This includes the following:

- direct written (or oral) explanations

- guided questions to help students recognize "how, why, and when to use strategies" (Ryder & Graves, 2003, p. 178)

- models to be followed, analyzed, or criticized

- mental modeling "to share the reasoning about strategy use in a natural, realistic context" (Ryder & Graves, 2003, p. 178)

When students are provided with enough modeling and coached practice at the initial stages of the learning process, they will be ready to use the strategies independently. This supportive instruction helps students progress in their use of strategies "from the role of active observers to autonomous learners" (Reppen, 2002, p. 322). At this stage, students are encouraged to ask their own questions in order to critically analyze the texts or to make intertext conceptual linkage, to construct their own outline, and to practice mental self-talk to monitor their learning of a specific skill or strategy.

This synthesizing module can be used as a separate course or can be embedded within a general research writing course. The general framework of this synthesizing module is based on the following assumptions:

- Synthesizing is a cognitive process that involves the utilization of topical knowledge as it deals with processing of information from different sources.

- Strategies need to be learned and applied in order to process multiple-source input successfully before trying to construct a meaningful output (Purpura, 2004).

- Strategies need to be reinforced "over new texts and tasks" so that "there is transfer of training from one type of text or task to another" (Janzen, 2002, p. 288).

- Reading skills are essential for the development of academic writing skills.

Miniproject Procedure

The synthesizing module has been presented in the writing course in seven sequential stages.

Stage 1: Introducing the Miniprojects

Students are introduced to the purpose of the synthesizing module so that they can engage in a meaningful learning experience. An analysis of synthesis models helps students visualize how integrated information is presented in written models. Students also look at each model critically to investigate the effectiveness of the presentation of integrated information, to pinpoint weaknesses, and to suggest possible methods of improvement. Last, the teacher and the students anticipate problems with application and negotiate approaches to facilitate the learning process.

Stage 2: Prewriting

As a prereading activity, students are presented with a question or a statement about a specific topic. The class discusses the issue to answer the question and to reflect on the statement while activating their prior knowledge and preparing to compose a research question. Then they are presented with three or four short texts on the research topic. As the module progresses, students are expected to search for some or all of the source texts. Working in small groups, students construct a tentative outline for a short essay that attempts to answer the research question.

Stage 3: Analyzing the Text

Students are asked to confirm that the information in the texts is relevant and appropriate for supporting their argument as it is stated in the outline. They work in small groups, using graphic organizers to help them understand the relationships of the ideas and to decide what information should appear in their essays.

A variety of activities in the synthesizing module are designed to facilitate critical analysis of texts. One of the most useful is asking questions that promote higher levels of thinking in order to

- identify the text's underlying structure by investigating its primary patterns of organization (e.g., how are the concepts and ideas presented?)

- understand the message of the text and evaluate how it is argued

- identify the author's purpose and tone

- connect effectively to what is read

Stage 4: Asking Questions

Sets of questions can be designed to help students comprehend each text, understand its underlying structure, and make cognitive connections. In the first few miniprojects, the questions are stated or generated by the teacher. Using "question stems designed to focus on the signal words" (Ryder & Graves, 2003, pp. 182–183), the teacher can train students to ask their own questions to analyze the texts and identify types of text structure. These include three levels of cognitively engaging types of questions developed by Pearson and Johnson (Ryder & Graves, 2003): text-explicit, text-implicit, and script-implicit questions. Text-explicit questions are aimed at comprehending the surface meaning and locating specific information (e.g., What kind of problem do Arab learners encounter when pronouncing the consonant $/p/$?). Text-implicit questions are devised to enable students to comprehend the underlying structure of the text in order to recognize conceptual relationships, such as causal, contrasting, or complementary (e.g., What kind of argument does the author present to support his claim against the issue of "political correctness"?). Script-implicit questions facilitate deeper understanding of the text and engage students in higher level thinking when making logical connections between the concepts and ideas presented in the text or in other sources (e.g., How do the author's claims relate to the ideas in source 2)?

Stage 5: Taking Notes

While analyzing the texts, students take notes from their sources and record the information gathered on the synthesizing grid (see Table 1). Some of the activities, especially at the initial stages, include partially written graphic organizers to help students recognize how information is organized and developed. Synthesizing also helps students make conceptual links to their own ideas and thoughts. The grids reflect the working plan of the essay; each grid deals with a point or an

Table 1. A Synthesizing Grid

(Section number of outline)			
Student's background information	**Source 1:** (Bibliographical information) Author: Date: Etc.	**Source 2:** (Bibliographical information) Author: Date: Etc.	**Source 3:** (Bibliographical information) Author: Date: Etc.
a. (Student's notes)	a. (Notes on source 1)	a. (Notes on source 2)	a. (Notes on source 3)
b. Any modifications to student's notes	b. interpretations, reflections, and conceptual linkage	b. interpretations, reflections, and conceptual linkage	b. interpretations, reflections, and conceptual linkage

argument from the outline and is numbered accordingly. The grid is divided into columns, and each column is further divided into "a" and "b."

The notes taken from the different texts are used to identify intertextual relationships. Students examine the type of information in each text and predict how it will contribute to their own argument and to those of other texts, discussing whether the texts have contrasting ideas, complementary information, or different reasoning.

At this stage of the process, students are encouraged "to vocalize their thoughts and describe logical connections among ideas" (Ryder & Graves, 2003, p. 214). When first introduced, the synthesizing grids are supplied with guided questions or half-written notes to help students visualize intertextual relationships. As the synthesizing module progresses, students fill in the grid themselves, with the teacher assuming a supportive role.

Stage 6: Composing the First Draft

The next step is to practice putting the integrated information from the grid into meaningful statements that support the student's argument and point of view. Here students are presented with some questions that lead them to consider a variety of appropriate sentence structures and choice of words that convey specific rhetorical relationships. For example, students are asked

- How can this piece of information support your argument?

- What form of support is used: definitions, examples, causes, effects, contrasts?

- What verbs can be used to express causal, contrastive, and time relationships?

- How can the information from different sources be connected?

- Is it better to quote, paraphrase, or summarize the gathered information?

After students practice the construction of synthesized sentences that present supportive information from the different sources, they write a rough draft expanding the first main point in the outline. Students repeat the same procedures for the other main points of the outline. Then they follow a checklist to make sure that the concepts and ideas are linked coherently for a smooth flow of information. At this stage of the writing process, the teacher's comments and peers' feedback will have a profound impact on the development of students' essays.

The reading activities done earlier will raise students' awareness of how information is organized and presented. In fact, text structure not only contributes to text understanding, it also enhances the coherence and the structure of their own writing (Goldman & Rakestraw, 2000).

Stage 7: Revising, Editing, and Publishing

The process of drafting and revising is recursive. Students may need to write a second draft to incorporate any writing improvements, resulting in their editing the final writing product before publishing it by displaying it on the bulletin board, on the class's Web site, or in a bound collection of essays. They can even share their composition with other students in the class by reading parts of it aloud. In this way, they feel that they are writing for an authentic purpose and audience.

It is recommended for effective learning of skills and strategies to have students reflect on the final product of their writing. This self-reflection can help students evaluate their own writing and monitor their progress. As explained by Stoller (2002), "students can reflect on the language they mastered to complete the project, the content they learned about the targeted theme, the steps they followed to complete the project, and the effectiveness of their final product" (p. 117).

REFLECTIONS

Teaching critical analysis of texts took more time to practice than I initially expected, probably because most of those students had not previously analyzed texts. In addition, language intervention exercises (adapted from Stoller, 2002) were provided for some students as means of support during the language demands of each stage of the synthesizing process. Topics included using discourse markers signaling textual relationship or introducing in-text references.

However, the extra time was well spent. The writing portfolios of the students who took the synthesizing module show a gradual improvement in their writing skills in general and in the integration of source information in particular. It is believed that the miniprojects improved students' writing and provided them with a sense of achievement because each writing project was done in a relatively short time, which allowed for a continuous recycling of strategies. Most learned how to synthesize information from multiple sources and internalize appropriate strategies to help them investigate a research question, read and analyze texts critically, make intertext conceptual linkage, and produce a coherent piece of writing. In addition, the activities in the synthesizing module encouraged students to become independent learners who could work effectively with others.

Amina M. B. Megheirbi has served as an assistant professor of English at the University of Garyounis, in Benghazi, Libya, since 2000. From 1982 to 2000, she was an English instructor at United Arab Emirates University in Al-Ain, UAE.

CHAPTER 9

A Process–Genre Approach to Teaching Writing to Medical Science Graduate Students

Miao Yang

This chapter introduces how a genre–process approach to teaching writing was used with a group of medical postgraduates at a Chinese university. Detailed descriptions of the writing class are provided with some concrete examples of tasks and materials, demonstrating how a genre-based approach to writing can be used to engage students with the process of writing and with genre, such as writing for specific audiences or purposes.

CONTEXT

The students in the English writing classes were postgraduate medical students at a university in southeast China ranging in age from 23 to 35. Most of them had passed a national English exam, the results of which are recognized as certificates of English proficiency level for non-English majors in China. There were two classes, with a total of 72 students.

Teaching English writing has always been an arduous job in China. Although these students were in the postgraduate course, their previous experience of English writing was limited to examination writing, where they produced 150–200 words in short, timed essays. The teacher typically begins the writing class by reviewing linguistic information, such as the usage of transitional words or different ways of developing paragraphs. This is followed by the students' mirrored practice of writing similar texts. In the final step, the teacher grades the students' compositions. Most of the time, the writing process ends as soon as the drafts are finished, providing little or no opportunity for students to revise. This way of teaching writing is seen by the majority of students as boring and ineffective. To cite a student's comments (from a March, 2004, e-mail): "I have to write for the exam. But English writing is never interesting to me ever since middle school. We are always taught to write in the same way. It does help in the exam. But the more I write, the more I hate writing. It's so boring" (cited in Yang, 2005). It is a challenge to teach English writing to students at any level, but it is especially difficult to teach English writing to students at an advanced level.

A small-scale research survey (Yang, 2005) on students' writing needs showed that as students' academic levels ascended (from undergraduate to postgraduate), their writing needs changed from examination writing to academic writing and writing for communicative purposes, such as e-mailing or messaging. Moreover, students were not satisfied with the product approach to writing, which prevailed in the examination-oriented teaching context in China. The survey suggested that a product–process approach would be more suitable to teach intermediate level students and a process–genre approach would be more appropriate for advanced students.

In another study (Yang, Badger, & Yu, 2006), two sets of undergraduates wrote English essays on an identical topic, one group receiving feedback from the teacher and the other from peers. Collected data revealed that students used both teacher and peer feedback to improve their writing, but teacher feedback was more likely to be adopted and led to greater improvement. However, peer feedback was associated with a greater degree of student autonomy. Therefore, even in the Chinese culture, which is said to give great authority to the teacher, there is a role for peer feedback.

To further understand the students' ideas about writing feedback, the feedback questionnaires used in the second study with the undergraduates were also distributed to the postgraduates before designing the writing curriculum. Altogether, 79% of the postgraduates thought teacher feedback was useful or very useful in revision, and 68% took the same view of peer feedback; in addition, 76% would like to have both teacher feedback and peer feedback before revising.

CURRICULUM, TASKS, MATERIALS

Based on our research, a genre–process writing curriculum was developed for advanced students in our program, combining genre analysis activities with activities that are normally used in the process approach. Corresponding teaching tasks and materials were designed.

A Process–Genre Approach: Theoretical Underpinning

Although the process approach, with its emphasis on the writing process, learner interaction, and the importance of both self-discovery and cognitive development, has been very influential in second language (L2) writing instruction, its limitations have been broadly discussed (e.g., Horowitz, 1986; Hyland, 2002, 2003a;

Raimes, 1991). From a social-constructionist perspective, Hyland (2003a) comments that the process approach "represents writing as a decontextualised skill" (p. 18), can "disempower teachers and cast them in the role of well-meaning bystanders," "fails to make plain what is to be learnt," tends to "draw heavily on inaccessible cultural knowledge," which relies on "hidden mainstream American values," and finally, "lack[s] . . . engagement with the sociopolitical realities of students' everyday lives and target situations" (p. 19). Hyland considers genre to be a social response to both process and text. As he points out,

> Genre-based pedagogies rest on the idea that literacies are community resources which are realized in social relationships, rather than the property of individual writers struggling with personal expression. . . . The teaching of key genres is, therefore, a means of helping learners gain access to ways of communicating that have accrued cultural capital in particular professional, academic, and occupational communities. (p. 24)

The combination of process and genre approaches to writing highlights the best in both. The emphases on the recursive writing process and revision activities in the process approach involve students in negotiation and interpretation of meanings and help them avoid the danger of using genre as a static and product-oriented pedagogy (Flowerdew, 1993). At the same time, the explicit instruction of genres fills a gap in linguistic knowledge that is often found in English as a foreign language (EFL) students. To a certain degree, genre-based pedagogies coincide with the Chinese culture of learning, which honors teachers and texts with an authoritative status and attaches great importance to learning through imitation and memorization.

The combination of two approaches is not eclecticism. Instead, it reflects the kind of "cultural continuity" (Holliday, 1997) that helps bridge traditional and innovative forms of teaching. It appears to be the most appropriate approach to writing instruction at our university.

A Process–Genre Writing Curriculum

Tribble (1996) also draws on the strengths of both process and genre approaches, represented by his model modified here (see Figure 1). The model combines process writing activities with genre-based activities. It shows how content, context, process, and language knowledge interrelate and how they can be realized in practical classroom procedures. For example, the teacher can organize prewriting activities that depend solely on the students' knowledge of the world, or the instructor can do some preparatory work on the related genre by collecting corpus data for the students to work with. The students can begin their study of the genre either before the writing, or they can start in a process writing cycle and later have recourse to genre analysis whenever they feel a lack of sufficient information about the text or context. In this way, both the teachers and the students can draw flexibly from the resources of process and genre approaches.

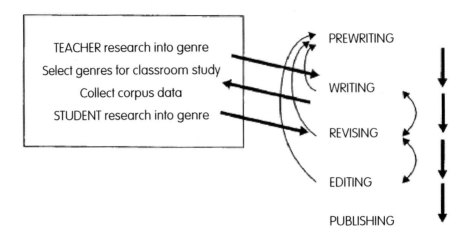

Figure 1. A Model of Process–Genre Writing Activities (based on Tribble, 1996, p. 60)

Because the writing course was scheduled for one 16-week term and either the process or the genre approach was new to most of the students, expectations for significant student progress in writing seemed impractical. In cases such as this, the teacher can "make learners aware of how genres differ one from another and within each other, and how they can go about discovering these differences" (Flowerdew, 1993, p. 309). It would be beneficial if the students began to enjoy writing, had some ideas of the recursive yet motivating processes of writing, and knew what was expected from their writing for specific communicative purposes. The writing curriculum has the tentative objectives of helping students

- realize that writing can be a process of self-discovery and self-expression

- develop various strategies when offering and receiving feedback, either from peers or teachers, and use feedback effectively when revising

- develop the strategies of corpus data collecting and genre analysis

- establish concepts of audience, purpose, and discourse community in specific writing tasks

To ensure that students' abilities develop in proper sequence, some principles were followed in selecting writing topics and organizing classroom instruction:

- The writing topics were arranged from informal to formal (i.e., students began with personal writing and, toward the end of the term, began to write academic content).

- The focus of instruction switched from process at the beginning of the course to genre at the end.

- In genre-based instruction, teacher-initiated genre analyses were gradually replaced by student-initiated genre analyses.

Within 16 weeks, five writing rounds were arranged, and five genres were introduced (life stories, summaries, film reviews, argumentative essays, and abstracts).

The topic for each genre was selected according to the students' interests and immediate needs (see Table 1). For example, taking the national postgraduate entrance examination was a life-changing decision for most of the students. Writing about the life stories that led to that decision involves self-reflection and self-expression of authentic feelings. As medical students, they had been involved in laboratory animal testing; thus, an argumentative essay about testing animals was a topic relevant to their lives. As postgraduates, they would eventually have to publish articles in academic journals, so learning how to write an effective abstract required necessary training (even if they publish their articles in Chinese journals, they have to prepare an English abstract).

It may be noted that the key genres in Table 1 cannot be categorized as key genres for medical professionals except the last one, the abstract. Actually, the writing of other genres served as fluency writing practices that allowed the students to move gradually from informal writing to formal writing, and the teachers could, therefore, shift the instruction focus from process to genre. Moreover, as will be discussed later, the writing course serves as the transition from the general English course to the English for specific purposes (ESP) course; therefore, academic genres are not the focus.

In each writing round, prewriting activities included discussing in groups, reading, or free writing about materials pertaining to the writing topic or genres. Then genre analysis was conducted and corpus data introduced, followed by

Table 1. Key Genres and Writing Topics for the Writing Course

Key Genre	Writing Topic
Life story narrative	Why I chose to become a postgraduate medical student
Summary	Write a summary for the essay "Managing Stress."
Film review	Introduce and comment on a film you liked.
Argumentative essay	Address the issue of animal testing and ethics. Should it be outlawed, or is animal experimentation necessary in order to develop new medicines and advance scientific knowledge?
Abstract	Write an English abstract for an article to be published in a medical journal.

discussion on the rhetorical forms and genre structures. The students wrote their own essays after class and sent them to a public e-mail box, where they were free to read each others' assignments. This can be viewed as the pre–peer-review stage, when reading and appreciating others' writings are optional and flexible according to students' own schedules. The next class provided peer response activities guided by a feedback checklist, which was then followed by revisions of their own drafts. The second drafts were sent to the public e-mail box again, at which time the teacher provided individual feedback via e-mail. Students then finished another round of drafting.

Preparing Process–Genre Writing Tasks and Materials

One challenge I experienced was the availability of appropriate classroom materials. A readymade textbook featuring the genre–process approach was not available. The textbook that had been ordered for the students did not intentionally include genre information, so I decided to selectively use parts of their general English textbook as a starting point and search for related materials from other sources.

The following sections present how five major groups of activities were implemented in the writing course. In addition, for some tasks, examples are provided with specific materials.

Prewriting Activities

An initial obstacle was to change the students' approach to writing. Previously, students had been expected to begin writing as soon as they were assigned a topic, which limited their imagination and gave them the impression of writing for writing's sake. To motivate the students and make writing an "education process" rather than a "training process" (Flowerdew, 1993, p. 306), a variety of activities were completed prior to writing. Included in these prewriting activities were watching videos, discussing in small groups, fast reading, and free writing. Sometimes, several tasks were done if relevant materials could be found. For example, four prewriting tasks (see Figure 2) were employed before the writing of the first topic: What led you to pursue postgraduate study in medicine?

The prewriting activities helped create the social context in which language production takes place. In this way, the teacher adopted a sociocognitive approach to teaching genres by making use of activities usually associated with the process approach.

Peer Feedback Activities

The students were placed in groups of 3–5 members and exchanged drafts. They commented on each other's drafts by referring to a peer feedback checklist with suggestions for commenting on the peer's writing. They were told to take notes during their peer feedback sessions for later use in the revision process.

Task Example 1

1. The students watched a CNN video, which featured a 6-week science program offered by California Institute of Technology for students from minority families.

2. The students read a related passage and answered comprehension questions.

3. The students free wrote for 10 minutes about key life events that finally led to the decision to enroll as postgraduates.

4. The students joined in a group discussion in class to exchange their decision-making experiences about returning to school.

Figure 2. Prewriting Tasks for the First Topic

(Examples of peer feedback activities and the feedback checklist are provided in the appendix.)

Teacher–Student Conference

Although teacher feedback was provided for each student during every writing round, after three writing rounds, I found that some students could not utilize the feedback in revision, causing identical writing errors to reappear. To enhance revision strategies, teacher–student conferences were arranged. Before the conferences, each student's drafts and final texts were collected and major problems analyzed. During the conferences, I discussed the problems with the students and gave suggestions for revisions and corrections. The students also talked about any difficulties they had in writing. The conferences were time consuming, but it was time well spent. In the writings that followed, some students made obvious progress, especially in editing.

Genre Analysis Activities

Flowerdew (1993) suggests six activity types that might help students focus on the process of genre learning rather than the end-products of specific genres. In this writing course, the first three types were practiced, including: (a) using the results of genre analysis, (b) "metacommunicating" (talking about instances of genres), and (c) doing genre analysis (Flowerdew, 1993, p. 310).

According to Tribble (1996), genre analysis activities can involve learners in the process of both adoption and adaptation of different genres as they respond to the texts they encounter. Such activities help learners avoid uncritically imitating a prescribed model. For example, the students first joined in a discussion about the important parts of an introduction paragraph of an argumentative essay. They then read a sample introduction paragraph and identified those important parts. In another case, they reordered a jumbled conclusion paragraph and discussed the results (see Figure 3 for examples of genre analysis tasks).

Task Example 2

1. Read five argumentative essays and finish the flowchart. (The flowchart is designed with blanks and arrows for the students to fill in terms that can summarize various parts of an argumentative essay.)

2. Can you identify the structural formula of an argumentative essay?

3. What variations can be found?

4. Describe two or three ways of developing an argument you can find in these texts.

Task Example 3

1. Reorder the jumbled sentences into a coherent paragraph.

2. A structural slot displays the sequence of the moves in a paragraph. What structural slots can you find?

3. How can they be used in your writing?

Task Example 4

1. Connectives make an argumentative essay coherent. In this argumentative essay, the connectives are missing. Fill in the blanks with proper ones.

2. Identify the logical relationship of the sentences, using connectives.

Figure 3. Genre Analysis Tasks

At the beginning of the course, I initiated more genre analysis. However, the students became more involved in self-initiated genre analysis as the course proceeded. In the last writing round, the students collected samples of abstracts published in both international and Chinese journals. They analyzed and compared the corpus texts, discussed these in groups, and presented their findings to the class. Then, armed with the analysis findings, they began to write abstracts for the articles that they were planning to publish.

Explicit Grammar Instruction

Although grammar instruction was not considered in the initial stage of curriculum implementation, it turned out to be a necessary and useful course component. As similar mistakes appeared in the students' writings multiple times, the teacher decided to present mini grammar lessons. Most of the time, the lessons were given as time allowed between activities or at the end of the class. Supplemental grammar exercises, such as multiple choice and gap-filling, were sent to the public e-mail box for the students who needed further practice. Special attention was paid to verb tenses. Students were reminded that past events are best expressed in past tense, even when some of the information is still currently true but that when discussing plans and present actions, however, the present or future tense is more appropriate. When genre-based instruction became important as the course progressed, the grammar of specific genres required more explanation in the class. For example, the instruction of connectives, pronouns, and referencing words was an important part in the instructional activities during the discussion of argumentative essays. The usage of passive voice was emphasized when writing abstracts.

REFLECTIONS

The students welcomed the new process–genre approach to writing, and their motivation increased. For the first time, writing was not for the exam; instead, it was a social and collective act for sharing opinions and professional writing with their teacher and classmates. Moreover, the essays were not final products to be marked; rather, the process of writing was a journey of self-reflection, critical thinking, problem-solving, and idea-sharing. Sample texts were no longer objects of imitation.

Genre-based pedagogies will gradually play a more important role in the latter stage of curriculum development, and more genres in the medical profession will be introduced and practiced so that the medical graduates will be better pre-pared for their careers. Furthermore, if the course is offered regularly for future students, the writing teacher can gradually collect more sample texts of specific genres and build a corpus of appropriate medical academic writing. This corpus of texts could then become a permanent resource for use in the teaching program. Moreover, if the writing course is extended to include one more term of study, the teacher can then focus more on key genres in the field of medicine and make the course more ESP oriented.

The writing course based on a genre–process approach is a good example of how students' writing needs can be addressed and their writing interests can be aroused, resulting in a budding interest in their own academic writing. In addi-tion to the process approach, genre-based pedagogies can be utilized to cultivate the academic literacy of students in different professions. A genre–process writing course for advanced students could serve as an effective extension of the general English course and provide a transition to ESP-oriented courses.

Miao Yang is an associate professor at Shantou University Medical College, in Quangdong, China. She has been teaching English at the tertiary level for more than 10 years. Her research interests include L2 writing, classroom interaction, and curriculum development. She is presently a doctoral candidate at the Chinese University of Hong Kong.

APPENDIX: SAMPLE LESSON PLAN

Yearning to Learn: Why I Chose to Become a Postgraduate

Section 1: Prewriting Activities

1. Watching for Writing: CNN video

2. Reading for Writing: Essay "School Days"

3. Free Writing: What happened that led to your decision to continue your education? What are your reasons for returning for more schooling? Write everything that comes into your mind. Keep your pen moving for 10 minutes. Pay more attention to ideas than to grammar and vocabulary. Remember to keep your free writing for planning and outlining.

4. Speaking for Writing: In group discussion, explain how and why you decided to continue your education as a postgraduate student. Tell your group members your story. Ask questions to discover more of others' stories.

Section 2: Writing Techniques

1. Using Dialogue in the Story: Include dialogue to make your story more memorable and to guide the readers' attention to the most important or emotional aspect of the story.

2. Writing a Unified Paragraph: Provide unity by initially stating the main idea and expanding upon it throughout the paragraph in an effort to make the topic of the paragraph clear. Give only information and examples that are directly related to the topic, and avoid discussing anything that is not directly related to the topic.

Section 3: Writing After Class

1. Planning Your Writing
Review the free writing, class discussion, and readings you have already completed on this topic to get ideas. Jot notes about important things you want to include. Make a list of the steps in the story.

2. Writing Drafts
Write a story of at least 350 words in which you tell about what made you decide to continue your education as a postgraduate student. Bring your draft to the class next week for review activities.

❏   What specific title would you give your classmate's essay?

❏   Do you believe you will think about his or her essay later, when you are not in class? Why or why not?

❏   Find a word, phrase, or sentence in your classmate's paper that you particularly like. Circle or highlight it. And tell him or her why.

❏   Was there anything you disagree with or didn't understand? Explain.

❏   Did you get any ideas for your own essay by reading your classmate's essay? Explain to him or her.

❏   Are there conversations that highlight the whole story? If not, can you suggest ways to include them?

❏   Does your partner use tenses correctly? Does the story have a time frame?

Note. Partially adapted from Weidauer. *Tapestry Writing 3*, 2E. ©2000 Heinle/ELT, a part of Cengage Learning, Inc. Reproduced by permission. www.cengage.com/permissions

Feedback Checklist

Section 4: Peer Feedback Activities

1. Find a partner in your group.

2. Exchange your drafts of the story.

3. Talk about each other's draft based on the feedback checklist.

4. Jot down your partner's comments for later use in revision.

Section 5: Revision

1. For homework, revise your drafts, using your partner's comments and ideas you got from the review activities. Send your final text to the public e-mail box. Feel free to read others' drafts and give comments.

2. Revise your drafts again after you receive more feedback from your peers and the teacher. Then send your final texts to the public e-mail box again.

CHAPTER 10

"It May Be Possible" to Teach the Use of Hedging in EFL University Writing

Jingjing Qin and Erkan Karabacak

A quick look at editorial pieces, journal articles, and academic papers written in English reveals that these texts are interspersed with words such as *may, might, can, could, would, seem, suggest, propose, speculate, possibly, presumably*, and so on. These words permit writers to hedge, thereby modifying or mitigating their statements. The use of hedging is an essential feature in Western academic writing communities, where tempering scientific claims or personal viewpoints is expected. Hedging with carefully selected modal verbs, adverbs, and adjectives, for example, shields writers from making a firm commitment to the truth–value of propositions or claims.

According to the research, English as a second language (ESL) and English as a foreign language (EFL) writers consistently fail to modulate claims in their academic writing, and they are generally unable to handle subtle linguistic features well (Bazerman, 1988; Hyland, 1994; Hyland & Milton, 1997). There are various possible reasons for ESL and EFL writers' failure to grasp this elusive, yet essential, linguistic feature in academic writing. One plausible explanation, proposed by Hyland (2000), holds that second language (L2) writers tend to be inattentive to the use of hedging in academic readings, thereby ignoring hedging in their own writing. Salager-Meyer (1997) states that even if ESL and EFL writers notice hedging devices in academic readings, they are prone to weigh hedged statements or interpretations as facts. Given the prevalence of the use of hedging in academic writing and ESL and EFL writers' negligence of this feature, we hold that it is the responsibility of writing teachers to teach this important linguistic feature explicitly in order to make students aware of its role in English academic writing. As Schmidt (1990) argues, some degree of noticing linguistic input is necessary before writers can internalize it.

This chapter's focus is a description of a set of learning activities developed by Jingjing Qin, the first author of this chapter, through Hot Potatoes (Ameil & Holmes, 2006). This user-friendly software program allows the development of various types of online exercises, such as multiple-choice, short-answer, jumbled-sentence, crossword, matching and ordering, and gap-fill drills. By using this electronic tool, teachers can provide EFL university writers with focused exercises illuminating the use of hedging in academic articles, thus heightening their awareness and understanding of this essential writing skill. Most importantly, the chapter will suggest ways that teachers can help their students utilize hedging in their own writing. Note that these activities are designed particularly for university EFL English majors who have already had some experience in reading and writing academic papers. We recommend that readers take their own teaching contexts and their students' levels of proficiency into consideration before adapting these activities for their own instructional settings.

CONTEXT

Numerous studies have indicated that novice ESL and EFL academic writers seem to have problems with the use of hedging in their academic writing. Hinkel (2005), for example, has shown that ESL writers tend not to use hedging when necessary, and even if they use hedging devices, they employ a severely limited range. In a retrospective think-aloud study conducted by Hyland (2000), EFL undergraduates were found to be unaware of the use of hedging in academic texts. Partly due to its subtlety, hedging has received considerably less attention than many other linguistic features in academic writing instruction (Hyland, 1994).

In the EFL university context in China, more emphasis has been given to academic writing in recent years, especially for English majors. According to the *National College English Curriculum for English Majors in China* (China Higher Education English Teaching Committee for English Majors, 2000), by the end of their 2nd year of English study, students are required to write a short essay of 150–200 words within 30 minutes. The essay is evaluated for its coherence, organization, use of language, and grammatical accuracy; however, no mention is made of the use of hedging in academic writing. This is understandable because these novice writers struggle with elementary writing skills such as forming a controlling idea, organizing information, maintaining coherence, and using appropriate language, so no attention is left for the less obvious feature of hedging. Nevertheless, in order to enhance the quality of students' academic writing in general, it is imperative to teach them how to hedge. Furthermore, with the opening up of China's university education to the outside world, more and more EFL undergraduates will further their studies in English-speaking countries, where the use of hedging in academic writing is highly valued to show one's writing sophistication.

In light of the need for explicit teaching of hedging, Qin designed learning activities for two academic writing classes of 2nd-year English majors in China and then uploaded them to a Web site for easy access. By the time the instructor implemented these lessons, the students had already taken academic writing courses that had taught them how to use a variety of organizational modes, such as narration, description, and exposition. According to the writing curriculum, the students were then expected to learn how to write argumentative essays. Introducing the use of hedging at this time was especially appropriate because in writing argumentative essays, writers are expected to propose their own points of view and introduce others' ideas and claims, making hedging both useful and necessary. The following section describes the activities designed for these students with some insights into their experiences.

CURRICULUM, TASKS, MATERIALS

Learning Activities

The activities are based on the following sequenced steps:

- prompting students to see the real need for using hedging in their academic writing

- heightening their awareness about the use of hedging in authentic academic journal articles

- applying the use of hedging in reading and writing activities

- peer editing each other's papers for the use of hedging

- providing feedback and guidance on the edited papers

First, Qin asked students to write an argumentative paper after reading two editorial pieces, which had opposing views on the same controversial topic, that is, *whether the spread of English is a prerequisite for China's internationalization*. In the argumentative paper, students were asked to examine the opposing views presented in the two editorial pieces. Then they were asked to evaluate, weigh, and combine the opposing views to support their personal position. This argumentative writing task required the students to use hedging in an authentic manner in order to reference others' views, refute others' opinions, and express their own ideas.

Second, awareness-raising activities, which can be viewed on Qin's (2007) link, exposed the students to the use of hedging in academic journal articles. These activities, which Qin developed from an article written by Rot (2007), gave students the chance to see how expert writers use different forms and functions of hedging in their academic writing and, in particular, how hedging devices are used to tone down their own propositions or deny others' claims in a socioculturally appropriate way. These awareness-raising activities took various forms, such as multiple-choice questions, where students were asked to identify the most socioculturally appropriate statement (see Appendix, Example 1) and matching activities, where students needed to match different forms of hedging with the contexts provided (see Appendix, Example 2). The texts used for these activities came from authentic journal articles in applied linguistics and were chosen particularly for English majors. For students in other disciplines, we recommend choosing authentic texts according to the students' needs and interests. Through these activities, students can understand the role of hedging in the academic community.

In the third step of the process, students were prompted to move from comprehension to production of the target feature by undertaking reading and writing activities. The reading activity took the form of gap-filling, where all the hedges in an academic text were removed, and students were asked to fill in the gaps with appropriate forms of hedging (see Appendix, Example 3). Hints were provided when necessary. The writing activities took the form of short-answer questions, where students were asked to rewrite some sentences to make them more socioculturally appropriate by using hedging, or, conversely, to rewrite sentences to make them more assertive and hedge less (see Appendix, Examples 4 and 5). These activities reinforced what students had learned about hedging by asking them to utilize it in real reading and writing tasks.

Fourth, students were asked to edit the argumentative papers that they had written by conducting a peer review to check for the use of hedging. The instructor reminded students to pay particular attention to the places where the use of hedging was desirable, such as when refuting others' views and proposing one's own ideas. This activity prompted students to apply what they had learned when critiquing each other's work.

Finally, the instructor collected the students' original and revised versions of their argumentative papers and provided feedback and guidance on the use of hedging in their papers.

Students' Feedback on the Learning Activities

The instructor decided that it would serve the students' best interests to direct their attention explicitly to hedging during informal conferences. First, the oral feedback revealed that the majority of the students were not aware of hedging before these lessons; in fact, they had never even heard of the term *hedging* before. Their lack of knowledge of this feature could be easily seen in their original versions of argumentative papers, which illustrated their inadequate linguistic resources to point out opposing views or to propose their own views. Students reported that through these learning activities, their awareness of hedging in academic writing had been greatly heightened, and they appreciated the opportunity to learn about a linguistic feature that is highly valued in English-medium academic settings in general.

Second, the students recognized the importance of equipping themselves with an inventory of strategies for using hedging in different contexts and for different purposes, such as how to hedge one's own claim or how to refute others' propositions in a socioculturally appropriate way. Some students jokingly commented that when they tried to propose their own views or challenge others' viewpoints before, they did not realize that what they had written was inappropriate and that they might have imposed their own views on readers without showing them proper respect. For example, at the end of an essay one student wrote, "Pay attention! Do not forget our culture." By forcefully admonishing his audience to accept his point of view, he failed to take his readers' point of view into consideration.

Third, students also reported that their recent training had changed the way they read academic journal articles. By paying attention to how expert writers used hedging in academic articles, students were better able to use it in their own writing. Admittedly, it can take time and practice for students to master such a complex and nuanced feature as hedging. Therefore, we have found that they need constant reminders to pay attention to the use of hedging in academic reading and also to use it in their academic writing.

REFLECTIONS

As Hyland (2002) argues, there is no clear-cut answer to what constitutes the best method for teaching writing because it depends on the specific instructional context. The learning activities reported in this chapter are designed to provide the following benefits:

- addressing an important and yet underrepresented linguistic feature in academic writing (Hinkel, 2005), thus providing a valuable contribution to the field

- using authentic journal articles as texts for the learning activities

- sequencing well by beginning with awareness-raising activities and then introducing reading and writing activities to students' writing tasks in a real writing class

- creating an authentic need for using hedging by asking students to write an argumentative paper based on two source texts with opposing views

- reflecting current writing teaching theory, namely, process writing, by asking the students to peer edit and revise their papers

There are some potential challenges associated with developing activities for the use of hedging in academic writing. First, it is time-consuming to design learning activities because texts must be selected carefully from authentic journal articles. Second, the use of hedging in academic writing is subtle; thus, hedging may prove challenging for students to understand and use properly. Third, students may come from different disciplines using different patterns of hedging. In other words, hedging is contextually oriented and discipline appropriate or specific. Fourth, different sections of a journal article may employ different hedging patterns.

Despite the challenges, we believe that students with academic aspirations need to learn how to use hedges in their academic writing. Considering the complexity of the use of hedging in academic writing, it is imperative for writing instructors to make a commitment to teach this essential feature to ESL and EFL students so that they can thrive in the English academic writing communities.

Jingjing Qin teaches at Nanjing University, Nanjing, China. She has broad research interests in writing in English for academic purposes contexts, writing assessment, and second language acquisition. She has presented and published papers on academic writing, writing assessment, instructed SLA, and heritage language learning.

Erkan Karabacak teaches at Nanjing University, Nanjing, China. His main research interests are corpus linguistics, terminology, and English academic writing.

APPENDIX: SAMPLE AWARENESS-RAISING ACTIVITIES

Example 1: An example of a multiple-choice question

Directions: Choose the sentence that is more socioculturally appropriate.

   a. What becomes clear is that not only are the cognitive mechanisms involved in reading comprehension and lexical acquisition different, they might even be in conflict.

   b. It is clear that not only are the cognitive mechanisms involved in reading comprehension and lexical acquisition different, they are even in conflict.

Example 2: An example of a matching activity

Directions: Match the different forms of hedging with the contexts provided.

Readers _____ be wholly consumed by word encoding processes, not permitting sufficient attention for reconstructing the text. (can, might, will)

Example 3: An example of a gap-filling activity

Directions: Fill in the gaps in the following passage with appropriate hedges.

Research has repeatedly _____ that encountering an unfamiliar word in a text or even comprehending it in its context _____ not lead to an initial assignment of meaning to the orthographical representation of the word. Accordingly, it is well _____ that comprehension and learning are not the same phenomenon.

Example 4: An example of a short-answer question

Directions: Rewrite the following sentences to make them more socioculturally appropriate with the use of hedging.

> **Sentence:** Repeated visual enhancements have no effect on strengthening word encoding.

> **Possible answer:** Repeated visual enhancements seemed to have no effect on strengthening word encoding.

Example 5: An example of a short-answer question

Directions: Rewrite the following sentences to make them more assertive and less hedgy.

> **Sentence:** Textual input is generally assumed to be an important source for L2 lexical development.

> **Possible answer:** Textual input is an important source for L2 lexical development.

CHAPTER 11

Service Learning and Writing With a Purpose

Denise Vaughn

A copy of *Teaching as a Subversive Activity* (Postman & Weingartner, 1969) has traveled around the world with me since my undergraduate days as a teacher in training. It seems the book was meant to make readers think about schools, education, and teaching in order to inspire teachers to make learning more relevant and meaningful for students. A recommended act of subversion is to write the following questions on a piece of paper and post them where they can be seen every day before teaching: What am I going to have my students do today? What is it good for? How do I know?

I have come a long way since I first read this book, beyond doing something because it feels intuitively right or simply teaching something because the approach is new, innovative, or reported to be more meaningful. So it is with service learning. Although a case may be made for service learning on philosophical grounds, it supports and is supported by what we know about teaching and how we are being asked to teach today, decades after we were encouraged to be "subversive" as teachers.

Service learning is both a philosophy and a learning method. It is experiential learning that engages the student in service at a nonprofit organization within the community to support the learning goals of a course. As they learn, students engage in critical, reflective thinking about their experience, and thus, they develop and deepen an awareness of society and various communities within it; in particular, they gain an understanding and awareness of marginal populations. Engaging in a service-learning project leads students to make connections between subject matter and community issues and experiences (Butin, 2005). In the process, this civic engagement is the basis for the development of citizenship and leadership skills, as well as other important life skills (Parsons, 1996). English as a second language (ESL) learners, in particular, can benefit from service learning in these same ways while also gaining confidence in their ability to communicate in English. Moreover, they acquire experience that is relevant to academic coursework and future careers. Furthermore, the goals and objectives of service learning are congruent with U.S. federal and state standards for adult basic education, based on *Equipped for the Future* (2004). The National Institute for Literacy developed *Equipped for the Future* (EFF) in order to standardize adult basic education in the United States by providing a framework to help instructors and institutions identify and respond to students' needs and personal goals as members of their own families, their communities, and the work force.

CONTEXT

Service learning has been successfully used with ESL learners in an intensive precollege writing course. Students must select a project, complete required paperwork and forms, record activities for regular submission to their instructor, and write a final report. Although the number of hours of service a student must perform varies from program to program and with the purpose of the service, students in the writing course must commit to and complete 16 hours of service. Students can choose a service site from files maintained by the college service-learning office, or they may select a project on their own, with consultation from their instructor or guidance from the college service learning coordinator.

Theory–Practice Connection

Despite the fact that ESL learners are living in the United States, language and cultural differences often make it difficult for them to become involved in their school and their community. As a result, they tend to make friends primarily within their own language or cultural groups and may be slow to develop the communicative competence and confidence that allow them to interact with native speakers of English or to get involved in school activities. Service learning offers a means for students to be involved in communities outside of the classroom, to establish peer working relationships with diverse populations, and to have ample opportunity to practice language skills in real-world settings. However, service projects and writing must be gauged to the proficiency level of learners. In the classroom and through the experience, learners learn to discuss and cope with product and process, technique, and purpose.

The EFF Content Framework (2004) describes the Four Purposes for Learning for the adult learner:

- **Access**: To gain access to information and resources so that adults can orient themselves in the world

- **Voice**: To express ideas and opinions with the confidence they will be heard and taken into account

- **Action**: To solve problems and make decisions without having to rely on others to mediate the world for them

- **Bridge to the Future**: To learn how to learn so that adults can be prepared to keep up with the world as it changes (Teaching/Learning Toolkit, n.d.)

Meeting State Language Requirements

According to EFF, teaching should focus on real-life experiences so that what is learned and discussed in the classroom can be easily transferable to the learners' lives. The Washington State Adult Learning Standards (2006) are based on EFF standards and are used to communicate the skills and strategies taught and performance expected of students in ESL reading, writing, speaking, and listening. The writing curriculum is based on EFF's writing standards, *Convey Ideas in Writing*, and covers the following components:

- Determine the purpose for communicating.

- Organize and present information to serve the purpose.

- Pay attention to conventions of English language usage, including grammar, spelling, and sentence structure, to minimize barriers to readers' comprehension.

- Seek feedback and revise to enhance the effectiveness of the communication.

The state standard and components are the same for all levels of ESL, but they vary according to expectations of specific levels. Therefore, the grammar and vocabulary taught at the highest level of study are more extensive than those taught at the lower levels, and are specified at the local program level. The writing standard articulates the skills that are necessary for adults to be successful in their lives in the United States as family members, in their various communities, and in their careers. Service learning offers an effective means of developing and mastering those skills.

Writing and Learning

Most writing is written to be read; powerful writing often comes from experience; writing is learned by writing; we don't know what we really think until we write our ideas. These are common accepted principles about writing, and ESL instructors emphasize these concepts in one way or another through the textbooks chosen and activities created for students. Furthermore, to write successfully, learners must master the mechanics of grammar, syntax, and process in order to communicate ideas clearly and fluently.

To inspire content, personal experience is often a theme in ESL texts, and students' experiences are expanded upon to connect with community and global themes. For academic writing, learners must learn how to do research and how to incorporate external ideas and viewpoints into their written work. These are all very complex tasks that can take years to master; however, most learners do not have the luxury of unlimited time for study or unlimited money for tuition. In addition, having grown up in other countries, ESL learners have limited background knowledge of U.S. society, culture, or various social conditions and problems when compared to their U.S.-born peers. This adds another dimension that affects comprehension of a text or content area. The service-learning experience helps students develop background knowledge through conscious, mindful, social engagement that creates content for thought, reflection, and writing that is personal yet objective. At the same time, students learn language and techniques necessary to describe the experience clearly. With the kind of reflection that is integral to service learning, students receive direction and guidance that allow them not only to express critical thinking skills they already have but also to develop these skills further according to academic English standards. Because of their involvement in service projects, ESL students become interested in and excited about an expanding understanding and awareness of life in their new country and, thus, are motivated to write about what is both personal and meaningful.

CURRICULUM, TASKS, MATERIALS

Service-learning programs exist in various forms, depending on the college or school they are affiliated with. A project may be part of a curriculum, or it may be a credit-bearing class in and of itself. The nature of a program and the part that service learning plays determine the role a student must take in contacting a service site and establishing the terms of service. In a general ESL classroom, a teacher or other support staff may take the primary responsibility for finding service sites and establishing expectations and terms of service. In this case, service may involve an entire class or groups of students dedicated to projects with specific goals and objectives. The teacher or other support staff contacts an agency and negotiates timelines and project parameters.

Students in an academic, college preparatory writing program are more likely to have the communication skills necessary to set up service sites independently, with guidance from their instructor or service learning office. Because ESL learners usually have little, if any, experience in a U.S. college environment, every aspect of the service-learning project provides significant learning—from deciding to do a project to submitting the final report.

To further explain the service-learning program, our coordinator, an enthusiastic supporter of the program, visits the classroom to give examples of projects other students have completed. She describes resources available to help students select their projects and invites them to meet with her in her office. She has compiled a list of sites where other ESL and EFL learners have served and distributes materials that describe students' obligations and responsibilities.

Students are generally inclined to do projects in areas connected with their future career or choice of major. For instance, those interested in nursing may work in nursing homes with the elderly. A student interested in majoring in biology found a good fit at a nonprofit animal shelter. On the other hand, some students aspire to acquire credentials to resume occupations they had in their own countries, so they look for office work in their previous fields. Some would like to gain confidence in using English and, for this purpose, have served in daycare centers. Parents have used this option as an opportunity to serve at their own children's schools. Others have done service in their own countries and have been influenced by their parents' or other people's experiences. They are drawn to a variety of community services, such as food banks, tutoring, and public health. With the combination of the support of the service-learning office and the students' own motivation and ambitions, a wide range of service projects emerge. However, service can only be performed at a nonprofit organization and, as this is an ESL class, it must involve interacting with staff or clients in order to enhance and develop both communication skills and cultural competency.

The first challenge for a student opting to do a service-learning project may be contacting the site. After consultation with his or her instructor or the service-learning coordinator and being coached about how to approach a site supervisor, a student may decide on a site and make several phone calls but get no response. Equally troubling, after finally getting a response, the student might discover that the agency needs to approve a student prior to doing service or do a background check. Some agencies require longer terms of service than what a student can offer. This is problematic because the clock is ticking, and the deadline for establishing the site is approaching. Each delay requires communication and, perhaps, renegotiation. This is a challenge for both the instructor and the student. Therefore, an instructor must decide how much flexibility and freedom of choice can be allowed in this process.

When a site supervisor has been contacted and has given approval or accepted the student, the student must submit a contract to the writing instructor with a brief description of the service project, including the agency's contact information, the supervisor's name and signature, and the work schedule. Upon completion of the project, the student must submit a timesheet signed by the supervisor and an evaluation of the site. It is also the student's responsibility to give the supervisor the evaluation forms that need to be completed and returned to the college. Communicating with an onsite supervisor, negotiating terms of service, and taking responsibility for required paperwork are challenges for the student at this second stage of the project.

Finally, students engage in the actual project and writing assignments that they must submit. Students are highly motivated because they have chosen projects that are relevant to their own fields of interest. They are expected to keep a journal or log of service as it occurs. They are to describe what happens each time they do service. This is to include tasks performed, as well as interactions with staff and those served at the site. There are two reports due during the term and one final report at the end of the term. The reports summarize significant occurrences during their service. In addition, students must reflect on their experiences.

To assist them, students are given a list of questions from the Service-Learning Program Faculty Manual (2004) developed by the service-learning office as a guide:

- What did you find most interesting about your service-learning site on the first day you were there? What surprised you the most?

- What was the worst or most difficult thing that happened to you while you were working at the service site? Tell what you learned from the experience.

- What was the best thing that happened? Tell what you learned from the experience.

- How do other people at your service site view you? Has this perception changed over time?

- Has there been anything disappointing about your service experience?

- If you were the supervisor of your service site, what problem would you identify and how would you attempt to solve it?

- Rate yourself from 1 (low) to 10 (high) for your performance. Why did you rate yourself the way you did?

- What have you learned about yourself from your service-learning experience?

- How could you improve your individual service contribution?

- Have you taken any risks at your service site? If so, what did you do? What were the results?

- Have you changed any of your attitudes or opinions about the people with whom you have worked?

- What would you change about your service assignment that would make it more meaningful for you or other service-learning students?

- What have you learned about yourself while doing your service project?

- Has your experience influenced your career choice in any way? (p. 25)

Students are required to choose one or two questions for each report. In their final reports, they not only reflect on their service, but they also do a self-assessment.

Assessment

Assessment includes both the fulfillment of the service-learning contract and its expectations, along with a satisfactory completion of the intensive precollege writing course.

Nongraded

Paperwork that students must submit includes various required forms, including:

- contracts that specify project site, supervisor, and duties
  - — one copy goes to instructor
  - — one copy goes to service-learning coordinator
- timesheet signed by site supervisor that proves completion of 16 hours of service
- evaluation from the service site
- student evaluation of service experience

Graded

Assignments include three typewritten reports to reflect the beginning, middle, and end of the project, as well as a journal.

- The first report summarizes the process of setting up the project, what is expected of the student at the service site, and reflection.

- The second report summarizes what activities take place at the site and describes significant incidents. Students are advised to consider different reflection questions than those used in the first report.

- The final report summarizes the student's assessment of his or her performance. Students are instructed to use the reflection questions that are evaluative; they also grade their service.

- The journal, in which details of each service session are recorded, serves as notes for the formal reports.

Reports are evaluated according to how well students follow directions, use logical paragraph organization, and express themselves in standard grammar. Students are allowed to rewrite when necessary, to include what may have been missed, to make corrections, or to clarify any confusion. The ultimate objective is for students to be able to write, format, and present an academic report documenting their service requirement.

REFLECTIONS

Students develop their skills in written English at the sentence level through intensive class work and at the organizational level through various writing assignments. Through the combination of teacher feedback and self-reflection, students become more aware of what they can do and what they need to do to make continued progress. The style of reporting required for their service-learning projects prepares students for reports that many will later do in their careers.

More significant is the communication and social and cultural learning that take place and, of course, the unexpected learning. Examples of student reflection and evaluation include the following:

- A Japanese student found a nonprofit animal shelter in preparation for a degree in biology. Upon final reflection, he declared that he had learned from his supervisor what it means to be a good boss.

- A Nigerian mother had her first experience being a coworker while serving at her child's school.

- A Taiwanese student had previously thought that because children are simple, their language would be simple. She learned otherwise at a daycare center.

- A young Vietnamese immigrant described experiencing her first job interview at her service site.

- A young Somali woman got over her fear and loathing of small children by working in an after-school program at a refugee women's center.

- Two Taiwanese sisters, inspired by their parents' volunteerism, served at two different food banks so that they wouldn't speak in Taiwanese to each other.

- A Somali mother of four, who was employed at a nursing home, served at a different nursing home, feeding and caring for patients with dementia.

- Four young Ethiopian women aspiring to be nurses served at a nursing home that was being shut down amidst controversy. They were asked on occasion to distribute information about the closure to passers-by near the nursing home, which was located on a college campus.

- A Chinese student continued the project he'd worked on in high school (developing after-school programs about global warming). Now in charge, he learned the difference between being a leader and being a team member.

Through service learning, students get involved with U.S. citizens, experience improved self-esteem and confidence in English, and enjoy personal satisfaction. Through their actions, they express personal commitment to helping others and to understanding various aspects of diversity, whether related to age, socioeconomic status, or racial identity. They are challenged by the responsibility they take on to contact and communicate with service sites, to describe and discuss the experience in English, and to reflect on and contemplate their learning. As the instructor, I am humbled each term by students who choose to do a project that involves more time and effort than are required in other courses and to do it with such sincerity. With each step toward completion, students are given the opportunity to explore who they are more fully, which normally results in discovering that their identity is much more substantive than simply being a nonnative speaker of English. Some who have been the receivers of service are now able to be providers. They develop English communication and writing skills through meaningful and purposeful tasks and challenges outside the classroom. Furthermore, these skills are transferable to future careers and facilitate active involvement in community life, the primary objectives of standards-based adult education.

Denise Vaughn was first a social studies teacher, and she used her credentials to support working, living, and traveling abroad. She has lived and taught in Japan, where she obtained her master's of education. She now lives in Seattle, Washington, in the United States, where she teaches ESL at a community college.

CHAPTER 12

From the Classroom to the Boardroom: Grammar and Style Across Genres in ESL Professional Writing

Jennifer Haan and Karyn Mallett

INTRODUCTION

A cursory examination of professional writing textbooks indicates that most relegate the examination of grammar and style to the end of the writing process. How can instructors incorporate rhetorically effective grammar and style instruction in their professional writing (PW) classrooms, especially those designed for future business professionals who are English language learners? Is it even a good idea to include grammar and style instruction in English as a second language (ESL) PW syllabi? Are grammar and style issues in the PW classroom the same as or different from those issues covered in non-ESL business composition courses?

Specifically, this chapter is concerned with the application of second language (L2) writing theory and principles to the particular rhetorical and grammatical expectations faced by ESL students in and beyond the PW classroom. We aim to provide ESL colleagues at the postsecondary level with applicable, rhetorically situated real-world components for their business writing classrooms. These situated assignments have been designed to address the appropriate purpose, audience, and context of real-life situations in business. Throughout the chapter, readers will find the following information: detailed descriptions of each project, examples of student-generated writing, discussions of how to address genre-specific grammar and style issues common in the ESL PW classroom, and reflections on how other instructors might use and adapt the tools provided here.

CONTEXT

Theoretical Context

The curriculum and materials provided in this chapter have been shaped by sound theoretical principles. The first is that genre-based instruction provides an effective framework in the PW classroom. PW and business writing instructors who effectively incorporate real-world projects into the ESL classroom foster students' critical awareness of language usage within a variety of rhetorical contexts. Writers learn to write better when they address their audience appropriately, when their texts have a clear purpose, and when the context for writing prepares them for the kind of writing they will do after leaving the classroom setting. This rhetorical approach to writing instruction is supported by researchers, including Blakeslee's (2001) article, in which real-world assignments are recognized as "useful transitional experiences that bridge classroom and workplace contexts for students" (p. 170). For, as Blakeslee points out, the value of such projects is that they introduce students to workplace practices and genres "while also allowing students to address a variety of audiences" (p. 170).

Further, a focus on real-world projects is substantiated by McEachern (2001) who argues that "not even the best-written case study or end-of-the-textbook-chapter-exercise can duplicate the rhetorical complexity that comes from a real human reader trying to solve real problems using a real document" (p. 211). Wickliff (1997) also suggests that client-based group projects in introductory technical communication courses force students to negotiate, to renegotiate, and often to negotiate again the evolving rhetoric of an extended writing task while stopping short of the level of workplace involvement required in internship or cooperative education experiences. As each of these researchers points out, rhetorically situated writing assignments provide students with the opportunity to discover real business-world aspects of professional writing by challenging them to interact with authentic texts and actual people.

In addition to our commitment to rhetorically situated writing assignments, the second overarching principle that guides this chapter stems from L2 writing research and the recognition that "L2 writing pedagogy may be most effective when it directs writers' attention toward macro- and microlevel textual concerns, including audience expectations, patterns for producing unfamiliar rhetorical forms, and tools for improving lexicogrammatical variety and accuracy" (Silva, 1993a, p. 670). L2 composition teachers offer their learners the greatest benefit by devoting "more time and attention across the board to strategic, rhetorical, and linguistic concerns" (Silva, 1993a, p. 670). Within ESL PW, it is important to address the linguistic or lexicogrammatical issues, not as isolated issues without meaningful context, but rather to look at them as they arise within rhetorically situated genres (Grabe & Kaplan, 1996; Leki, 1991). Examining language features in a rhetorical context provides a framework for instructors to approach grammatical issues and helps students to "discover that grammar and its related topics are not ancillary to language but represent language in action" (Petit, 2003, p. 66).

This emphasis on teaching grammatical principles as "purposeful rhetorical moves" (Cook, 2001, p. 154) is particularly helpful in business writing courses for nonnative English speakers (NNES). It has been rightfully recognized by Silva (1993a) and other L2 writing researchers that the expectations should be different for ESL writers in comparison to native English speaking (NES) writers "on writing tasks and tests that are designed for NES writers" (p. 671).

Yet, outside of the ESL classroom, professional, business, and technical documents are expected to meet a high level of professional scrutiny in terms of macro- and microlevel accuracy. Moreover, in many professional contexts, written documents are the only means by which safety, legal, contractual, and instructional materials are conveyed to consumers. These factors make the PW writing and teaching context unique.

In order to address these concerns, PW curricula for ESL students must include ESL-specific strategies (e.g., understanding key words and business idioms in order to recognize company ethos), ESL-specific rhetorical concerns (e.g., in addition to understanding the basic principles of audience, context, and purpose for writing, ESL students need to consider how style may be perceived by NES as a series of rhetorical choices), and linguistic concerns (e.g., individualized feedback in terms of grammar and style). With these guiding principles in hand, then, these materials integrate real-world tasks while aiming to meet the varied cultural, linguistic, and rhetorical needs of ESL PW students on both macro- and microlevels. This chapter addresses these issues and provides theory-driven, practical materials based on instructors' own reflections and experiences as PW instructors in the university ESL classroom.

Local Context

Materials for this chapter were originally designed to be sensitive to the rhetorical, linguistic, and strategy-writing needs of university-level international ESL students at Purdue University, in the United States. In order to meet the needs of this international student population, the university requested that the English department create a business writing course intended specifically for NNES. The textbook for the course, *Professional Writing Online* (Porter, Sullivan, & Johnson-Ellis, 2009), is organized according to genres, with the instruction of rhetorical principles included as an essential element of each genre.

CURRICULUM, TASKS, MATERIALS

In order to develop the materials used in this chapter, we collected student-generated writing samples from ESL PW students over the course of several terms, using these documents to construct PW curriculum and assessment materials. Although we taught three projects each term, materials for this chapter come primarily from two projects: the employment project and the community-based service-learning project.

In terms of the data gathered for the employment project, we examined students' first and final drafts of cover letters and resumes. For the community-based service-learning project, we analyzed the first and final drafts of students' white papers, which are research reports used in the business setting to inform others about products as well as to advertise them. In addition, we read students' memos in which they reflected on their experience and critiqued their own progress throughout both projects. Finally, we also collected survey information concerning the students' demographic information and reflections on their own writing needs, questions, and concerns.

In the sections to follow, readers will find strategies and materials that have been designed in response to the data collected during each of these projects. Although we hope that these materials will be useful for other instructors as they appear here, the main message of this chapter is that each ESL PW classroom will differ in terms of student enrollment, demographics, writing needs, program goals, available resources, and so forth. Thus, the tools included here are only a starting point, and instructors are encouraged to view their own PW classrooms as fertile ground for research and materials development.

The Employment Project

Typically the first project in the term, the employment project is an individual assignment that requires students to research and respond to a job posting. This project reflects a real-world context because it requires students to search for a potential job or internship in their field, to analyze the job advertisement rhetorically, to research the company that is hiring, and to tailor their application materials accordingly. Within the rhetorically situated framework provided by the employment project, student-generated resume writing provided several opportunities for addressing genre-specific grammar and style issues in the PW classroom. We identified and classified these sample student resume and cover letter issues, keeping in line with the theoretically grounded claim that ESL writing instructors need to address both macro- and microlevel textual concerns.

Macrolevel Textual Issues in the Resume

In general, macrolevel concerns for the resume were recognized as content issues. Specifically, many of the students included culturally and professionally inappropriate background information such as height, age, and family information. They also were more likely than NES to include less relevant experience, such as church and military activities. Additionally, students in the ESL class often used rhetorically inappropriate job descriptors, such as "Participated in praise events in Friday large group events. Helped build a church. Copying and faxing." The content of these descriptors was unrelated to the context of the particular job requirements. For example, the descriptor "helped build a church" might have been useful in a resume for a job in the building and construction field, but not toward an internship in sales. In order to address these macrolevel textual issues, instructors can emphasize the cultural and professional context of the job application process in the United States, showing the students how to select and include pertinent experience to impress potential employers.

Microlevel Textual Issues in the Resume

In addition to the content and culturally based macrolevel issues in the students' resumes, the samples showed a number of pervasive microlevel grammatical errors. The most common of these included inconsistent sentence fragment formation, inaccurate verb tenses, and unprofessional word choices. This genre gives instructors an opportunity to address these issues within a rhetorically situated context.

Grammatical Construction of Fragments

One of the grammatical constructions unique to the resume is the construction of "grammatically correct" sentence fragments. Because applicants are required to convey a significant amount of information about their previous experiences in an easily scanned format, bulleted sentence fragments are commonly used. These fragments, however, have a particular grammatical structure. Many of the ESL students, having never been taught how to create such fragments, had a difficult time knowing how to write them. Not only did students struggle to create meaningful fragments, but they also failed to approach the grammatical structure in a consistent manner. This led to a lack of parallel structure that could be confusing to the reader. Consider the following example:

- Chairperson of social events group

- Being responsible to maintain daily account

The generally accepted grammatical structure of job descriptors in a resume is a fragment that begins with a verb, leaving out function words, such as articles. In this example, the student is trying to show the experience gained from working in an extracurricular organization, but because the descriptors do not follow the appropriate grammatical conventions, the information is unclear. A better construction would be

- Chaired social events group

- Maintained daily account

This structure allows the reader to scan the information quickly and easily, while retaining the grammatically appropriate construction.

Parallel Structure

Because job descriptors used in a resume often begin with verbs and participles, instructors should review verb tense and parallel structure. In the example in the previous section, the student could have used present participles, rather than the past tense:

- Chairing social events group

- Maintaining daily account

This would also be an appropriate grammatical construction, as long as it is consistent throughout the document. Instructors can use these stylized sentence fragments to discuss parallel structure and to practice using various tenses and aspects, which will be useful for the students when writing in a variety of genres.

Word Choice

The resume must also emphasize the applicants' skills and experiences as specifically and precisely as possible. It is also, therefore, particularly important in this genre for students to pay attention to accurate and professional word choice throughout the document. The verbs and keywords that students use should be positive, specific, relevant, and varied, and they should serve to showcase the students' abilities. While writing their resumes, students encountered problems with generalizations and redundancy. Many students, for example, used vague phrases such as "worked as." Although this phrase is not unprofessional or ungrammatical, per se, it is not precise enough to highlight the applicant's specific accomplishments. Students would be better served describing the kind of work that they did. Instead of "worked as cashier," they could write "served customers, maintained daily financial balance, and contributed to pleasant and hospitable environment" to showcase some of the specific skills that were gained while working at a cash register.

Additionally, many students struggled with redundant verbs and verb phrases. Some of the most commonly used verbs included *assisted, assured, helped*, and *ensured*. Instructors can help students avoid such redundancies by working with them to expand their vocabulary to include more specific terms that are relevant to their field.

Macrolevel Textual Issues in the Cover Letter

The types of macrolevel textual issues that were examined in the cover letter can best be described in terms of cultural transfer, as well as a misunderstanding of the needs and expectations of the audience for this genre. As was the case with resumes, students often included inappropriate information in their cover letters, such as their age, personal information about their family members, their beliefs, and their personality traits. In the surveys, many students indicated a lack of understanding of how the content of the cover letter and resume differed from similar documents used in their own countries. Additionally, most of the cover letters focused on college experiences and character, rather than work experience. This tendency might have been due to a lack of relevant work experience.

To address these issues, instructors can emphasize the ways in which the cover letter must meet the expectations of its audience. Whereas the resume provides job applicants with the opportunity to showcase their education, skills, activities, and experiences, the cover letter provides them with the chance to reflect on specific ways in which these experiences and attributes make them the most suitable candidate for the desired position. Teachers, then, can focus their instruction on connecting the experiences that the students have delineated in their resumes to the needs that the potential employers discuss in their job advertisements and other corporate materials. Finally, some classroom comparative genre analysis might be a helpful tool to show students some of the differences between the genre of the cover letter in the United States and similar employment documents in other contexts.

Microlevel Textual Issues in the Cover Letter

To create rhetorically effective cover letters, it is valuable not only to address macrolevel textual problems but also to examine the types of microlevel errors in the students' texts. Because the genre of the cover letter requires prose writing, as opposed to the bulleted lists of the resume, the types of grammatical and stylistic problems that the students exhibit differ. The grammar and style issues in students' papers included run-on sentences, lack of variety in sentence structure, incorrect use of business idioms, and lack of professional language.

Sentence Structure

In their survey responses, many students indicated a lack of understanding of sentence structure issues. In particular, they voiced questions relating to the use of commas, semicolons, and other punctuation marks within complex sentences. A study of sample students' cover letters revealed that this difficulty had resulted in an excessive number of run-on sentences. For example, consider this typical sentence from a cover letter: "I am a junior year standing management student in Purdue University who are studying on both management and accounting and my previous work experiences are reasons that make me a great applicant for working with XXX Company." Possibly, when this student wrote the cover letter, he or she may have simply converted the bullet points from the resume into a single sentence. The result is an incoherent, poorly punctuated run-on sentence. A general way to approach this problem in the ESL PW classroom is to review the basic components of clause structure. This approach will allow instructors to discuss the appropriate use of commas and semicolons, and how to punctuate coordinating conjunctions.

Cover letters that did not contain run-on sentences often suffered from stylistic, rather than a grammatical, sentence structure errors. These letters contained numerous simple sentences, beginning with the same word or group of words, such as "I believe" or "I am." Such sentences, while grammatically correct, lack variety. A review of clause structure can help students to incorporate varied sentence structure into their cover letters, thus enhancing their readability.

Business Idioms

Teaching the cover letter in an ESL PW course also provides an opportunity to integrate vocabulary and idiomatic expressions. Idioms are often taught in isolation. In the PW context, however, there are a variety of business-related idioms that, when used appropriately, can enhance students' communicative ability. One student, for example, wrote in his cover letter, "I am a self-motivate and have a people person" rather than "I am self-motivated and a people person." Expressions such as these effectively describe the traits that a person can bring to a company, but they must be used correctly.

Professional Language

Finally, an examination of the students' cover letters revealed that they often had difficulty describing their previous experiences, traits, and expectations in a clear, confident, and meaningful manner. Some students showed their lack of confidence by using excessive hedging or begging in their cover letters. For example: "If, by any chance, I am given an occasion." This stylistic word choice conveys uncertainty rather than confidence. It demonstrates that the student is unsure of his or her qualifications. On the other end of the spectrum, many students use adjectives that are too informal or unprofessional to express their confidence and enthusiasm as a job applicant. For example, one student wrote, "I am an extraordinarily talented person . . . a wonderful bonus to the experience." These statements show confidence, but their tone is too informal. Instructors can use these statements to show how vocabulary choice affects the tone of the document and, therefore, contributes to the overall ethos of the writer. Students who pay attention to their language choices can create a confident, professional cover letter.

Reflection on the Employment Project

As the examples here show, the genres involved in the employment project provide instructors with a number of opportunities to address rhetorically situated, contextualized grammar and style errors. Although it is not always feasible to teach a wide variety of grammatical concepts in a PW classroom, addressing these issues as they arise within particular genres can help students to recognize the interplay of their language choices, the purpose of their documents, and their intended audience.

The Community-Based Service-Learning Project

Turning to different project, in community-based service learning, students work in groups with actual clients to produce promotional materials for various local businesses or other organizations. This type of project allows the students to work with an actual client in a real-world small business or nonprofit organiza- tion, thereby enhancing the validity of the rhetorical situation and providing students with hands-on experience outside of the classroom. The students work with clients to understand their goals and then create a PW document to meet the clients' needs. In order to accomplish this, the students first create a white paper, which is a type of research paper, delineating the type of document that would be most appropriate for the goals of the client. For instance, if a client were interested in updating advertising, the students would then research the type of campaign that would be most appropriate and present that research to the client in a white paper. They would then create a proposal for the project, write a con- tract that the client and the group members sign, and then keep the client and the teacher informed through memos and progress reports. At the end of the project, students create a usability guide, ensuring that the client can continue to use their document without the students' help, and create an electronic presentation for the class describing their project.

Macrolevel Textual Issues in the White Paper

Inappropriate Shifts in Audience

Student-generated white papers contained a number of macrolevel textual problems that were likely due to students' unfamiliarity with the white paper as a genre. Because the white paper is a type of research paper, students transferred their understanding of the generic academic research paper to the white paper assignment, resulting in confusing shifts in audience awareness. For example, one group began its white paper with an enthusiastic description of a local restaurant. The description was detailed but introduced the business to a reader who had never seen or eaten at the restaurant. However, later in the same paper, the group shifted and began addressing the client, the restaurant owner, directly. In this case and many others, students showed that they were aware of the general compo- nents of a research paper, but they were uncertain how to write for a real and specified audience.

Unblended Collaborative Writing

In addition to inappropriate shifts in audience awareness, other macrolevel textual concerns were the result of collaborative writing. The majority of student groups decided to divide the work of researching and writing, so the result was often unblended and unbalanced. For example, while one author depended heavily on research to support his claims in his own section, his coauthor made no refer- ence to any outside texts. In a different group, each writer referred to the client's organization from a different perspective. One writer wrote about the business as a familiar place and used language that assumed things about readers' familiarity as well, while another author wrote more formally about the business. Further, beyond obvious writing style differences among the authors, white papers also needed to have unified formatting. Instructors can use these types of style shifts to address writing concepts such as voice and person.

Unincorporated Visual Texts

Finally, the third major macrolevel concern with the white paper stemmed from students' efforts to combine visual text with written text. In general, when students aimed to incorporate images, charts, and tables, the resulting document lacked professional quality. Students often chose images that did not complement the written text by simply decorating the written text, or they did not incorporate the visual text within the written text (e.g., a chart or a table was not analyzed or referred to directly within the written text). In each of these cases, students needed to revise their white papers on the macrolevel by rethinking how to be rhetorically effective within the specific business genre.

Within the genre of the community-based service-learning project, instructors can address many of these macrolevel textual issues in the ESL PW classroom. It may be helpful to introduce the genre of the white paper with a discussion about audience, an exercise on collaborative writing, a lesson on using systematic typography, and a review of how to integrate visual texts effectively. Not only will addressing such macrolevel concerns earlier in the project allow students to avoid such textual concerns before they negatively impact the professional quality of their work, but the discussions will also help students to understand the components of the genre.

Microlevel Textual Issues in the White Paper

In addition to macrolevel textual concerns in the white paper, student-generated work showed microlevel grammatical and stylistic errors that tarnished the overall professional quality of their work. At the sentence level, a variety of grammatical errors were produced, and parallel structure was again an issue that required further attention.

Grammatical Errors

As is appropriate in many ESL writing courses, surface-level grammatical errors may be addressed through individual feedback. In the case of the rhetorically situated project outlined here, PW instructors can approach these errors with a discussion about professional ethos and the impact grammatical errors may have for consumers who are trying to utilize a business document in order to purchase a product or use an item correctly (e.g., a manual, a spreadsheet, a report). Take, for example, the following paragraph in which students were clearly attempting to articulate their project goals to their client:

> Our group propose to the organization to help them creating good advertising and the first step that we should take is by choosing what kind of advertising method that will help the organization promote the event. In this paper, we research common type of advertising for an event such as posters, brochures, open booth, message on

> white blackboard around campus, E-mails, Television, and windows display. Provided some advantages and disadvantages for all of those in order for the organization could decide which method the best for them.

Here, missing verbs and subjects, subject–verb agreement, verb tense, and singular and plural nouns need to be addressed at the microlevel. Although no one's writing is error-free, the frequency and variety of errors here decrease the readability of the paragraph and impact the group's professional ethos. Instructors may want to address grammar errors earlier in the project instead of waiting until the editing phase. Further, approaching the topic of collaborative writing may be a helpful way for students to be encouraged to review and provide continuous feedback to their peers.

Parallel Structure

In addition to the frequency of grammatical errors, students continued to have a problem with parallel structure. In many of the white papers, students included lists of bulleted items so that they could summarize information quickly. Though this was a good rhetorical move, given the genre of the white paper and the context in which white papers are typically read, the lack of parallel structure throughout the white papers made it difficult to scan the lists, as is evidenced in this example:

- "Advantages of using reminder on chalk/white boards to advertise:"
    — "It will catch many people's attention as it is a large room."
    — "This is cheap, no cost at all."
    — "Can be colorful and well designed."

Here, students were trying to summarize the advantages of a particular advertising method so that the client could make an informed decision about promotional documents. However, on the microlevel, students needed to rework the bulleted items to make the information more accessible. Put another way, students needed to be aware of the relationship between consistent parallel structure and the degree of a document's readability. Instructors may want to address this microlevel topic directly, providing well-written and poorly written examples and asking students to record the length of time it takes them to read or scan different samples.

Reflection on the Community-Based Service-Learning Project

The community-based service-learning project is multifaceted and challenging. Throughout, students are required to work collaboratively with an actual client in order to produce an authentic promotional document. By the end of the project, students have been introduced to a number of real-life business genres and have come to appreciate the ways in which a written product conveys professional ethos. This finding has been reflected in students' memos in which they commented on their progress throughout the project. Students felt that they understood these business genres and were prepared to construct such documents once they left the classroom.

REFLECTIONS

Based on their sample writing and survey data, it is clear that students benefit when PW instructors directly address grammar and style concerns in the ESL classroom. Furthermore, students' own reflections at the end of each course confirm the need for instructors to integrate real-world projects in a way that raises students' awareness of the legal, professional, ethical, and practical issues common in the business and technical worlds. The materials presented in this chapter are difficult to construct without a good supply of student writing and without the support of a PW program. By sharing these strategies, we hope to encourage other ESL instructors to develop research- and theory-driven PW materials to meet their own students' needs.

Jennifer Haan is a doctoral candidate in the English as a Second Language program at Purdue University. She has taught professional writing for native and nonnative speakers, for both university students and adult learners. Her interests include program administration, institutional language planning, and second language writing.

Karyn Mallett is a doctoral candidate in the English as a Second Language program at Purdue University. She has taught ESL courses at the university and community college levels, including professional and technical writing for native and nonnative students. Her interests include second language writing, educational language policy, and advocacy.

Enhancing Critical Writing Skills

Discourse Analysis: Bridging the Gap Between Linguistic Theory and Classroom Practice in Writing Classes

Peter McDonald

Although discourse analysis (DA) is a method of linguistic description that has practical pedagogical value (McCarthy, 1991), many of the ideas that are contained in the DA literature have not been fully applied to intermediate writing classrooms. This is unfortunate because DA offers key theoretical concepts that can easily be applied to existing curricula to create tasks that will offer students fresh and exciting ways to analyze their classroom texts. Moreover, once students have achieved an awareness of textual structures, DA can help students move beyond analyzing everyday classroom language and allow them to deconstruct authentic texts. Most importantly, by empowering students with the knowledge of how to deconstruct texts, DA gives students a new awareness of textual structures that can be applied to their own writing, which will significantly improve their ability to create texts successfully. Finally, because DA is an interactive approach to writing, it can be used to create a communicative learning environment that supports discovery learning.

CONTEXT

The teaching context described in this chapter is a 1st-year writing course in a university in Japan. The students are English majors who have graduated from Japanese high schools, so most of them have not been introduced to a pedagogical approach that includes DA. Rather, both my own experience and the literature (Burden, 2005) suggest that Japanese students are more familiar with teacher-centered classrooms where translation methods are taught. However, the approach used at my university is based on research that suggests language learning should be communicative and should be studied across the traditional boundaries of lexis, semantics, and discourse (Brown, 2000, p. 362).

This holistic approach dictates that language cannot be broken down into a traditional "atomistic" system (Cook, 1989, pp. 82–83), where language is separated into components that are mastered over time (Rutherford, 1987), but rather language is learned by using a top-down approach that studies the inter-related levels of language in context. This is, however, a complex process requiring students to hypothesize about language based on the data being studied, as opposed to learning the formal rules of language and then applying them to the data. This approach, then, embraces a consciousness-raising (C-R) approach (Rutherford, 1987). The course is designed, therefore, to build on students' knowledge about English and to introduce them to the C-R learning strategy.

In order to do the activities outlined in this chapter, two features of DA must be examined: (a) an awareness of the common patterns found in all texts and (b) an awareness of critical approaches to reading and constructing texts.

Awareness of Common Patterns in Texts

The first factor of DA relevant to the classroom is analyzing common textual features contained in all written language because they provide an understanding of underlying elements in linear prose structures. Knowing how to use and recognize common structural patterns allows writers to create texts efficiently and, likewise, enables readers to navigate, interpret, and understand texts successfully (Hoey, 2001). However, for second language (L2) learners accustomed to a traditional instructional approach, the reciprocal relationship between the writer and the reader may not be fully realized because common textual features may not be immediately apparent. This chapter introduces three of the most common textual features: genre analysis, patterns in text, and textual cohesion; then it explores how these can be effectively utilized in writing.

Defining Genre Analysis

Genre analysis, which studies the underlying organization of texts, suggests that the creation of successful texts involves the writer exercising a series of language choices. The types of choices are naturally constrained by the genre the writer has chosen or has been assigned. For example, the schematic, lexical, and syntactic choices used in creating paragraphs for an academic essay are fundamentally different from those used for advertising. Applying Swales' (1990) definition of genre, the select community that reads academic essays will impose different discourse constraints on the writer. Readers of academic writing would expect formal language and a well-balanced discussion of the topic; in contrast, readers of an advertisement would expect informal, persuasive language with no intention of balancing the discussion.

Understanding the Problem–Solution Text Pattern

Hoey (2001) points out that most patterns in texts adhere to "culturally popular patterns of organization" (p. 122). Perhaps the most common pattern, found in everything from ancient folk tales to modern movies, is the problem–solution pattern (Labov, 1999). In this pattern, a series of narrative stages can be explored by answering four basic questions: (a) What is the situation? (b) What is the problem? (c) What is the solution? and (d) What will the result be? If the result is negative, the readers return to the first question and recycle through the process until a positive result is realized. If the result is positive, the narrative ends. This pattern is not a fixed rhetorical structure but rather one that appears with many variations in nonnarrative genres, such as academic writing or advertising texts.

Defining Cohesion

Cohesion refers to common textual patterns that work across sentences and phrases. Because all readable texts manifest cohesion, it is very easy to recognize. For example, in the previous sentence, *it* refers the reader back to the word before the comma, *cohesion*, and, therefore, links the two sentences. This type of link is known as *anaphoric pronoun reference* (Halliday & Matthiessen, 2004). These types of patterns are clearly shown in the text in Figure 1. Here, numerous examples of anaphoric reference are italicized. Also, in sentence 6, there is an example of an *exophoric reference* (boldfaced), which is commonly used in academic writing to introduce supporting information from primary or secondary sources. Other examples of cohesion include reiteration, or repetition (larger type), and parallelism, or equal grammatical structures (underlined).

Deforestation is a serious problem because forests and trees aren't just pretty to look at, *they* do an important job making the earth's environment suitable for life.

2) *They* clean the air, store water, preserve soil, and provide homes for animals.

3) *They* also supply food, fuel, wood products, and paper products for humans.

4) In the past fifty years, more than half the world's rainforests have been destroyed.

5) Today the forests of the world are being cut down at a rate of fifty acres every minute!

6) **Scientists say** that if deforestation continues, the world's climate may change, floods may become more common, and animals will die.

Note. From *Success with College Writing: From Paragraph to Essay,* by D. E. Zemach and L. A. Rumisek, 2003, Tokyo: Macmillan Language House. Copyright 2003 by Macmillan Language House. Reprinted with permission.

Figure 1. Examples of Cohesion in Paragraphs

Awareness of Critical Approaches to Discourse

After identifying the underlying patterns and features in texts, the second factor of DA relevant to classroom instruction involves the application of textual knowledge to evaluate a text. This is done in two ways: (a) looking at the text's underlying "textualization," and (b) applying the findings of critical discourse analysis (CDA).

Awareness of Textualization

Textualization refers to evaluating whether or not a writer's language choices are communicated successfully (Johns, 1994). In this approach, a written text is seen as representing only one set of possible choices (Coulthard, 1994, p. 10), arrived at from a limitless number of other possible choices. This position of judgment is important for L2 writers because it empowers learners with the knowledge that the final set of choices in a text, be it a published text or their own writings, may not be the best available options.

Awareness of Critical Discourse Analysis

For many researchers and practitioners, DA should include not only an analysis of the text's linguistic properties but also an analysis of the ideology and values that underpin the creation of a given text (Jaworski & Coupland, 1999). Thus, CDA has been challenged (see Widdowson, 1995, for an overview). However, aspects of CDA are relevant because students' writings and classroom texts are in themselves genres and are judged for both their linguistic merit and the ideology and values represented in the text. Bakhtin (1999) explains, "There can be no such thing as an absolutely neutral utterance" (p. 128), so it follows that neutrality is impossible in either the students' own writing or in their assigned texts. Therefore, in order to create successful writing, students must be made aware of the ideological implications of the words they choose.

CURRICULUM, TASKS, MATERIALS

The curriculum, tasks, and materials are designed to support what White (1988) refers to as a textbook-based "hybrid" (p. 111) curriculum, where the textbook dictates the pace and the content of the course, but where teachers are expected to supplement the textbook information with suitable activities. The discourse activities outlined in this chapter, then, are designed to supplement and support existing textbook-based curricula.

Task 1: Introducing the Problem–Solution Pattern

The first discourse activity is to introduce students to the problem–solution pattern by having them ask the four basic problem–solution questions about a text. The second step is to have students recognize the narrative pattern in their classroom texts, as illustrated in Table 1.

Table 1. The Problem–Solution Template Applied to Classroom Texts

Directions: Complete this table by filling out columns 2 and 3 from the information you have learned from reading the paragraph on page 51 of your textbook.		
Problem–Solution Pattern	*Explanation*	Textbook Chapter 7 The Problem–Solution Paragraph (page 51)
What Is the Situation?	*Topic of the paragraph*	Something must be done about deforestation.
What Is the Problem?	*Deforestation*	(1) Deforestation is a serious problem because forests and trees are not just pretty to look at; they do an important job in making the earth's environment suitable for life. (2) They clean the air, store water, preserve soil, and provide homes for animals. (3) They also ……
What Is the Solution?	*Use less paper* *Recycle* *Reuse* *Reduce*	(7) One solution to the problem of deforestation is to use less paper. (8) If you use less paper, fewer trees will be cut for papermaking. (9) How can you use less paper? (10) One answer is to reduce your paper usage by using both sides when you photocopy, write a letter, or write a paper for the school.
Result? (positive)	*You can help*	(15) If you follow the three Rs—reduce, reuse, and recycle—you can help save the world's rainforests.

Note. From Success with College Writing: From Paragraph to Essay, by D. E. Zemach and L. A. Rumisek, 2003, Tokyo: Macmillan Language House. Copyright 2003 by Macmillan Language House. Reprinted with permission.

As Table 1 shows, students are to identify the topic of the text. In the next stages, they must clearly signal the problem and the solution, and finally, they must determine how the pattern ends with a positive outcome. The numbers in parentheses refer to the order of sentences in the assigned paragraph. Again, this is not a fixed rhetorical structure but rather a common pattern that may appear with many variations used to enhance writing.

The template provides an excellent approach for introducing students to key patterns in texts. For one, it is a model that can be replicated, providing students with a guide for their own writing. However, reproductive language work cannot teach the complexity of text creation. In fact, when students rely on simple models, they often become confused and feel constrained when expressing their own complex thoughts or arguments. Therefore, students need a greater awareness of how the problem–solution pattern actually supports text construction.

Task 2: Analyzing the Problem–Solution Pattern in Texts

Task 2 concerns the Discourse Dialogue Matrix (see Table 2), which works on the principle that all texts contain underlying cohesive dialogue that can be projected into question form (Hoey, 2001). Thus, the discourse questions represent

Table 2. The Discourse Dialogue Matrix

Discourse Questions	What Is the Situation?	What Is the Problem?	Why Is That a Problem?	Why Are Trees Important for Life?	What Is Happening to the Trees?	Why Is That a Problem?
Row 1 Answers to discourse questions	*Something must be done about deforestation*	*Deforestation (1)*	*Pretty to look at/ makes the environment suitable for life (1)*	*Helps air, water, soil, animals, supplies food, fuel, products/ paper (2, 3)*	*Destroyed/ cut down (4, 5)*	*Climate change, floods, death to wildlife (6)*
Row 2 Writer's moves	None: *The main idea is not directly stated*	States the problem	Explains problem	Supports with examples	Supports with statistics	Supports with expert opinion

the underlying dialogue inherent in the previously discussed problem–solution paragraph.

First, students are given the discourse questions and asked to fill in the answers, which is best done as a pair-work discovery activity. After students discuss the potential answers among themselves and summarize their findings in Row 1, they compare their answer with the teacher's (shown in italics). Then the students complete Row 2, which asks them to think about what discourse moves the writer makes (e.g., in the first sentence the writer states the problem, in the second the writer explains the problem in detail).

Having asked students to deconstruct the paragraph at the macrolevel (top-down) across the paragraphs, the next stage is to deconstruct it at a microlevel (bottom-up) across sentences and phrases. Asking students to find the cohesion elements within the paragraph, as shown in Figure 1, can help to accomplish this. Cohesion can show students that the writer repeats the same ideas using different words or patterns and illustrates the point that writers use many different ways to say the same thing. This activity should help students understand how they can utilize relatively simple grammar structures efficiently across texts.

Overall, this task introduces students to the complex writing process of crafting well-constructed paragraphs and shows them that common features of writing are to expound and support ideas. The matrix in Table 2 can easily be adapted to students' own writing by asking them to create a similar paragraph about a different problem, using the discourse questions and the discourse moves as a foundation for their ideas. Once they have created their own paragraphs, the matrix can also be used for peer correction, allowing students to apply the discourse questions to their classmates' writing.

The writing that students initially create is only one possible set of choices, or one textualization, but it may not be the most successful. Choosing another textualization by rewriting, based on their classmate's deconstruction of the original paragraph, should improve the initial texts. Thus, by providing facilities to gain more informed choices, students are able to improve their writing skills. Students should be reminded that all writers, be they first language (L1) or L2 students, must revise and rewrite. Moreover, they should also be reminded that the basic principles, which are to project monologues into dialogues, to support points using a variety of devices, and to link ideas across paragraphs using cohesion, are important writing skills that are easily transferable to other writing contexts.

However, if students are to create successful texts, they must also be made aware of the fundamental differences in schematic, lexical, and syntactic choices offered across different genres. Nunan (1999) explains that students need to explore language as a "set of choices" (p. 137). This exploration can be accomplished by applying a genre approach to classroom writing. Students need to know that they are writing for a specific discourse community (e.g., the "experts" are their teachers and other potential examiners). Each community imposes constraints not only on the form of writing but also on its content. Thus, students who are asked to answer a comparison essay are writing in a specific genre and, therefore, making a different set of language choices than students who are writing to answer a classification essay question. Therefore, for students to write successfully, they need to be made aware of language choices that underpin certain genres.

In order to gain this awareness, students should be introduced to nonclassroom language. Textbooks and teacher-created examples are composed of texts produced solely by teachers and textbook writers for the "imagined readers" (Coulthard, 1994, pp. 4–5) of L2 students. Ultimately, the students must be able to create texts that are to be read by the imagined readers of L1 examiners. In other words, the students' textbooks were created for a specific discourse community, but the texts created by the students themselves will be addressed to a different discourse community. Bridging this gap involves introducing nonclassroom language taken from a variety of genres to support classroom language. Examples on how this can be done are provided in Task 3.

Task 3: Supporting the Textbook With Authentic Materials

Task 3 shows how authentic language from different genres can support the textbook without overwhelming the students. Students are given a small text, an advertisement for a financial company (see Table 3). They are asked to discover, using their basic problem–solution questions, the similarities and differences between this new text and the academic text used to discuss deforestation. The texts are clearly different; the advertisement displays the common advertising features of a casual but persuasive tone, simplistic sequencing of words and phrases,

Table 3. Advertisement for Financial Company

Problem–Solution Pattern	Advertising Text
Situation–orientation	Looking to buy a home in Japan?
Problem	Need a mortgage?
Solution	Talk to Banner Financial service representative.

Note. From advertisement for Banner Japan K.K., 2006, *Metropolis Magazine.* Reprinted with permission.

and numerous rhetorical questions (Woods, 2006). Surprisingly, however, the advertising text and the academic text also have similarities: The problem–solution pattern is strongly signaled, the interactive writer–reader relationship is clearly illustrated by the question and response patterns, and they both contain lexical signals.

There is enough information in this small text to allow students not only to hypothesize but also to rehypothesize about discourse as more information is discovered. Students could be encouraged to create simple advertisements as follow-up writing activities. Once this is accomplished, students can rehypothesize by using more complex texts, many of which can easily be found online. For example, a quick online search of *deforestation* produces countless examples of the problem–solution pattern in a variety of genres, such as process and comparison–contrast. Using authentic resources will improve students' understanding of the common discourse features, and, therefore, improve their approach to creating their own successful texts. Finally, once students have been introduced to authentic texts, they can begin to develop a critical approach to creating texts, as seen in Task 4.

Task 4: Adding a Critical Approach

The final task (see Figure 2) shows students how to evaluate writing for successful textualization as well as the ideological values that underpin texts. These critical questions are follow-up activities based on the successful completion of Tasks 1–3 and are best introduced in discovery–discussion tasks.

First, the students are being asked to express their genuine feelings about the model readings they are being encouraged to read and emulate. It is also a good idea to have students keep a record of their evaluations so that they can build an awareness of how their impressions and preferences change over time. Question 2 is designed to show students that both context and audience change the text's construction. One way for students to become aware of this concept is to compare the textbook example of the problem–solution pattern (created for the discourse community of L2 learners) with an authentic text that gives a more complex view of the issue. For example, an online article (http://earthobservatory.nasa.gov/Features/Deforestation/) discusses deforestation

1. How do you feel about the issues raised in the reading assignment?
2. What is the writer's purpose? (Why was it written? Who was it written for? Who was it written by? Where was it published?)
3. What is the writer's main idea?
4. What devices does the writer use to make each point and achieve the purpose?
5. How successfully do you feel the writer achieves the purpose?

6_____5_____4_____3_____2_____1
VERY   **REASONABLY**   **NOT AT ALL**

Figure 2. Increasing Critical Awareness

from the point of view of the discourse community of subsistence farmers (NASA Earth Observatory, 2007). For this community, the language contained in the textbook may be objectionable because its solutions to deforestation might create an economic crisis in their community. Thus, asking the students to examine the text in its context can make them aware that language choices play an important ideological role in the text's message.

Question 3 increases students' awareness that most texts contain a finite point that can be summarized succinctly. Unless this point is clearly discernable and cohesively expressed, it is unlikely that the writing will communicate its message successfully. Question 4 is a review question, so the students' answers can illustrate how far they have progressed from sentence-level comprehension to discourse-level processing, which, in turn, helps the teacher format future lessons to meet student needs. The last quantitative evaluation question helps students think in less general terms by reassuring them that L2 students are entitled to make evaluative judgments. Again, keeping a record of these judgments should help them focus on ways to develop their own writing. Moreover, students should begin to realize that not all L1 texts represent the most successful textualization. This advanced evaluative approach can easily become part of the everyday activities in the classroom. Moreover, these types of C-R questions can be applied to all texts, and they also serve as a basis for peer- and self-evaluations of student writing.

REFLECTIONS

This chapter assumes improved skills if the writing curriculum incorporates two features of DA: (1) an awareness of common textual features, such as genre, the problem–solution pattern, and cohesion; and (2) an awareness of critical approaches that analyze text creation. These features of DA are not intended to replace or challenge existing approaches to writing. Rather, they work best while supplementing them. Since genres already exist in the classroom in both student writing and textbooks, expanding the genre study is relatively easy to do. Articulating the problem–solution text as a pattern, using it to deconstruct existing texts, and then reapplying it to construct new texts can also make a positive difference in the way students construct their own texts. Cohesion can be seen as another way for students to look at how the grammar patterns they have already studied in previous learning contexts work in building texts. Finally, critical approaches to learning are standard classroom expectations for both teachers and students as they offer evaluation, feedback, and peer correction. Including DA in classroom instruction offers additional ways to develop these practices.

That DA is already widely used in the classroom is also evident in recently published textbooks, many of which already contain DA ideas to support their underlying pedagogical approach. However, not all instructional information accompanying the textbooks contains an adequate explanation of the theoretical ideas employed by the authors. Therefore, in order to fully utilize DA ideas in the classroom, teachers might need to research available DA literature.

Although the tasks and materials are presented in a linear fashion, they also work well as supplementary activities presented periodically across the curriculum, working in conjunction with other classroom materials. One way of introducing DA tasks and materials, if the teaching context does not permit a fuller treatment, is to use them in the same way as communicative textbooks use "grammar boxes" to focus on form. DA activities are excellent recourse to support students who can process the standard classroom exercises quickly and have extra time to work independently on a new challenge. Moreover, DA can be used when individual learners need additional support to address writing weaknesses.

However, although a DA approach to writing is beneficial, introducing it in the classroom might create challenges. The students' reading level is a consideration because if students cannot read well, they cannot be expected to create detailed hypotheses about text construction. Therefore, it is best to introduce detailed text analysis only after students have successfully comprehended the text. In order for discovery techniques and the DA approach to learning to be successful, the reading materials must be understood by the students, or the desired pedagogical outcome cannot be achieved.

A second challenge is the students' flexibility. It is important to recognize that each classroom contains students with different learning styles (Richards & Lockhart, 1996). Consequently, many students, no matter what their educational background, may prefer teacher-led explanations over discovery techniques, so careful consideration needs to be taken if all types of learners are to benefit.

Finally, because DA is a theory of linguistic description rather than a pedagogical approach, it can appear overly complex. For example, this chapter has focused on only the problem–solution pattern. There are other patterns, such as comparison and contrast, cause and effect, and classification. Moreover, it is common for texts to display a general pattern along with combinations of the other patterns. This might confuse students who are uncomfortable with ambiguity.

With these reservations in mind, as this chapter has shown, the findings of DA can be successfully applied to the writing classroom to produce a pedagogically sound yet pragmatic way to help students bridge the gap between traditional teacher-centered classrooms and a challenging DA instructional method. Indeed, used wisely and consistently in an existing curriculum, DA can greatly improve students' awareness of text construction and help student writing become richer, fuller, and more communicative.

Peter McDonald has 13 years of teaching experience in a variety of teaching contexts. He has taught in Greece, India, and the United Kingdom, and is currently teaching in Japan while his classroom research is being done through the University of Birmingham, in England. His interests include how to use discourse analysis and systemic functional grammar in the classroom.

CHAPTER 14

A Case for Writer-Generated Annotation

Holli Schauber

This chapter makes an instructional proposal for the use of a student-generated annotation system as one way to raise awareness about clarity, cohesion, and coherence in English for academic purposes (EAP) writing courses. The ideas in this chapter are framed from several perspectives: (a) the development of strategies that contribute to resourcefulness in evaluating, monitoring, and explaining one's own writing; (b) the promotion of attention to text-based signals of clarity, cohesion, and coherence; and (c) the use of the students' own writing to achieve these two objectives. Learner-generated annotation supports these goals.

After an initial overview of annotation and its role and rationale in the present EAP context, this chapter reviews the sequence of practical initiatives comprising the annotation system with reference to how students can use annotation to elucidate their sentences' purposes and the criteria by which they can glean clarity, cohesion, and coherence. This is followed by some concluding recommendations, benefits, and remarks.

CONTEXT

The context in which this annotation technique took shape is a required 16-week undergraduate English as a second language (ESL) basic composition course at a university in Switzerland. The students were Swiss and non-Swiss native speakers of French, Swiss German, Italian, Spanish, Polish, Romanian, Arabic, Turkish, Greek, Ukrainian, Russian, Farsi, Korean, and Chinese.

CURRICULUM, TASKS, MATERIALS

Annotation and EAP Teaching

Although annotation is sometimes used within current approaches to EAP writing instruction, especially when autonomy and self-monitoring may be emphasized, a review of the literature reveals no precedent for how learner-generated annotation might be effectively and reliably used to

- raise awareness about clarity, cohesion, and coherence within the writing process itself

- contribute to EAP writer autonomy through self-monitoring

- arm EAP students with the language forms and features to help them make informed decisions as writers

Writer-generated annotation can be understood as isolating, summarizing, labeling, identifying, and recognizing the meanings and purposes of sentences and their relevant elements both within and across sentences and paragraphs. Annotation as a tool for learning in writing has typically been used to identify sentence roles and meanings accurately within a text and to invite teacher feedback on written drafts. In the former, the learner relies on a given set of constructs to apply to an existing text (often from a textbook), while in the latter the learners annotate their own texts to signal difficulty, request advice, or invite commentary. In both cases, the learner decides what merits annotation by using an existing and predetermined set of constructs. Charles (1990) used an annotation technique to call attention to problem areas within students' texts through their questions and comments to teachers. A decade later, Cresswell (2000) reiterated that purpose but added the idea that annotation increased learner control. More recently, Xiang (2004) found that learners who engaged an annotation system to self-monitor aspects in their writing increased their involvement with the writing process.

Annotation builds on the cognitive process of noticing text-based features, along with serving to raise students' consciousness about the aspects of the text that concern distinct language forms, functions, and purposes. Brown (2005) proposed a self-evaluation technique involving preexisting annotated writing samples for students to use as part of an independent learning opportunity. Although these approaches differ from the annotation system proposed here, they do, nonetheless, highlight its importance as a strategy for promoting self-monitoring within the writing process. The annotation technique described in this chapter relies exclusively on writer-generated constructs (labels for identifying sentence meanings and purposes) prompted by the students' own writing. Generating these constructs is contingent on the production of new drafts.

Annotation's Role in the Curriculum

Annotation is one of many approaches used in my basic composition class in order to explore features of clarity, cohesion, and coherence, which are core course objectives. A defining principle of the course is that the interplay between those three constructs and the techniques to promote awareness about them in EAP writing should naturally include a form of learner initiatives for accountability.

For this reason, annotation was selected as one of the analytical tools students should use because of the intimate way it permits them to take stock of the inherent sentence- and paragraph-level purposes and meanings contained in their writing. It asks them to examine the local and global elements within their work that signal and contribute to clarity, cohesion, and coherence. Conducting a metadiscourse examination increases the resonance of the technique and the impact it can have on their writing. Hyland (2005) refers to this point as writers confirming their own stance while indicating an allegiance with their readers.

The writer-generated annotation system described in this chapter draws on an integrated view of EAP writing and acknowledges the nexus between how text is shaped, for whom, and why. It respects the individual and personal nature of text, and by asking students to explain and justify their work from that perspective, it promotes students' abilities to critique, analyze, and negotiate the content and language forms that contribute to the effectiveness of their texts. Within that framework, annotating text augments the control EAP students have over their own writing and intensifies the intimacy they experience with their texts as both readers and writers. It likewise contributes to an overt awareness of the inner workings of the text, a core curricular goal in EAP instruction. The annotation system meshes well with the curricular demands of a 16-week ESL basic composition course that presents students ample opportunity to explore and practice ways to achieve clarity, cohesion, and coherence as part of a more global examination of the relationships that sentences and paragraphs convey within an academic essay.

Before introducing the idea of annotation to students, it is necessary to settle on a set of understandings and explanations about clarity, cohesion, and coherence. Clarity refers to the notion that ideas are expressed fully, explicitly, clearly (Leki, 1995), concisely, and directly (Williams, 2003). Although both coherence and cohesion are understood to be the lexical glue that binds text together through unity, organization, focus, logic, and signposting (McCarter, 1997; Reid, 2000; Spatt, 2003.), more pointedly, cohesion is the vehicle by which elements in text are linked together through the use of pronouns, repetition, substitution, and other devices (Halliday & Hasan, 1976; Raimes, 2002b).

A cornerstone of this curriculum involves using this annotation technique to provide EAP writers with a concrete means for understanding how clarity, cohesion, and coherence contribute to meaning-making within a discipline-specific community that has expectations about structure, appropriateness, voice, and style. Apprenticing the forms, functions, conventions, and disciplinary expectations that signal this participation requires that teachers expose their students to these sources of information.

Inspiration

The sentence annotation technique described in this chapter was inspired by *A Book on Writing* by Sam McCarter (1997), which includes a series of form and meaning-focused exercises intended to shore up students' practical understanding about writing for academic and general purposes. Among the tasks included in the text are exercises that ask students to apply a pre-existing set of constructs (sentence-purpose labels) to a given set of individual sentences that, when stitched together, form a unified but brief text. While the EAP students did these exercises, it became evident that they would profit enormously from that type of exercise if it were taken several steps further. By customizing the system to produce a personalized version, every time a student applies the technique a new set of labels is generated. These labels grow organically from students' writing, reflections, and explanations. Since my initial use of the technique, more than 100 students in my classes have gained better control of the writing process and of the strategies, language features, and text-based signals that contribute to overall clarity, cohesion, and coherence. The annotation technique has proven to be a powerful writing tool, endearing it to the writers and their readers.

Practical Initiatives

After addressing why the annotation system makes good pedagogical sense, its implementation can be discussed. The annotation technique can be divided into a three-task sequence.

Task 1

Beginning with a set of consciousness-raising, guided questions to sensitize learners to the idea of critically examining and annotating their own writing, a bank of questions is initially proposed or modeled by the teacher. After a short period of time, students are asked to generate their own set of questions as part of an in-class group task. This results in a list of questions that students then use to scrutinize their own work. Students' responses to these questions result in the list of purpose labels they can draw on for the annotation. Each new draft yields a new set of constructs for annotation that represents the development of their text. The questions are intended to encourage students to consider and inventory the local and global purposes of their sentences and to pay attention to how the language supports or detracts from those intentions. See Figure 1 for some of the questions that have emerged from that effort.

Task 2

Students then generate a list of constructs to reveal the purposes that sentences can fulfill. These constructs build on the guided questions and draw on sample

---

Does this sentence signal the writer's opinion?

What is the new information in this sentence, and what old information does it build on?

Has the writer achieved cohesion and coherence? How do you know?

Is this sentence a conclusion, a recommendation, or a result?

Does this sentence add emphasis, provide more detail, or indicate a contrasting position? What words in the sentence signal its reference to the previous idea?

Figure 1. Classroom Questions for Consciousness-Raising

sentences from their own writing. To help students practice and apply the annotation technique, the class isolates examples of the different types of sentences contained in their work (see Figure 2). They are then weaned off of the guided questions, and in the third task, they are asked to generate their own questions addressing a variety of prompts that elicit critical thinking. A sample list of annotation labels is provided in Appendix A. While generating the functions list (see Figure 2), the students also elucidate the criteria for achieving clarity, cohesion, and coherence.

Task 3

Finally, students annotate sections of their own texts to yield an authentic set of purpose labels and explanations for their decisions. Building on Task 2, students are asked to explain why they labelled each sentence as they did and what particular aspects of the sentence alerted them to that label. This is undertaken as a group task, followed by a full class discussion of some of the examples. Once the sequence of practice tasks has been completed, students begin the annotation process as part of a homework assignment.

Task Synthesis

The combined set of tasks is intended to help students

- develop an awareness of the meanings and purposes of different sentences

- determine and recognize the signs and lexical markers in their sentences that pin down meaning, purpose, clarity, cohesion, and coherence

---

1. a cause	5. a contrast	9. a false analogy	13. a rhetorical question
2. a challenge	6. a criticism	10. a process	14. a reiteration
3. a comparison	7. a definition	11. a purpose statement	15. a generalization
4. a concession	8. a description	12. a recommendation	16. an explanation

---

Figure 2. Language Functions

- consider the relationships between sentences

- notice the presence or absence of coherence and cohesion within and between sentences and paragraphs

- clarify sentences (activating nouns, using parallel construction, etc.)

Recommendations

In addition to the practical considerations already listed, the following guidelines are recommended.

- Begin the process of annotation as a guided set of exercises that serve as a progressive set of building blocks. This enables the teacher to introduce students to the goals, rationale, and language of the annotation task as part of a hands-on implementation of the annotation scheme.

- Frame the entire annotation process with several overarching questions: What is the purpose of the sentence, and has it achieved the objective of its label? What is the signature feature within the sentence that elucidates the label? Have clarity, cohesion, and coherence been achieved? (See Appendix B for sample questions.)

- Focus on the sentence purposes and their meanings, their signature features as sentence types (e.g., interrogatives, declaratives); their supporting roles (e.g., facts, suggestions, anecdotes, illustrations, examples); their roles as text markers; and the contributions they make to the overall clarity, cohesion, and coherence of the text.

- Have students label each sentence in a designated paragraph using one or more of the following constructs: its purpose (e.g., topic sentence); its markers of clarity, coherence, and cohesion (e.g., transition signals, active voice, pronouns); its relationship to other sentences; and an explanation of why it has received the designated label (see Appendix C).

- Acknowledge that sentences can have more than one function and can be meaningful in a variety of ways.

- State the purpose of the sentence and justify its particular meaning. When students begin to expose the purposes and meanings of their own sentences, it allows them to be more mindful of the value of their choices in achieving their goals. It likewise helps them notice whether the words they've chosen best fulfill the original intentions of their sentences and paragraphs.

- Practice using the "insert comment" function in Microsoft Word to make the task of annotating their work more efficient, better organized, and easier for revision.

Four Benefits of Annotation

Benefit 1: Improved Revision

An obvious benefit of writer-generated annotation is its natural alliance with the revision process. Because the system grows organically from the student's own writing and the constructs they generate as labels, natural opportunities for revision are exposed. Because identifying and explaining their labels are key to the annotation process, they can revise on the basis of whether they have achieved their intended purpose and in light of the feedback they receive on their annotations.

Benefit 2: Learner Autonomy

Annotation of this type facilitates and contributes to opportunities for learning, self-monitoring, and assessment (self and peer). It builds as well on the benefits of active learner involvement that contributes to learner autonomy in ways that allow students to make informed decisions as writers.

Benefit 3: Lexical Awareness

By calling students' attention to the function and purpose of individual sentences, students develop a deeper understanding of the subtleties and nuances of particular lexical items that are prone to arise frequently in an academic essay.

Benefit 4: Writer Role Awareness

This approach contributes to the students' evolving understanding of the roles they and their texts play when coming into contact with others and the control they can assume over their communicative effect.

REFLECTIONS

This chapter has described a system for annotating sentences that draws on EAP student-generated constructs to demonstrate students' understanding and appreciation of the roles sentences and paragraphs occupy in their texts and how elements within and across these boundaries are connected to issues of clarity, cohesion, and coherence. This system works well because it is adaptable to the competence level of the students, to the curricular objectives of the course, and to the larger program, into which the development of this knowledge and these skills fits. Moreover, it draws on the importance of arming students with the strategic know-how and language-based resources that are essential tools for effective and independent writing. When students begin to take a hard and intimate look at their writing in ways that ask them to make meaningful discoveries, they learn to be more mindful of the requirements for achieving their goals.

The annotation system has the potential to inform other adult instructional contexts where learner autonomy is emphasized and in which practitioners seek a reliable, innovative, and context-sensitive means for helping ESL learners strengthen their understanding and competencies as writers. The system was developed because of the instructional opportunities it presented and because of the learning capital it affords ESL writers.

Holli Schauber is a lecturer and researcher in the English as a foreign language teacher preparation program in the Institute of Secondary Teacher Education at the University of Geneva in Switzerland.

APPENDIX A: STUDENT-GENERATED ANNOTATION LABELS

- a bridge
- a cause
- a challenge
- a comparison
- a concession
- a conclusion
- a contrast
- a criticism
- a definition
- a description
- a fact
- a false analogy
- a generalization
- a hasty generalization
- a process
- a purpose statement
- a question
- a recommendation
- a reference
- a reiteration
- a repetition
- a result
- a statistic
- a summary
- a supporting detail
- a supporting quotation
- a thesis statement
- a topic sentence
- an anecdote
- an effect
- an example
- an expansion of a previous idea
- an explanation
- an expletive
- an illustration
- an introduction
- an opinion
- an organizing sentence
- an organizing word (transition)
- background information

APPENDIX B: SAMPLE CRITERIA FOR
SENTENCE CLARITY, COHESION, AND COHERENCE

- Does this sentence build new information on previous information?

- Does it repeat key terms or ideas?

- Does it make use of synonyms?

- Does it use transition signals?

- Are the actors performing the action?

- Could the nouns be converted to verbs?

- Does the action appear early in the sentence, and do we know who is performing it?

- Is there parallel construction across similar word class items?

- Is there subject–verb agreement?

- Does the punctuation in the sentence help the reader?

APPENDIX C: SAMPLE STUDENT ANNOTATIONS

Academic English Class 6—Summary Writing

The author writs about the languages skills (1). First (2) he explains that, according to a neurolinguistic research, the polyglot people make function more the brain as a person who speaks only one langue. The study of Albert and Obler (1978) points out that same part of the brain of persons knowing various languages is well developed (3).

(1) Purpose: "writs about"

(2) Transition signal: "first" signals sequence, report statement; "he explains" = pronoun for coherence

(3) Support: "the study"

In the second part, the author continues augmenting with psycholinguistic studies, that the polyglots can express themselves with more facility. He gives examples, referring first the report of Lerea and Laport (1971) and Palmer (1972), that, as well, they have a better memory by listing and second, referring Slobin (1968), that they have a better intuition to understand the meaning of the new words.

The third example is about the study of Feldman and Shen (1962), who observed that the low-income two-languages-speaking children can learn easier new label as the low-income one-language-speaking (4). The last example (5) giving from the author is about the study of Peale and Lambert (1962). They found (6) that a child of ten years old, who speaks French and English, shows better capacity in linguistic abstraction as a child, who speaks only French o only English.

> (4) Example: "the third example," a comparison "can learn easier new label as the"

> (5) Another example: "the last example"

> (6) Explanation, coherence: "they found" builds new on old. Comparison: "shows better ... as a child"

The author concludes telling, that the acquisition of a second language is a very good reason to improve of the mental skills, in addition to the professional advantage.

Explanation of the Annotated Student Summary

In the previous sample of a student-annotated text, only two paragraphs were targeted for annotation. Students can choose which portions of their texts they want to annotate. In this case the student chose to annotate aspects of the summary that were discussed in class as part of our exploration of summary writing. Each set of annotations will be explained.

- The first annotation (1) focuses on the purpose of the original article and the student acknowledges that understanding through the label *purpose* and the words *writes about.*

- The second annotation (2) contains several labels: *transition signal, report statement,* and *pronoun reference for coherence.* In the student's interpretation and presentation of that sentence, she understands those elements to be represented by *first, he explains* and *he.*

- In the third annotation (3), the student labels her sentence purpose as *support* for other research by focusing on *the study.*

- In (4), the annotation label focuses on an *example* and a *comparison.* These are represented by *the third example* and *can learn easier new label as the low-income.*

- Another *example* is labeled in (5) as *the last example.*

- In (6), the student labels several purposes for the sentence: *Explanation, coherence (they found* builds new on old), and *comparison (shows better . . . as a child).*

In the event that there is disagreement with a student's annotation, feedback is provided that challenges the label or requests further evidence. The feedback will also call the student's attention to elements that are erroneously labeled, missing, or unclear. Attention is also drawn to sentences or sentence elements where cohesion, coherence, and clarity are present but not annotated.

Utilizing Technology in the Writing Curriculum

Wiki Writing Web: Development of a Web Site to Improve Writing Motivation in Exam Courses

Christopher A. Baldwin

Wiki Internet technology provides a quick and easy way to set up and edit Web sites and is being used more frequently by teachers around the world, as is evidenced by its inclusion in the increasingly popular Moodle course management system (Dougiamas, 2008). This chapter examines the development of a Web site to motivate teenagers to improve their writing skills in preparation for the Cambridge English for Speakers of Other Languages (ESOL) Preliminary English Test (PET) and First Certificate in English (FCE) exams (University of Cambridge ESOL Examinations, 2005, 2007a).

This chapter examines theories of writing development, including feedback and error correction issues; these are then applied to computer-based writing instruction. In addition, the structure of the site will be discussed, as well as its implementation and reactions from students and teachers.

On this Web site, writing exam questions are posted. Then students upload their answers, which can be edited online by their peers and teachers. This project, therefore, takes a social constructivist view of writing development, by encouraging peer review and correction and by applying the Vygotskyan principle of the zone of proximal development (ZPD) (Vygotsky, 1978). This chapter serves as a model for any teacher looking to add an extra dimension to writing classes, both in terms of the specifics of the Web site design and in the underpinning theory which can be applied to other content and contexts.

CONTEXT

The courses described in this chapter take place in a private language school in northern Italy, specialising in young learners, 4–19 years old. In the high school department, the students study for the Cambridge ESOL PET and FCE exams by attending lessons after normal school hours. Students in these courses are generally highly motivated and take these exams 1 or 2 years earlier than their classmates do. The courses last 2 years for PET, followed by 2 more years for FCE. Most students take both courses. In the 1st year, the courses focus on developing linguistic ability in all four skills: reading, writing, listening, and speaking. The 2nd year of study concentrates on specific exam skills and preparation.

Many students say that the writing exam is the most difficult to prepare for, yet teachers are hesitant to teach writing because of their own lack of experience as writing instructors. One way to help teachers and boost students' motivation to improve their writing skills is to include an online component. Krajka (2000) states that "with the help of selected websites or other on-line techniques, writing instruction can be made more interesting, appealing, motivating and authentic" (Introduction, ¶ 2).

The question addressed in this chapter is how a specially created Web site can make the teaching and learning of writing more interesting and motivating within the context of exam courses. This chapter will first look at the literature to examine how to develop writing skills, how to present feedback, how to correct errors effectively, and how to analyze exam washback. The literature review will also consider the use of computers in the writing classroom. All the above points will be synthesised to help create a Web site to develop students' exam writing skills and to encourage teachers to develop their teaching skills.

CURRICULUM, TASKS, MATERIALS

Writing Feedback

Hedgcock and Lefkowitz (1996) note that teacher response is the principle means by which students understand their development as writers. Keh (1990) highlights the role of the student in peer feedback, noting, too, the importance of training students to give feedback. It follows that any writing materials should encourage both teacher and peer review. By using computer-based materials, this aspect of peer and teacher review can be developed more easily than by using pen and paper. A text on paper can be comfortably read by only one person at a time, but a text uploaded onto the Internet can be reviewed by an entire class.

Guerrero and Villamil (2000) invoke sociocultural theory and Vygotsky's (1978) ZPD to help explain why peer correction is effective. The ZPD is the difference between what a learner is able to do with and without help. This help can come from the teacher, but it can also come from peers as they can offer suggestions during the revising and editing process. However, Guerrero and Villamil (2000) note that when students work together, they sometimes produce incorrect editing decisions, which again emphasises the importance of teacher correction on final drafts.

Davidson and Tomic (1994) and Keh (1990) discuss the importance of not focusing exclusively on surface errors, such as grammar and spelling, to the exclusion of what Keh calls "higher order concerns" (p. 296), which include the development of ideas and the overall structure of the text . Davidson and Tomic also note the advantages of using computers to encourage students to revise on a global level, as well as on a sentence level, because it is more expedient to cut and paste text on a computer screen than to rewrite whole segments of an essay on paper. Students need to know how to revise texts on both a surface level and global level, so this issue should be addressed by computer materials designers.

Error Correction

It has been shown that both teachers and students can correct surface-level errors, but whether they should or not remains controversial. If they should, how exactly should errors be corrected? This is an area of much controversy in the field of second language (L2) writing, notably because of an article by Truscott (1996), which strongly argues against correcting grammar in students' texts. His argument is that correcting grammar causes students to avoid writing difficult structures, thus limiting their expression. He also states that students who receive grammar correction spend less time writing than they could because they spend the bulk of their time focusing on error avoidance. He contends that time spent producing new texts is more beneficial. This contention is strongly refuted by Ferris (1999), who claims that Truscott understates the evidence in favour of error correction. Both authors cite the same studies but draw opposing conclusions. Truscott and Ferris agree on one point: More research is necessary.

With this controversy in mind (to cite Ferris's, 2004, title, "What do we do in the meantime?"), how should writing teachers treat students' errors? Six suggestions for error correction, which encourage high-quality self-correction and raised student awareness of potential problem areas, have been suggested by Ferris (2004, pp. 59–60).

Writing instructors should

- correct errors competently, incorporating correction in course planning

- use indirect feedback to encourage problem-solving and self-editing

- understand that different types of errors need different treatment

- require students to revise their texts after feedback

- give extra grammar instruction, tailored to students' needs, and combined with other error treatment methods

- encourage students to keep error charts, to monitor progress and heighten awareness of weakness

Ferris' suggestions can be easily incorporated into computer-based writing materials.

Washback

The courses under consideration all lead to standardised exams, so students need to learn how to pass the exams. Whether or not this also helps them to develop their language skills depends on the washback effect from the exams (Prodromou, 1995). This is the effect exams have on learning, which influences the teaching methodology employed and the materials used. Prodromou stresses the importance of avoiding repeating dry exam questions. Instead, he suggests that teachers breathe life into materials to encourage a high level of learner input, which he sees as the key to transforming negative into positive washback. This can be brought about by computer-based writing materials in that they are easily adaptable to students' real needs and wants. An exam writing question given on an aged photocopy without any explanation as to why it is important would probably lead to a dry lesson and a negative view of writing. The same question presented on a computer screen to students who have learned how to approach such questions and who expect both positive learning outcomes and the enjoyment of correcting other students' work will likely result in positive lessons and washback.

Using Computers in the Writing Classroom

Research has suggested various ways for using computers to help students develop writing skills; for example, Krajka (2000) writes about the benefits of Internet writing lessons because materials are current and because students display increased motivation. Also, Hertz-Lazarowitz and Bar-Natan (2001) studied elementary school students whose writing improved more by having learned from a combination of computer-mediated instruction and cooperative learning rather than by having been taught by either the product or process teaching method. Matsumura and Hann (2004), however, warn about the dangers of computer anxiety, indicating that students with lower computer skills prefer face-to-face feedback. They note, however, that computers can have a motivating effect. It is important to note that the students' work in their study was not anonymous, which discouraged many students from posting their work on the Internet. Davidson and Tomic (1994) discuss ways to help teachers overcome their fear of computers in the writing classroom by not worrying about becoming computer experts. Teachers need, instead, to view the computer as a simple classroom tool.

The e-Materials

Computer techniques have much to offer the writing materials developer. For this project, the goal was to develop a Web site that incorporated the preceding points in materials for students and teachers.

One type of Web site that is very flexible and easy to set up is a wiki site. Every page on a wiki has a built-in text editor, so students and teachers can type directly onto a Web page, which, when saved, becomes available on the Internet. This text can then be edited by other students or teachers. Links can easily be made to other pages, and pictures can be uploaded to liven up the site. The most famous wiki is the Wikipedia (Main Page, 2008), an encyclopaedia created and edited by Web users (see LeLoup & Ponterio, 2006, for a description). Godwin-Jones (2003) describes a wiki as a "collaborative environment which is more naturally suited for collaborative on-line projects" (p. 15). A wiki component is also included with the educational platform Moodle (Dougimas, 2008). A search on a wiki site, such as http://www.seedwiki.com (Tyler, 2001), shows that many teachers are using these types of sites. Anderson (2004) describes a wiki project to help new participants in a master's teaching ESOL programme, whereby students post information on the site that they have found to be useful relating to the course.

Description of the Site

The site, *Big Ben Exam Writing*, was named after the school. The site has three main sections: FCE, PET, and Teachers' Page (see Baldwin, 2006). The FCE and PET parts are similarly organised. There is one exam question per month for the course on a page, followed by pages for students to write their answers. As wiki pages are all editable, anyone can add comments and corrections to students' answers (see Appendix). How this is implemented depends on individual teachers. This site can be used to correct content issues and surface level errors; thus it is adaptable to both sides of the Ferris–Truscott debate. However, considering Ferris's (2004) point that students want their errors to be corrected, and the aim of the site to motivate students, a colour code that highlights grammatical errors in red, capitalisation errors in green, lexical errors in purple, and spelling errors in yellow has been suggested.

Teachers can use this or other codes adapted to their students' needs to highlight errors in the appropriate colour and then can make general comments under the text. This method conflicts with Chandler's (2003) findings that "both direct correction and simple underlining of errors are significantly superior to describing the type of error, even with underlining, for reducing long-term error" (p. 267). The correction method used on this Web site is "underlining-plus" to give students help in identifying errors. The proposed system follows Sugita's (2006) advice: "Clarity is the first thing to bear in mind in writing a comment" (p. 35). The site is, however, flexible, which allows teachers to take their own stance on the matter of correction and on whether to concentrate more on sentence-level issues or global concerns.

The pages can also be edited by fellow students, who can correct or highlight errors. This aspect of the site promotes a social constructivist view of writing development in that it encourages peer revision. Teachers are advised to have students write anonymously to diminish the problem of anxiety, and it encourages group possession of the work: One person starts, but many others collaborate in order to produce a finished text.

The fact that the pages are editable leads to a process view of writing development, with many drafts being written of each answer. An interesting feature of wiki sites is the ability to view old versions of the page, thus making it possible to see how the text evolves over successive drafts. This feature can be used as a type of error correction chart, as mentioned by Ferris (2004, p. 60). By helping students keep track of the errors they made, they may master correct usage of specific structures. A combined process–product approach can also be fostered in that students are able to look at answers written by other students and edit them before attempting to write their own answer. Reflecting on Badger and White's (2000) suggestion of combining the approaches, it would be good to alternate between students acting as editors before writing, and then acting as writers before editing. Students can also be encouraged to rewrite their original texts to incorporate the changes in order to foster acquisition of the correct forms, in line with Chandler's (2003) results.

Piloting and Implementation

The site was piloted with a group of 1st-year FCE students who wrote answers to an exam question. These answers were first commented on by the teacher–researcher. Then they were shown to another group of 2nd-year students so that they could revise the text. After this trial, several technical problems were solved, and the structure of the site was improved to allow for expansion throughout the year. The piloting proved to be vital to understand more fully the classroom dynamics of using the site.

The site was then launched school-wide after holding a short training session with the instructors of the exam courses. Teachers were shown how the site works, and its editing capabilities were demonstrated. A summary of this information was included in a teachers' page included on the site.

In the Classroom

Preparing the site is the first stage. It is necessary to have different answer pages for each student or pair of students, which must be created before the lesson. These pages contain brief instructions on how to use the editor, a function which can be copied and pasted quickly. Answer pages can be created with the name of each student, or more generic pages with the type and number of the question could be used.

A typical lesson using this wiki for the first time would start with students being told about the computer program; then they would have a chance to answer their first exam question on the Web site. They can see both the question and answer on screen at the same time. It is necessary to ensure that students open different answer pages because one page cannot be edited by two separate computers at the same time. The teacher next explains how to save work, and answers are then typed onto the answer page.

Once all the students have finished their answers, they are then directed to review their classmates' pages for ways to improve the text. This can be done in many ways depending on the aim of the lesson and each teacher's philosophy regarding error correction. Students can be encouraged to look at how completely the question has been answered, the construction of the text, and the grammar. Grammatical problems can either be highlighted or corrected in another text colour. After the changes have been saved, the original author checks the suggestions and makes necessary revisions. Any new language learned can then be recorded in notebooks or on a personal wiki page.

Outcomes

The purpose of this project was to design computer-based materials to improve motivation of students in writing lessons. Students were asked to answer a questionnaire about their experience with the computer-based writing. Their responses showed a very positive reaction to the site overall, with very few negative opinions; however, this reaction was mainly due to the editing of other students' work than to writing itself. This reaction was observed in the classroom in the form of very positive lessons, especially during the correction stage. The more negative answers were from younger students, whose exam dates were in the distant future, thus suggesting a more positive washback from those with impending exam dates. It is expected that the use of the site will increase as the exam becomes imminent. The site has achieved its objective of increasing the majority of students' motivation to write.

Teachers' opinions were sought during informal interviews after they had used the site in one lesson. Attitudes were universally positive about the site, finding that it helped produce interesting and stimulating lessons. They all reported that the most enjoyable aspect for the students was peer correction, with one teacher saying that her students were looking forward to checking their work at home to see if anyone had edited it. Some teachers felt uneasy about using computers, but the training session helped to show the simplicity of the site, which reassured them. One teacher said that it made teaching writing more interesting by providing an additional teaching tool. Another teacher commented that she was very busy and didn't have time to read the teachers' page, thus highlighting the importance of the training session, which explained the different correction methods available to them.

Students' comments also included technical points about the text editor, requests for a greater variety of questions, and requests for explanations of errors, not just corrections. This desire for explanations reflects the findings of Ferris and Roberts (2001); however, the flexibility of the site allows it to be used with a variety of correction methods that could be more explicit in error explanation. A problem highlighted by one student is that errors in the original text can be removed completely, which makes learning from mistakes more difficult. The site still allows access to old versions of answers, but it would be helpful if teachers and students left the errors visible, as in the example in the appendix. Several younger students mentioned adding games or quizzes to the site to help motivation.

REFLECTIONS

Successes

The site has been successful in its two primary aims of increasing both student motivation to write and teacher motivation to teach writing. Part of the success of the site could be explained by students feeling honoured because the Web site had been created specifically for them. The feedback, given by whatever means, was considered positive, thus aiding motivation and possibly leading to acquisition of clear, communicative writing. This result agrees with Perpignan's (2003) observations that "it is therefore not the explicitly conveyed messages and their encoding that should be focused by teachers and researchers, in order to generate better conditions for feedback effectiveness, but the intentions which inspire them and the means which promote them" (p. 271).

This observation underscores the value of a social constructivist view of writing development, where peer reviewers and teachers are not there to find faults but to help, especially when considering "L2 acquisition as a situated, co-constructed process" (Young, 2004, p. 519). This view can be fostered by computer-assisted language learning according to Ortega (1997), a vital aspect of this site because it would not work if students only corrected, without posting their own work. Therefore, students must become part of the group both helping and being helped to become better writers.

Drawbacks

The site requires the use of the Internet, which in this school is available to students, but two students usually have to share a computer. This arrangement is sometimes beneficial in the social constructivist view, but it is sometimes negative in that working individually helps develop learner autonomy. Most students in this context have the Internet at home, but when there are technical problems it is difficult for students to complete their homework. Pen-and-paper writing work can be done anywhere, but this site requires an Internet connection and the ability to type, aspects that could discourage its use. The one-question-a-month format of the site proved difficult to maintain in a busy school environment. A second version of the site could instead offer questions thematically, relating to type of writing required (e.g., formal or informal letters, reports, articles, or story writing).

The Future

Computer-based editing programmes can also be considered as a tool to help both teacher and student development. One important area raised in this project is that of correction. Most of the teachers at the school have relatively little experience as writing teachers; thus, they do not have their own personal theory as to how to correct writing errors. Experience with this site could help them to develop a position. Keh (1990) and Min (2006) note the importance of training students to give peer review feedback, an area that has not been examined in this project. Another aspect that has not been addressed is whether the site actually helps students improve their writing skills. If it does, what kind of writing instruction and which correction method are most effective? A longitudinal study to monitor the effects of use of the site and its various correction methods, as proposed by Ferris (2004, p. 56), would be useful. In the future, the site could be expanded in many ways; for example, sections could be added to help develop other skills, such as reading and exam techniques, and pages could be added for other exams, such as the Cambridge ESOL programme's Certificate in Advanced English exam (University of Cambridge ESOL Examinations, 2007a).

Christopher A. Baldwin is a freelance teacher and teacher-trainer based in northern Italy, working in private and state schools, teaching adults and young learners. He holds a master's degree in teaching ESOL from Aston University, in England. His professional interests include computer-assisted language learning and written error-correction strategies.

APPENDIX: A STUDENT'S FIRST ATTEMPT

Hi alex, i'm happy to have recived your letter that i have just read. On 25th december i left home and i went to the montains with my parents and my friends. There i have a small house in Val di Fiamme since when i was 2 years old. I really enjoyed myself because i went skiing with all my friends and also because i could get up late in the morning and i could relax myself. The weather was really good because it's sunny and not too cold and so i could sunbath. One evening my parents and all our friends went for dinner in a "baita" on the snow; there was very cold when we were going there with motosnows,it was very exciting. There we ate tipical food and we danced tipical music but the more exciting thing was the return because we saw the sky with all it's stars, which were shining.

Write back soon

With love

After two student edits, the first in bold italics (blue on the original site), and the second in underlined italics (red on original).

Hi Alex, *I*'m happy to have received your letter that *I* have just read. On 25th December *I* left home and *I* went to the mountains with my parents and my friends. ~~There~~ *I* have *had* a small house *there*, in Val di Fiamme, since ~~when~~ *I* was 2 years old. I really enjoyed myself because *I* went skiing with all my friends, ~~and also~~ because *I* could get up late in the morning and *I* could relax ~~myself~~. The weather was really good because it~~'s~~ *was* sunny and not too cold and so *I* could sunbathe. One evening ~~my parents and all our friends~~ *we* went for dinner in a "baita" on the snow *with all our friends*; ~~there was~~ *it was* very cold ~~when we were~~ going there ~~with~~ *by* motosnows, it was very exciting. ~~There~~ *We* ate typical food *there* and we danced _to_ typical music, but the ~~more~~ *most* exciting thing was _coming back_ because we saw the sky with all ~~it's~~ *its* stars, which were ~~shining~~ _twinkling_.

Write back soon.

With love

CHAPTER 16

A Chain Story Blog

Najla Malaibari

The expansion of Internet technologies has created new opportunities for the English language learning (ELL) classroom. One such advancement is the Web log, or "blog." With the advent of numerous software programs that instantly update and publish Web sites, blogs (online personal journals) have become increasingly popular (Blood, 2002). Blogger, a free blog hosting service released in 1999, has become a mainstay for people who post blogs. Although the use of these new technologies to enhance learning in the ELL classroom has yet to be determined fully, it is important to explore new and effective ways to use them to improve the English language learning process both in and out of the classroom.

Developing new and exciting ways to foster writing in the ELL classroom has always been a challenge for teachers. This chapter introduces a chain story activity that has ELLs combine writing (scheduled blog postings, comments, and captions) with online supplements or Web tools, such as images, audio files, and Web site links. This activity was devised for students to prepare and produce their own written language in a safe environment where they can benefit more concretely from critical analysis, reflection, and directed feedback. It was created with the aim of bolstering student confidence and satisfaction in free writing and expression. Finally, in addition to promoting a sense of pride and ownership for the students, the instant publishing aspect of blogging allows for easy accessibility and acknowledgment not only from peers and teachers but also from the worldwide Internet community at large.

CONTEXT

A blog can be viewed as an easily updated diary with worldwide accessibility via the Internet. Blogging provides students with an environment that fully encourages written communication, along with the added benefit of building class rapport and camaraderie. As an alternative to the standard journal writing, blogging encourages students to experiment with imaginative and creative avenues of expression, rather than following prescribed writing "rules."

Additionally, blogs were chosen for this activity due to their user-friendly accessibility, easily manipulated format, and interactive nature (Johnson, 2004). Students can quickly learn how to create and maintain a blog, and they can effortlessly publish their work online (Blood, 2002). Giving learners the opportunity to create and manage individual blogs can provide them with a sense of belonging to and ownership in the Internet community (Campbell, 2004). This ownership can help learners foster a sense of pride in their work. Blogs can also be used as a collaborative tool that encourages learners to share resources and ideas through ongoing discussions. Additionally, peer editing and feedback can help learners improve their writing (Dieu, 2004).

CURRICULUM, TASKS, MATERIALS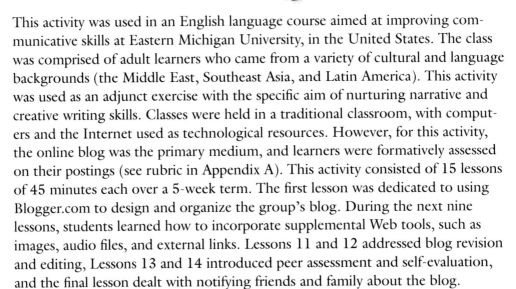

This activity was used in an English language course aimed at improving communicative skills at Eastern Michigan University, in the United States. The class was comprised of adult learners who came from a variety of cultural and language backgrounds (the Middle East, Southeast Asia, and Latin America). This activity was used as an adjunct exercise with the specific aim of nurturing narrative and creative writing skills. Classes were held in a traditional classroom, with computers and the Internet used as technological resources. However, for this activity, the online blog was the primary medium, and learners were formatively assessed on their postings (see rubric in Appendix A). This activity consisted of 15 lessons of 45 minutes each over a 5-week term. The first lesson was dedicated to using Blogger.com to design and organize the group's blog. During the next nine lessons, students learned how to incorporate supplemental Web tools, such as images, audio files, and external links. Lessons 11 and 12 addressed blog revision and editing, Lessons 13 and 14 introduced peer assessment and self-evaluation, and the final lesson dealt with notifying friends and family about the blog.

Students were assigned to groups of three, with each group responsible for devising and managing a collaborative blog on Blogger.com. At this beginning stage, each group determined whether or not members wanted their blog to be available to the world outside the classroom, but the blog had to include the entire class: The instructor and all classmates were added as members of each blog.

During the initial preparation of group organization, introducing resources for the supplemental Web tools and deciding which features are best to incorporate on the blog is critical to the success of the overall project. Once the blogs had been created and organized, the teacher asked each group to delegate which supplemental Web tool (an image, an audio file, or an Internet link) the individual members wanted to work with first. The teacher explained that each member would rotate experimenting with these Web tools so that each blog would have a minimum of three images, three audio files, and three external links. The teacher then presented the opening lines of the chain story to the class, which students used as their first blog posting. Then, "image file members" were asked to continue the chain story by posting a paragraph and a relevant image (or images) to their blog. The chain story would then continue, with the "audio file members" and "link members" each posting a paragraph and their respective supplemental Web tool. Learners were given sufficient time to formulate ideas and revise their writing as needed, posting their best drafts onto their blog.

Trial and error indicated that it worked best to start the chain story for the students with either an image or an audio file. These supplemental Web tools were used to introduce at least one element of the story by, for example, supplying a photo of at least one character or the setting, or adding an audio file with a snippet from a conversation or a sound effect. Additional prompts were not provided for the students, so students had full control of the storyline. Students were reminded that the primary goal was to keep the chain story growing, with each part and supplemental Web tool providing crucial links for the reader. (Unfortunately, permission to publish the chain stories was not collected from the students or university, so a sample chain story is not available for this chapter.)

It is also important to understand what tools students can use to create and maintain the eye-catching factors on their chain story blogs. Specifically, along with a great story line, these factors partly entail creating or finding supplemental Web tools such as images and audio files. Images, such as photos and drawings that belonged to the students, were either scanned or uploaded directly to the blog. Students also used properly cited, copyrighted images and copyright-free images found on Web sites such as http://www.office.microsoft.com/clipart and http://www.copyrightfreephotos.com.

In order to create audio files, some students used a microphone and Sound Recorder (found on any Windows-enabled computer, under "Entertainment" in the Accessories link of the Start menu), and then uploaded the audio file to the blog. Some students preferred to use copyright-free audio files found on Web sites such as http://www.webplaces.com/html/sounds.htm and http://www.freesfx.co.uk.

Along with each student group maintaining a blog, it is advisable to have a central classroom blog for the instructor. This can be used as a hub to post guidelines, rubrics, recommendations, highlights, etc. Also highly recommend is adding the Real Simple Syndication (RSS) or news-feed feature to the blog. This feature is provided by Blogger and effortlessly tracks and sends notifications of any changes and additions to all subscribers to the blog. Much like a news feed that scrolls the latest news event on the bottom of a television screen, an RSS feed provides an automatic update whenever anything has been added to a blog. This is a great timesaver for the instructor, as it avoids having to manually check each and every student blog for new posts, comments, photos, etc.

Placing an RSS for each student blog on the central classroom blog assists the instructor in two ways. First, by having a central RSS feed, the instructor is automatically notified of any changes made to any of the student blogs by simply accessing the central classroom blog, rather than individual student blogs. Second, in addition to helping with blog maintenance, the RSS feed can also help with grading, especially if daily blog participation is a criterion for students.

However, RSS feeds are not only beneficial for the instructor. For example, in order to keep better track of deadlines and updates, students can have an RSS feed dedicated to the central classroom blog. Students can also add an RSS feed for other classmates' blogs, which strengthens teamwork skills and encourages cooperation and amity amongst the class.

REFLECTIONS

Johnson (2004) found that blogs were a useful supplement in ELL classrooms, and, indeed, they were with this activity. According to student responses, most students found the activity to be exciting and felt that their writing had improved. Each group member was given an opportunity to use each type of supplemental Web tool. If the storyline started to wane, other classmates were asked to post "dramatic twists" to the plot or to introduce new characters.

By collaboratively working on a project, learners were not only able to hone their writing skills, but they were also able to see how writing connects individuals. Students also noticed that blogging had increased their curiosity about English Web sites, and the supplement Web tools (images, audio files, links) gave them more opportunities to read related articles and explore other Web sites and blogs.

By using the unique medium of a blog and by pooling multiple sources of information (their own creativity, as well as various online sources), learners were able to see their work published instantaneously, allowing them to see the results of their hard work and effort directly. Learners also enjoyed reading other blogs and felt even more confident when posting comments. They wrote more carefully because they knew that instant publishing was a part of blogging, and their blogs were open to real readers in cyberspace.

As for the setup and maintenance of the blogs, most students felt that it was quite easy to use Blogger, and most felt satisfied with Blogger's help sections. Students also interacted more with each other in class, swapping tidbits on how to change templates or background colors or the best way to upload audio files and images. Information gained from informal student responses revealed that some students felt that blogging had also greatly increased their computer and Web literacy.

Finally, because the students used the Internet on a daily basis (e.g., e-mailing friends and family back home, instant messaging, chatting), they felt that their blogs would be read on a regular basis by their friends and family, and, therefore, students felt compelled to produce the best quality of work possible. Some students even received comments (thankfully, all positive and encouraging) from readers outside of the classroom, which only further encouraged their writing and increased their excitement.

Overall, using blogs in an ELL classroom motivated students and spurred creativity. However, it should be noted that with very large classes (e.g., 20 or more students), teachers should pay particular attention to whether they want to have each student create an individual blog. It can be very taxing to monitor and assess such a large number of blogs on a regular basis, and the process can echo the drudgery of evaluating traditional journal writing. For this reason, it would be much more beneficial to have students collaborate on their blogs. In this case, there were teams of three people for each blog, resulting in only five blogs total for a class of 15 students. Students were each given an opportunity to write and interact with classmates, but the number of blogs to assess and monitor was greatly reduced.

Finally, in terms of assessment, a rubric detailing the requirements for the blogs was presented early in the project. Learners were then given the opportunity to discuss and revise the requirements, and a final rubric was voted and agreed on by all. The final rubric is found in Appendix A. Peer- and self-evaluations were also conducted. The self-evaluation form can be found in Appendix B.

Najla Malaibari teaches in the English language department at Dar Al-Hekma College, in Jeddah, Saudi Arabia. She has a master's degree in teaching English to speakers of other languages from Eastern Michigan University and a bachelor's degree in biology from the University of Michigan, both in the United States. In 2006, she was a recipient of the Teachers of English to Speakers of Other Languages Professional Development Scholarship Award.

APPENDIX A: ESL BLOGGERS' CHAIN STORY BLOG RUBRIC

Assignment of Points (maximum: 4 points per item)			
4	**3**	**2**	**1**
All requirements were met and exceeded.	All requirements were met.	One requirement was not completely met.	More than one requirement was not completely met.

Item	Requirement	Points
Name of blog	Blog has a creative and appropriate name that captures the spirit of the chain story.	
Chain story specifications	Each individual posting has a minimum of 250 words, submitted and posted on time, addressed to the correct audience, and is enjoyable to read. Language is appropriate for a university-level audience (writing can use an informal tone but must be grammatically correct).	
Formatting	Blog is presented using a neat format, with an easy to read font, a colorful and eye-catching display, and proper spacing.	
Supplements	For each posting, includes appropriate, properly cited supplements (three images, three audio files, three links, etc.) and meshes well with the story content.	
Comments	Each group member posted a minimum of four comments on other classmates' blogs.	
Invitation to friends and family	At least four invitations were sent to friends and families to check out the completed blog. Extra credit (2 points each) if a friend or family member posted a comment (if it's not in English—please translate and post)!	
Morale/pride in work	Evaluations were filled in and submitted. Student displayed pride in the work, and effort was put in to the project.	

APPENDIX B: ESL BLOGGERS' SELF-EVALUATION FORM

Self-Evaluation

Use this information to see how you may improve your writing and the project!

Please answer the following questions.

Title of Chain Story Blog: _____

Collaborators: _____

URL: http://_____

- What are some of your teacher's comments about this blog?

- What were some suggestions or comments from your classmates?

- Did you like using blogs? Why or why not?

- Did you feel that it was worth the time to learn about blogs?

- Will you continue using your blog? Will you tell your friends to start blogs too?

- Do you have any suggestions to make this project better for next time?

CHAPTER 17

Authentic English Through the Computer: Corpora in the ESOL Writing Classroom

Vander Viana

The challenge of how to choose words to convey specific meaning is common and recurrent in English for speakers of other languages (ESOL) classrooms. Learners and teachers generally have doubts when it comes to expressing themselves in a language other than their own. Another equally important concern is how to communicate one's ideas naturally, meaning that words are expressed in proper combinations to achieve a desired effect.

Historically, nonnative educators have had access to only their course books or other teaching and reference materials to solve their language problems (see Viana & Zyngier, 2008). As for students, they relied, in most cases, on their teachers' knowledge to solve language problems. Such a situation was clearly not the best environment for a number of reasons. First, books are limited by the information they contain. Second, intuitions are not reliable enough as "they describe what people *know about* language, or what they *perceive* language to be, rather than how language *is used*" (Tsui, 2004, p. 39). Finally, both course materials and intuition generally make use of oversimplified examples to get their points across.

This scenario had already been identified by Milton (1998):

> Conventional classroom methods are often inadequate for conveying to learners our growing understanding of language features, and inappropriate for providing learners full access to, or significant experience with, the features of target language behaviours and how particular features of their own production deviate from these targets. (p. 186)

On another note, what research shows about language may help teaching. Therefore, linguistic studies should inform pedagogical practices so that they yield more positive results. For this reason, this chapter draws on the principles of corpus linguistics, which holds that *corpora* (electronic collections of writing that focus on how words and phrases are used by speakers and writers of a particular language) must be the focus of study in any language.

Currently, some English language corpora from which teachers and students can benefit are available on the Internet for free. A corpus shows how language is used in real situations and puts an end to the so-called necessity of relying on a native speaker's intuition to tell what is commonly or rarely used in English. Online corpora and their exploration in the ESOL writing classroom are the focus of this chapter.

CONTEXT

First, it is important to clarify what is meant by *corpus*. According to Sinclair (2005), "a corpus is a collection of pieces of language text in electronic form, selected according to external criteria to represent, as far as possible, a language or language variety as a source of data for linguistic research." In the case of this chapter, the corpus to be used contains spoken and written texts by speakers of English as a first language.

Having access to the information contained in a corpus is not the same as reading a text. The latter takes place horizontally, from left to right, so that one may understand the main idea put forward by the author. Texts are generally a result of coherent writing (Tognini-Bonelli, 2001). A corpus, however, is investigated with the help of computer tools. One indicates a search word for the computer to generate *concordance lines*. As Conrad (2002) explains, "these listings display all the occurrences of a word or structure in a database, with a small amount of context on each side" (p. 75). It is by means of these lines that information is inspected. The concordance lines[1] for the search word *concordance* illustrate this point:

```
01  ost frequently appearing words in the 2,000 concordance lines was analysed with respect to their de
02  ractical problems associated with running a concordance program to study a wide range of syntactic
03    For such a massive study to be feasible, a concordance program which picks out tokens of the pron
04  ted by Gottesman and Shields (1972) found a concordance rate among identical twins (that is, the fr
05  that date had shown substantially different concordance rates for depression (68 per cent and 23 pe
```

This type of concordance line is referred to as *key word in context* (KWIC), as the search word is in its middle. It is exactly at this midpoint where the reading process should start. One should check for the existence of any patterns either to the left, to the right, or in both directions. Students should be reminded that they are not expected to understand the text as a solid piece of coherent writing or speaking because the samples of how a given word is used come from various sources. If this fact is not clarified from the beginning, learners may experience frustration while trying to work with corpus data because the lines taken

---

[1] Data cited in all examples in this chapter have been extracted from the British National Corpus (BNC) Online service (http://www.natcorp.ox.ac.uk/), managed by Oxford University Computing Services on behalf of the BNC Consortium. All rights in the texts cited are reserved.

together are meaningless. As Tognini-Bonelli (2001) puts it, a corpus is read in a fragmented and vertical way so that repeated events, indicating some kind of language patterning, may be found.

In the example, there are five concordance lines for the search word *concordance*, which were manually selected from the British National Corpus (BNC). The lines are organized alphabetically to the right of *concordance* in order to facilitate pattern identification. When followed by another noun, this word is commonly associated with *rate(s)*, *program*, and *line(s)*, to cite a few examples (see *Available Online Corpora* for an explanation of the BNC).

The introduction of corpus-based activities in the writing classroom brings about a shift in perspective because form is favored. Such a focus on form is necessary because some recent approaches to English as a second language (ESL) teaching have "been accompanied by a loss of accuracy, especially grammatical accuracy" (Granger & Tribble, 1998, p. 199). In other words, the use of corpora may help students become more accurate when it comes to expressing themselves in writing.

The corpus-based approach proposed here has been tried out with older teenagers and adults at private language courses in Rio de Janeiro, Brazil, but it may be adaptable to learners in other countries because the activities are not contextually bound.

CURRICULUM, TASKS, MATERIALS

After a period of formal instruction, students should already know which kinds of general combinations are possible in English and generally should be able to form grammatically acceptable sentences. However, this ability is not enough for full language mastery. According to Hyland (2002),

> L2 writers need to know what is typical rather than what is possible, and a concordance can both suggest the appropriacy of using one word rather than another in specific circumstances and indicate the rarity of true synonymy among semantically related items. (p. 123)

Such a gap in teaching may be filled by corpus-based work.

Available Online Corpora

Although several English language corpora have been compiled, most are not available on the Internet or for free. One example of a corpus that may be accessed online is the Bank of English. It started in 1994 as a joint venture between the University of Birmingham, in England, and HarperCollins Publishers. The corpus, which represents current spoken and written English, contains 524 million words from U.S., Australian, British, and Canadian texts. It is referred to as a *monitor corpus* because it continues to grow with the addition of new texts constantly. By subscribing to WordbanksOnline, one can have access to 56 million words from the Bank of English. It is also possible to check how it works by accessing the

Concordance and Collocation Samplers at http://www.collins.co.uk/corpus/ CorpusSearch.aspx. In this case, users do not have to pay any fees.

Another corpus, and perhaps the most famous one, is the British National Corpus (BNC). It contains 100 million words from spoken and written media. The former comprises a small part of it, totaling only 10%, whereas the latter represents 90% of the texts included in the collection. As its name points out, the data contained in the corpus came from 20th-century British English. The BNC, which was completed in 1994, represents a variety of genres of spoken and written media. It can be accessed at http://www.natcorp.ox.ac.uk. Only 50 concordance lines are generated each time a query is run, but the corpus may be purchased for unlimited access.

Another way to access the BNC is to use the search interface developed by Mark Davies, which is available at http://corpus.byu.edu/bnc. In this interface, users may have access to all concordance lines instead of just a random selection. The options in the site also make it easier for users to find what they want to know. One of them focuses on the genres users are interested in studying. In practical terms, this means that a work or a structure may be investigated, for instance, only in academic English. The examples provided in this chapter are from the whole corpus, which has been probed altogether.

Using Corpora to Improve Writing

In teaching writing in English, ESOL instructors encounter a common problem of students using an incorrect word whose spelling is similar to the right one, showing that maybe these learners are not aware of the differences in meaning. For instance, in writing about what may be done to save the world, one student argued that even those who are not rich may help other people by means of "human warming." When this student checked the adjectival collocations for the word *warming* in the BNC, he noticed that it is generally used with *global* as the randomly selected concordance lines show.

```
01   atospheric ozone, tropospheric ozone, global warming and acid deposition. Meanwhile the chlorine k
02   heat from the sun. On the other hand, global warming is likely to produce more precipitation over
03   l warming. Effective action to combat global warming must be international action. Again we have t
04   e environments on this planet (though global warming reports suggest this may be about to change).
05   e ozone layer is probably slowing the global warming trend. Dr Tony Cox, programme director for at
```

As a matter of fact, *global* precedes *warming* 599 times in the corpus. In addition, a closer analysis of these instances shows that they are not used to refer to what the student had originally in mind, but to a natural effect.

When looking up the expression *human warm** (the second term may be any word that starts with the specified four letters, so as to enable *warming*, if there is one instance), only one possible result is found: *human warmth*.

```
01   in terms of openness, emotional expression and human warmth are also important. Indeed, this latter
02   on't panic. I wasn't suggesting you betray any human warmth in your soul by sharing a bed --; simply
03   he wanted to achieve was an excuse to feel the human warmth of his arm against hers. There was no ot
04   e her beside me, her hand in mine; and she was human warmth, normality, standard to go by. I had alw
05   ngdom, Leo loves and is loved by Ustane, whose human warmth and generosity provide a contrast to the
```

166

An analysis of these lines shows that *human warmth* is the expression the student should have used in his original sentence to convey his meaning accurately.

Another problem in writing has to do with not knowing what the most appropriate collocation choice is. In this case, words are known, but what remains obscure is which word should be employed. For instance, once a student wrote about "a good way to happiness," and the teacher corrected it to "a good way to reach happiness." The question here is whether it is *reach* that should be used. The next 20 concordance lines contain the most commonly used verbs together with *happiness*. They were alphabetically sorted to the left of the search word to facilitate verb identification.

```
01  fame and fortune, but it still didn't bring happiness to Boris Becker. "Money buys you certain thi
02  like Willy Loman salesmanship did not bring happiness and fulfilment --; that they made a document
03  ected by the mistaken belief that they bring happiness and fulfilment. These "ills" of industrial s
04  is easy to believe that owning money brings happiness. Wealth can make life easier, but the things
05  en and she told him that the war had brought happiness to her and Chris. "I know it's wrong, Joe, w
06  that they were very happy. If money can buy happiness, what would you expect the relationship betw
07  | . It's true what they say, money can't buy happiness, thought the simple sergeant. He had noticed
08  ty side and broke into her money-box. To buy happiness for her darling, she bought a rather delight
09  r Isabel's, I fear. I only hope she may find happiness with Saul Quatt." "Well, hope it no longer!
10  o those countries, so that those people find happiness in their own lands. " Seats Percentage of vo
11  ness, and should you have the chance to find happiness, whether you are someone young starting life
12  , so there are opportunities for you to find happiness and fulfilment this year. The problem is tha
13  Carry-On actress Barbara Windsor, 55, found happiness with her 35-year-old husband Steve Hollings
14  king up the pieces of his life and had found happiness with another woman. It would be even nicer t
15  life at a time when she seemed to have found happiness with her new husband. Tourist is beaten to d
16  uld be congratulated on at last having found happiness again. TOAST TO BRIDE AND GROOM (SECOND MARR
17  d by longing; and the older woman, who found happiness with a poor drunken sot from her father's st
18  y parents and to the Brownie Law and to give happiness to somebody every day. Law 2 A Brownie think
19  evaluation of its total tendency to promote happiness, on the one hand, and to promote unhappiness
20  ciety generally. A number of ways of seeking happiness are possible, and discussed by Freud, first
```

The BNC shows that the most commonly used verbs are *find* and, to a certain extent, *bring*. The list of verbs also includes *buy, promote, seek,* and *give*. As a matter of fact, there are other verbs preceding *happiness* in the corpus, but they are used mostly once and, for this reason, will not be commented on here. It should be pointed out, however, that there is not a single instance of "*reach* happiness" in the corpus. This shows that the choice favored by the teacher is one that is not probable in common usage although the structure is grammatically possible.

These two examples provide a brief overview of how corpora may be used in the ESOL writing classroom. This chapter is intended more as an introduction to ESOL practitioners who are novices in the field rather than a comprehensive approach to how corpus linguistics may be applied to language teaching. (For more comprehensive volumes on this topic, see, for instance, O'Keeffe, McCarthy, & Carter, 2007; McEnery, Xiao, & Tono, 2006; Tognini-Boneli, 2001; and Tribble & Jones, 1990.) Students are guided through their own explorations of corpora in order to make appropriate word choices when writing. In the first stages of such work, teachers may propose questions based on their students' writing, but later on learners should generate questions about how English is independently used.

REFLECTIONS

There are several advantages in introducing corpus-based work both inside and outside the classroom. First, using a corpus provides unmediated access to language; that is, the examples of English usage have not been edited or contrived. In other words, corpora provide real and natural examples in the sense that they have not been invented to explain or illustrate a point. Rather, they have been stated or written by speakers in communicative situations. They exemplify language use and not what language is thought to be. Additionally, there are no restrictions on exploring how language is used.

Second, computers enable one to carry out corpora searches instantly. It is much faster and more reliable to probe corpora using computer tools than to perform this task manually. As Tognini-Bonelli (2001) puts it, the computer "has affected the methodological frame of the enquiry by speeding it up, systematizing it, and making it applicable in real time to ever larger amounts of data" (p. 5). The use of computers also presents very little difficulty (if any) to the new generations of learners because they are already technology savvy.

Third, using corpora as a resource in English learning is believed to foster students' linguistic command. Edge (1989) argues that "the more the students are involved in correction, the more they have to think about the language used in the classroom" (p. 27). Maybe *correction* does not always apply; perhaps *appropriateness awareness* is a better option because learners should be left some choice about whether or not to comply with suggested patterns of expression (see Oliveira, 2002). This is exactly the idea underlying the present proposal: If students are encouraged to reflect about language, they will be more involved with it.

There is a need, however, for investigations that compare traditional teaching methods and corpus-informed teaching practices in relation to students' achievement. Therefore, only in the future will it be possible to assess students' learning with the help of corpora. So far, what this approach promotes is a student-centered atmosphere, one in which teachers help students find answers to questions about English usage by themselves. Teachers serve as facilitators, showing students how to solve their language problems independently. This attitude may ultimately foster autonomy (Benson, 2001), one of the main goals of education.

ACKNOWLEDGMENT

I am grateful to Sonia Zyngier, who reviewed an earlier draft of this chapter.

Besides teaching English as a foreign language, Vander Viana's research interests are in corpus linguistics and distance learning. He has been a representative of the Association of English Teachers in the State of Rio de Janeiro in Brazil since 2004 and a member of the Research and Development in Empirical Studies Project since 2003.

Re-visioning, Revising, and Editing ESL Compositions

Revising the Revision Process With Google Docs: A Classroom-Based Study of Second Language Writing

Soo Hyon Kim

"But *why* don't they revise?" It is not uncommon to hear discouraged writing teachers lamenting that their students simply do not revise enough. No matter what steps teachers take, many of their students' subsequent drafts do not significantly differ from their previous ones, with the exception of a few words or punctuation marks sprinkled in or erased throughout. This kind of resistance on the part of students to perceive revision as a true re-visioning of their work can be troublesome for writing teachers who are writers themselves and know the value of thoughtful revising. Nevertheless, teachers lead students through the process of writing, intervening at each step with comments and instructional activities, hoping that their efforts to encourage revision will help students become thoughtful and reflective writers.

This chapter reports on one such effort and shares some insights gained from an English as a second language (ESL) class that experienced the writing process with the help of a Web-based collaborative editing program, Google Docs (2006; visit http://docs.google.com for more information). This computer-mediated approach to revision showed great potential in promoting substantive and effective revision in ESL students' writing when used for a clear purpose in classroom activities and when thoroughly integrated into the curriculum.

CONTEXT

Setting

The setting of this project was a noncredit requisite ESL writing course at the University of Illinois at Urbana-Champaign, in the United States. The ESL service courses at this institution are designed to help international students attain the English proficiency required to be academically successful in the United States. Twenty international graduate students with various language backgrounds were enrolled in the class, the majority being Chinese and Korean speakers, along with a few Spanish, Bengali, Russian, and Polish speakers.

The main purpose of the writing course was to familiarize ESL students with the conventions of academic writing in their new academic discourse communities. In class, students were introduced to the concept of writing as a process, and they were taught the basic features of academic writing, such as purpose, audience, and organization. Learning through meaningful interaction and collaboration was encouraged throughout students' writing processes.

Approach to Writing and Revising

The process approach to writing emphasizes the recursive, personal process that a writer undergoes when producing a piece of text (Matsuda, 2003). Revision is a key component of this writing process because it serves as a means to explore, develop, and nuance the writer's intent and meaning (Haar & Horning, 2006). However, many inexperienced student-writers have a limited understanding of revision, believing that it only entails surface-level "cosmetic" changes (see Perl, 1979, an oft-cited study on the composing processes of unskilled college writers). Furthermore, research shows that while first (L1) and second language (L2) writers share some characteristics in that they both engage in recursive processes of writing, generate and develop ideas, and try to express these ideas linguistically and effectively, L2 writers also have distinct features that make their revision processes more constrained and complex (Silva, 1993b). ESL writing teachers, in response, have searched for effective ways to facilitate and coach students' revisions. Traditionally, teachers have addressed revision by including handwritten comments on student essays, conducting student–teacher conferences, and supervising peer review activities.

Enhancing the Revision Process With Technology

New approaches to revision instruction in the ESL writing classroom stem from the development of computer-assisted language learning (CALL). The use of word processors has "had a fundamental influence on the ways we write, the genres we create, [and] the forms our finished products take" (Hyland, 2003b, p. 144). Today, people compose on computers more often than they write with pen and paper. Technology has provided tools for writers to use not only while composing but also during all stages of writing. For example, writers can post and receive feedback online via message boards and personal blogs, and they can also use online wikis to produce and revise text.

Google Docs, a relatively new computer writing application, has attracted the interest of teachers and researchers. Despite the fact that Google Docs' producers claim that the product encourages the writing-as-a-process approach, most writing teachers remain uncertain of its applicability and value. By speculating on the experiences of an ESL writing class that utilized Google Docs to aid students' revision processes, this chapter answers the following questions: (a) Does the use of Google Docs enhance the efficacy of classroom activities (teacher feedback, peer review, collaborative writing, and self-assessment) that facilitate students' revisions? (b) What are students' perceptions of the effectiveness of Google Docs as a tool for learning writing?

CURRICULUM, TASKS, MATERIALS

Using Google Docs for Revision

Google Docs is a free Web-based collaborative editing program that enables writers to produce documents, track revisions and changes, and collaborate with others in real time (see http://docs.google.com for a detailed description of services provided). While the familiar Web interface makes it possible for even first-time users to create and edit a document comfortably, a few characteristics set Google Docs apart from other word-processing programs. It enables users to save their texts in an online database, not a hard drive, so the files can be retrieved from any device with an Internet connection. Another unique feature is that it facilitates collaborative writing by allowing users to invite collaborators to view and edit the document simultaneously. When a collaborator makes a change to the shared document, the change automatically takes effect and becomes visible to both parties. This synchronous characteristic of Google Docs prevents different collaborators from making conflicting changes, and it also makes the cumbersome exchange of revised documents via e-mail unnecessary. Google Docs also saves all previous versions of a document so that users can revert to a previous draft if needed. Completed documents can be converted into more conventional formats, such as Rich Text Files (RTF), Microsoft Word files (visit http://office.microsoft .com for more information), or PDFs, or they can be published online to a designated site, such as a personal blog or Web site.

These functions initially attracted individuals who frequently collaborate with others and, therefore, need to track changes from one draft to another. In a pedagogical context, however, the characteristics of Google Docs are conducive to promoting students' communication about their writing with their teacher and peers, and, at the same time, draw students' attention to the revisions they made on multiple drafts of an essay.

The following section describes the four major tasks that this Web-based collaborative editing program contributed to: teacher feedback, peer review, revision self-analysis, and collaborative writing.

Teacher Feedback

Students were given an assignment to write a source-based, informative essay on a topic of their choice, preferably a topic pertaining to their academic field. The essays, ranging from 500 to 700 words, were to be written for a general, educated audience, and students were required to create at least two drafts.

Once a student completed the first draft of this assignment, he or she saved the essay as a Google Docs file. The student then sent the instructor an automated e-mail invitation (an electronic link directing the teacher to the student's Google Docs document) to become a collaborator, one who can view, edit, and make comments. After gaining access to the student's online document, the instructor provided written feedback about necessary revisions by using the "insert comment" function in Google Docs. To view the teacher's comments, the student simply logged on to his or her Google Docs account and accessed the teacher's comments. Because both the student and teacher had access to the same document on the Google Docs server, there was no need to send multiple documents back and forth during this feedback and revision process.

Peer Review

For the next assignment, each student was asked to write a 500- to 700-word persuasive essay on the topic, "Should the United States provide public education for the children of illegal immigrants?" The requirements for this assignment were similar to the previous one. Again, students produced their first drafts using Google Docs. Before making changes for the next draft, students engaged in a peer review activity in which they received comments on the content, organization, and language of their essays via "insert comment" from their peers. This followed the same procedure as the previous teacher-feedback process, the only difference being that the students invited peers as their main collaborators. Google Docs enables multiple peers to review an essay simultaneously, along with the teacher, who scaffolded and monitored the peer review in process.

Collaborative Writing

The last writing activity involving the use of Google Docs was a collaborative writing project. In groups of three or four, students were asked to produce a report on the documentation style (e.g., APA, MLA, Chicago) that is used in their academic fields. The reports were to include an introduction of the documentation style with general information on how to cite in-text sources and how to format reference lists.

Once a Google Docs document was created, each member of the group and the teacher were invited as collaborators. Then the writing of the individual sections of the final report was divided among group members. As soon as all of the sections were compiled online, the group members revised the report to synthesize and integrate the information into a coherent piece of writing. Most of the actual writing of this project was successfully carried out beyond the classroom walls because Google Docs enables students to monitor changes being made to the report. This freed up valuable class time for discussion among the members regarding the revisions that had already been made and those that needed to be made.

The final reports, ranging from 500 to 700 words in length, were evaluated on the overall quality of the group's report and fulfillment of requirements, on each student's individually written section, and on the revision contributions made by each student. The "revision history" function in Google Docs described in the following section made possible the tracking of each group member's revisions and participation in the group project.

Self-Analysis

After finishing each assignment, students completed a revision reflection worksheet provided by the instructor. This activity was designed to raise students' awareness of the changes (or lack of changes) made during the revision process. The changes were easily visible through the "revisions history" function of Google Docs, which provides information regarding the time, author, and content of the revisions made to the text. Also, the "compare revisions" function located in the "revision history" of Google Docs allowed users to merge and compare two documents with changes from the first to second document made more salient by the use of different colored text.

With the help of these Google Docs functions and the worksheet provided by the teacher, students were asked to analyze the revisions they made for each assignment. The following are examples of questions that were asked in the revision reflection sheet.

Does the comparison of your two revisions show that you

- made extensive or few changes in your essay? Give your reasons for making or not making changes.

- made changes to your content? If so, give an example of one of the major changes you made in the content of your essay. If not, explain why you didn't make any content changes?

- made changes to your organization (e.g., sequence of ideas, paragraphs, sentences)? If so, give some examples. If not, why do you feel your document didn't need any changes?

- made changes at the surface level (e.g., grammar, wording, typos)? If so, give some examples. If not, state your reasons.

REFLECTIONS

At the end of the term, analysis of student revisions and their reflections on the experience revealed that the use of Google Docs in students' writing processes was helpful in promoting and raising awareness of substantive and effective revision. The positive comments made on classroom activities using Google Docs were associated with Google Doc's synchronous characteristic. Students commented that they liked being able to access the document at any time through the Internet. Naturally, student reactions to the collaborative writing activity were the most positive, again due to the synchronous nature of Google Docs that enabled the students to share and keep their document up to date.

However, there still remain possible pitfalls to avoid when using this technology in the classroom. One student, for example, commented that while the "revision history" function appeared to be good for tracking revisions, "the existence of the function did not motivate" him to actively do so. This student comment is indicative of how important it is to integrate the technology into classroom activities effectively. It may not be so much the technology itself but rather the way that it is implemented that encourages effective revision.

Thus, for teachers, rather than expecting Google Docs to magically encourage revision in students' writing processes, it is important to examine the technology's characteristic features and be certain those components will serve the goals and objectives of the course. Following this, teachers should carefully design assignments to maximize the effects of using Google Docs.

Tips for Success

For students, prior training is essential. This training is most effective when it includes instruction on both the purpose and the actual mechanics of using Google Docs. Also, like any other classroom activity, it is better to introduce it early in the term and build upon its use rather than suddenly introduce it halfway through the term and then expect students to assimilate. In the same vein, it is imperative that students and their teacher have a shared understanding about the procedures and expectations regarding assignments or tasks using Google Docs, such as the number of drafts required and feedback deadlines.

Another way to ensure the success of using Google Docs to assist students' revision is to diminish the technological aspect by focusing on the purpose of the activity. For example, before training students to make comments on peers' writing or teaching them to use the "insert comment" function in Google Docs, it makes sense to introduce the concept of peer review and its rationale, especially if the idea of peer review is new to them.

Finally, gathering constant feedback from students and keeping their perceptions in check can prove to be much more helpful than expected. Teachers will not only be actively engaged in their students' learning process and in nurturing reflective learners but will also be challenged to find other ways to use technology to aid L2 writing students.

Future Development

Google Docs is constantly evolving, which has a profound impact on the way that it can be used in the classroom. One of the changes is its inclusion of a filing system that, compared to its old archive, makes it easier for users to organize documents. This shows potential for using Google Docs to implement e-portfolio assessments. The emphasis put on growth and overall development in portfolio assessments fits in well with this tool that allows teachers to provide appropriate guidance throughout the writing process. Again, what decides the effectiveness of technology's use is the teacher's ability to integrate it into the syllabus so that it can augment student efforts.

Implications

Although this chapter discusses the implementation of Google Docs in one particular classroom, it offers broader implications for CALL in other contexts as well. Despite the rapid developments taking place in educational institutions, one must bear in mind that it is ultimately the teacher's job to make sound decisions based on the existing social, cultural, and educational context. This chapter proposes that instead of becoming caught up in the frenzy of using cutting-edge technology in the classroom, it is important to adapt the use of technology in ways that complement the existing curriculum to the benefit of teachers and their students. With continued classroom-based research generated by teachers, it will be possible to develop a model of CALL that is effective, culturally appropriate, and responsive to the needs of L2 writing students.

Soo Hyon Kim is a doctoral student in the Second Language Studies program at Michigan State University, in the United States. She previously taught ESL academic writing at the University of Illinois, Urbana-Champaign, also in the United States, and also worked as a writing center consultant. Her areas of interests include L2 acquisition, L2 writing, and CALL.

CHAPTER 19

Great Expectations: Whose Job Is This Anyway?

Donald Weasenforth, Margaret Redus, and Nancy Ham Megarity

The expectations that English as a second language (ESL) writing students have of their teachers' and their own roles in editing writing are revealed in variations of the familiar retort "How can I work on my paper? You haven't marked it yet." This chapter is, in part, a response to students' views of writing teachers as "proofreading slaves" (Milton, 2006, p. 125). The overall discussion provides insight into how second language (L2) writing instruction can foster student autonomy in the proofreading and editing phases of the writing process. The focus of the discussion is an analysis of two key aspects of autonomy: *training* in knowledge and strategies; and *engagement* with personally meaningful resources. This analysis is framed by students' achievement in editing autonomy at the beginning and end of the term. What follows is a description of a supplement developed for a traditional ESL writing curriculum in Collin County Community College in north central Texas, in the United States, but which could be implemented in any L2 program to bolster proofreading and editing autonomy.

CONTEXT

The context for this discussion is an academic skills-based ESL program at Collin County Community College, where the main purpose of the program's writing curriculum is to prepare students to enter credit-bearing college or university classes. Students in the program represent a wide range of ages, from late teens to more than 80, the average age being 25. There are diverse ethnic backgrounds, the largest groups being Koreans, Thais, Hispanics, Russians, and Ukrainians.

The basic and intermediate writing courses provide instruction in composing paragraphs and essays. The advanced course continues instruction in writing essays but focuses on argumentation and aspects of research and documentation. Although elements of process writing have been incorporated in the curriculum of all three courses, the teaching of how to proofread and edit was barely existent until the addition of the supplement described in this chapter. Proofreading strategies were not mentioned, and editing practice previously consisted of grammar explanations and exercises, including the editing of prepared texts.

CURRICULUM, TASKS, MATERIALS

Learner Autonomy

Autonomy is seen as being synonymous with *independence*, the ability to do something on one's own. By definition, however, the act of learning entails engagement with external resources. Thus, learning cannot be a fully independent act. Even though independent learners do not remain independent of resources—human or otherwise—they can be seen as independent in terms of their knowledge and learning strategies. Students' knowledge discerns appropriate resources, and learning strategies allow students to employ resources to extend their knowledge independently.

Learner autonomy is, thus, a product of leveraging student independence to maximize the effects of their *training* and meaningful *engagement* with learning resources (Tudor, 2001). Training in *knowledge* and *strategies* provides students with tools to address relevant problems independently (Benson, 1997, 2001). For instance, to train students to proofread and edit their own compositions, instructors can provide contextualized grammar instruction and its application. Likewise, training in *learning strategies* allows students to think about how they learn, assess the effectiveness of their learning, and extend their learning autonomously (see Chamot, 2001; Oxford, 2003). Strategies relevant to proofreading and editing include tactics for identifying editing needs and monitoring success in addressing those needs.

In addition to providing training in knowledge and strategies, developing autonomy entails training students to engage themselves productively with *meaningful resources* (Tudor, 2001; Van Patten, 2003). Building a repertoire of support materials, such as grammar references and relevant Web sites, and knowing how to use them effectively represent significant steps toward editor autonomy.

Using Diagnostic Results as a Teaching Tool

Diagnostic tools are not always exploited to their fullest instructional potential, often being limited to determining students' course placement. However, instructors in this program pair writing diagnostics with other activities to guide students' self-assessments of desired proofreading and editing skills. These exercises are used to ascertain whether students are able not only to detect writing errors but also to diagnose and correct them (Flower, Hayes, Carey, Schriver, & Stratman, 1999; Grabe & Kaplan, 1996). Then the instructor can develop a road map of issues that can be addressed throughout the term and determine how to help students develop autonomy (Milton, 2006, p. 127; Reid, 2006).

Activities stemming from diagnostic tools and used throughout the course include

- asking students to use diagnostic results in creating a learning agenda for the course

- asking students to revise writing diagnostics to gain an understanding of expected progress and writing quality

- observing students writing in a computer lab to gain insight into strengths and weaknesses in technology-related skills

- returning the diagnostic tools to the students at the end of the term to highlight students' progress

- conducting open discussions of diagnostic tools to (a) determine students' familiarity with concepts, (b) determine students' attitudes about proofreading and editing strategies, and (c) establish expectations (both teacher's and students')

- discussing individual diagnostic results to assist students with establishing agendas leading to autonomous behavior

Training for Autonomy

Having diagnosed the types of training needed, instructors lead their students in an awareness of general academic expectations, of textual revision, and of specific editing strategies. These types of training lay a firm foundation for students' editing autonomy beyond the L2 classroom.

ESL students need an understanding of their general academic responsibility in a U.S. academic environment. The institutional expectations of the role of students in the United States may be quite different from what they have experienced in other educational systems (Flaitz, 2003, 2006; Foster & Russell, 2002). Primary areas in which instructors can guide students to active engagement in their own writing progress include an understanding of the (a) expectation of collaboration with instructors and classmates, (b) location of their current writing course in the English writing continuum, and (c) necessity of self-pacing for process writing.

Collaboration is integral to the teaching–learning process in higher education in the United States, so instructors encourage students to be proactive in seeking the types of help they want or need. Frequently, teachers promote the use of e-mail for questions on assignments and, to help students focus their communication, ask them to use specific subject lines. Instructors often request that students complete collaborative projects and schedule face-to-face conferences in order to discuss particular phases of a writing project.

The end point of ESL writing instruction is successful performance in U.S.

higher education, so instructors need to delineate the position of their current ESL course in their future English writing continuum. As noted by Foster and Russell (2002), higher education in the United States is unique in its delay of specialization. In most countries, students are admitted to a specific department of a university with a chosen major or career focus, but in the United States, students are admitted to a university and are expected to spend their first 2 years on general studies. Incoming ESL students may feel stymied because they do not realize that U.S. college students do not typically specialize until the 3rd year of study. They often do not understand that in the United States, general college composition courses are required during the first 2 years of college study. In other countries, writing instruction in higher education is focused on the genres of specific disciplines (Foster & Russell, 2002).

Autonomous writers understand the importance of self-pacing for successful process writing. Incoming ESL students may not comprehend a need for intermediate steps in composition. To develop this awareness, teachers reward timely performance of intermediate stages of a writing assignment and often treat successive revisions as discrete assignments. These practices help students experience and value the way individual parts of any writing assignment lead to a successful result.

Within the process approach, teachers guide students to autonomy in a variety of ways. They frequently ask them to produce only one paragraph of an essay at a time. Students are then expected to generalize new understandings to subsequent paragraphs. Instructors limit the number of major writing projects in the term to give students more time to work and rework various aspects of their projects. When students ask for feedback or assistance on content or linguistic features, instructors encourage them to state the request as specifically as possible. In the process of articulating concerns clearly, students develop deeper understandings of the processes they are working through.

Training in Textual Revision

Teachers use results of a diagnostic survey of students' proofreading and editing knowledge to train students to take responsibility for editing their own texts, often a turning point in their evolution as proactive writers. The surveys often identify apathy and time-management issues, but instructors find that many ESL students have been taught not to take responsibility for editing their own writing. Some students are aware of the need for editing but expect instructors to correct their errors. These students often view the writing instructor's role as editor of their texts. There are also interesting and often hidden cross-cultural reasons for students not taking on or being aware of the need for editing written text. A Bengali student, for instance, described her instruction in English writing as a series of lectures and assignments entailing the copying of texts prepared by proficient writers. She claimed that her responsibility was to learn from models by reading and copying them accurately. Similarly, an Iranian student noted that her instruction in English composition entailed the preparation of texts that she orally recited to her instructors, the assessment of her work being based solely on the oral presentation.

Because our students' taking responsibility for proofreading and editing of their own texts depends on their understanding of how writing is taught in the United States and of their role in the learning process—as well as their willingness to attend to this task—it is necessary to cultivate students' autonomy. Familiarity with sociocultural factors of writing instruction enables students to use the skills and knowledge previously acquired to maximize their learning in their new learning environment. L2 writers may also benefit significantly from an understanding of *cognitive aspects* of writing entailing recursive composition and evaluation, *social aspects* of writing, such as addressing academic audiences, and *cultural constraints* of writing, which include the responsibility of the writer vis-à-vis the reader, including attention to linguistic and rhetorical aspects of text (see Ferris & Hedgcock, 2004; Grabe & Kaplan, 1996; Weigle, 2002). Because the linguistic aspects of editing are primary concerns in L2 classrooms, this is the focus of the following discussion.

Language Errors: Developing Focus

In our experience, at the low–intermediate level of instruction more guidance is needed to help students identify and correct language errors in their own writing. It is not uncommon at this level to find students having difficulty editing even though the target texts may be prepared with a limited number and type of target errors. Bridging the gap between guided editing of prepared texts and editing of students' own texts involves

- a focus on the most critical errors, usually basic sentence-level errors in short texts

- guidance in the identification and application of language usage rules

- maintenance of a detailed progress record

Instructors, for example, prepare students to edit their own writing by identifying two or three generic errors and demonstrating possible correction, then returning previously completed writing and asking students to edit for the same errors in their written work. Common, basic issues, such as verb tense, word order, and word form, often require instruction. Students benefit from a controlled approach to editing at this level. If they are required to edit for verb tense, for instance, they are asked to identify all verbs in their texts and then verify that the correct tense is used. This practice allows instructors to monitor the in-class editing activity and address questions as they arise. Instructor guidance is tailored to (a) the type of error (e.g., rule-based or semantic in nature), (b) the gravity (e.g., level of stigmatization, effects on comprehension) of the error, (c) the purpose of the writing task, and (d) students' needs, which, in part, are determined by the students themselves.

A similar approach is used to focus on more individual errors. The instructor can identify one, two, or three types of errors that occur in each student's text (see Ferris, 2002, 2003; Ferris & Hedgcock, 2004). The error types are noted at the top of the student's paper and, when first using this approach, the instructor may also indicate the locations of the errors. Students are then asked to edit only for the identified error types. This approach mirrors the editing of prepared texts but is intended to move student editors toward an ability to edit their own texts, a more realistic task that fosters a greater understanding of language usage rules and, thereby, a higher level of editing autonomy.

Editing Logs: Reminding and Marking Progress

Important at all levels are the editing logs used after the identification and correction of errors and during proofreading of subsequent drafts (see Appendix A). After error correction, the students use the editing log to maintain (a) a record of the types of errors in each assignment, (b) an explanation of the nature of the error in the student's own words, and (c) at least one source (textbook, grammar reference, or Web site) that the student has used to correct each error.

This process helps students understand that many of the errors in their writing are not all different, but are actually recurrences of the same types of errors. This summarizing procedure allays some of the students' feelings of frustration and being overwhelmed. Once students complete the first set of entries in their editing logs, they use the logs to proofread subsequent drafts and papers. This use of the logs reminds students of the types of errors for which they need to proofread and the correction strategies they can exploit.

The use of the log is tailored to the level of proficiency. For example, the log at the low-intermediate level focuses on linguistic errors. At the high-intermediate level, rhetorical elements, including coherence and cohesion, are introduced; likewise, linguistic errors should reflect general control of basic sentence-level grammar. Rhetorical aspects of text, such as the provision of nonrepetitious conclusions and elements of documentation, are introduced at the advanced level. Linguistic errors are limited to clause-level concerns and more semantically based grammar issues, such as article usage and lexical choice (Folse, 2004).

The use of an editing log promotes autonomy through (a) guided student-selected errors, (b) a consolidation of information, (c) explicit self-reminders of common errors for which students need to proofread, and (d) a charting of the progress in language control throughout the term. Submission of the editing log is required with every final draft. The instructor may grade for completion of the editing log, and feedback on the log can be very helpful to student editors.

Fostering Independence Gradually

Another progressive thread throughout all levels of the program is a gradual disaccustoming of students from instructors' aid with proofreading and editing (see the discussion of direct and indirect feedback in Ferris, 2002, 2003). This breaking away from total dependence on instructors' feedback during the revision process can be accomplished in a number of ways, which should be used in tandem:

- The level of teacher guidance should taper off throughout the term. The instructor, for instance, may begin the term by reformulating some errors and marking and labeling other errors, then progress to simply marking errors, noting the most common ones, and requiring students to identify and correct those errors.

- To bridge the gap between students' knowledge of grammar and their ability to proofread and edit, it is helpful to recommend specific grammar-related solutions. For instance, to remedy short, choppy sentences, the instructor may suggest combining the sentences by using adjective clauses.

- To highlight the semantic consequences of errors, leading questions can be used in place of editing symbols. For example, in response to the article error in "'By One River Blood' is the popular song of war in Bangladesh," the instructor writes "Is there ONLY one popular song in Bangladesh?" In the process of correcting errors marked indirectly, students are led to think through the identification of errors and possible correction strategies on their own. Also, students are more likely to see the importance of correct usage as a means of clear communication.

Linking Errors and Their Effect on Comprehensibility

Providing an audience other than the instructor is an effective tool to emphasize the importance of taking responsibility for editing. The recommendations of a reader other than the instructor can carry more weight than those of the instructor, and they may corroborate the views of the instructor. Alternative readers are provided through peer review, coauthoring, and the use of Internet facilities, such as blogs and wikis. These activities promote collaborative learning with various audiences and encourage students to take responsibility for their own writing.

At the higher levels of instruction, it is very useful to ask students to respond to instructor comments on final drafts of assignments. Students are asked to correct errors and briefly explain their corrections, or they are asked to reflect on instructor comments and provide a summary, including a statement of what they learned in the process of their reflection (see Ferris & Hedgcock, 2004, and Reid, 2006, for examples). This exercise prompts student reflection on personally meaningful aspects of editing and often reveals misunderstandings of grammar rules and class discussions, which, in turn, can provide an opportunity for training.

Advanced students benefit from materials that spotlight the importance of editing in academic and professional contexts. Copies of professors' syllabi that note the requirement for well-edited texts are used to persuade students of the relevance of editing to other courses. Likewise, reports from business executives, especially those with hiring authority, about the impact of well-written resumes and cover letters are effective in encouraging student editors (e.g., The National Commission on Writing, 2004, 2005; Pope, 2005). In a more creative vein, using clips of Jay Leno's "Headlines" (Leno, n.d.) or David Letterman's "Small Town News" (Letterman, n.d.), provides a humorous way to underscore the results of poor editing. Leno's late-night talk show segment on NBC and Letterman's similar segment on CBS's late-night talk show both offer humorous views of poorly edited texts. Viewing excerpts from these segments with students is an amusing way to provide students with insight into types of errors to avoid, including errors in word choice, syntax, spelling, and integration of text and graphics. It also offers humorous reminders of the consequences of poorly editing text, including miscommunication, reader confusion, and embarrassment for readers and writers. The activity also provides opportunities for discussing and practicing revision and editing. These activities help students understand their role in the proofreading and editing of their writing and lead them to assume more responsibility when revising their work, both of which set the stage for leveraging students' full potential to extend their autonomy as editors of their own writing.

Training in Editing Strategies

The term *editing* is familiar to incoming ESL students, but they often lack an understanding of its full range. The reaction of a student named Lucia was provocative to instructors in this program. Early in the term, Lucia's instructor used the whiteboard to demonstrate his thought process as he proofread and edited an example paragraph. Lucia reported her surprise at such a proactive search for possible revisions. She had previously viewed the process as a simple matter of reading for comprehension and making changes that might emerge.

As the term begins, instructors engage students in a discussion of processes used to edit written work in their first languages (L1s) and the degree of success they have experienced. In addition, they guide them in discussing methods by which they have edited in English. Students then build general lists of procedures they anticipate using during the remainder of the class.

Building on existing student ownership of the process, teachers next introduce additional editing strategies. (Figure 1 is a student guide used in this program.)

Ferris (2002), Linville (2004), and Madraso (1993) also provide lists of strategies. Some of these strategies help students focus their attention on specific parts of the text or distance themselves from seeing the passage in its expected context. Other strategies are more specific to resolving grammatical issues. Students with numerous article errors, for example, first locate all nouns in a sentence and then check for inclusion of appropriate determiners.

To introduce strategies, instructors model them by using selected passages from student papers that they have altered for anonymity. Students then engage in class activities to try specific approaches for themselves.

Throughout the term, instructors interject focusing opportunities (Miceli, 2006). When students create new drafts, teachers have them select a method or

Editing Strategies

1. Read your writing **out loud** to yourself. By listening, you may *hear* mistakes your eyes miss.

2. Proofread your writing **several times**. Look for a *different type of error* each time.

3. **Ideas:** Read through your writing at a *normal speed*. Are your ideas clear and well organized? Can you summarize the content easily?

4. **Grammar:** Read your writing *slowly* several more times. You may want to use a ruler as a reading guide to focus your attention. Each time you read, look for a different specific grammar, vocabulary, or punctuation error that is usually troublesome for you.

5. **Sentences:** Read your writing *backwards* from one sentence to another. Make sure all the elements of the sentence fit together. Check the order of your words, left to right. Are there missing words? Do your verbs agree with your subjects? Do your verb tenses agree with the time words and context of your sentence?

6. Messages from your **spell checker** and **grammar checker:** Did you choose the correct word from the list your spell checker gave you? Have you researched the messages from your grammar checker?

7. **Formatting:** For your *final* reading, make sure you have formatted the paper properly. Check requirements, such as font size, margin width, and title page formatting.

Figure 1. Student Handout on Editing Strategies

two to use. Students record the techniques at the top of the draft, edit the paper, and then record how effective they found them to be and why. By experiencing a variety of strategies for a range of editing tasks, students build personal repertoires for meeting various editing needs.

Training for Interaction With Personally Relevant Resources

Training students to address general academic expectations, to take responsibility for their own texts, and to utilize editing strategies provides them with knowledge-based, tactical tools to extend their editing autonomy. It is also important to facilitate student interactions with relevant sources of linguistic and rhetorical information. The ultimate goal is that students can determine the type of information they need, locate it, and use it independently.

Resources for Linguistic Knowledge

Students often enter writing courses with limited experience using reference materials. Students anticipate using one English dictionary and perhaps one grammar book to meet all of their English writing needs. Instructors, therefore, hold the key to a world of other support materials. They engage students in exploring a range of dictionaries, grammar texts, writing texts, and Web site resources. Higher level students benefit from trying out desk reference options as well. Instructors seek to show students how much material is readily available and to help them become educated consumers of linguistic information. Instructors also caution students about the limitations of some types of sources, such as electronic translators, and demonstrate common deficiencies.

Evaluating Paper Materials

The first step to involving students in interaction with meaningful material is guiding them to evaluate the materials they already have. Students bring to class various dictionaries, grammar books, and writing texts from current and past studies. They also find and check out similar materials from the shelves of their school library.

An effective extension of the gathering of materials for classroom discussion is the establishment of an accessible campus site for a permanent collection of ESL resources. In the case of this program, the school library offered a small room with wall-mounted shelves. Teachers donate books, and the library earmarks funds for ESL acquisitions. The materials are labeled by level to help students locate information appropriate to their reading skills. The library staff catalogues the resources so that students can check materials out.

To encourage students to actively investigate and use various resources, instructors ask them to share instructional information for resolving specific editing issues with their classmates. The class then evaluates the qualities of these materials. Students record for themselves resources they find most useful and which they anticipate using.

Evaluating Online Resources

Instructors also highlight online resources. Appendix B offers a collection of teacher-preferred Web sites for writing and grammar instruction and practice. Also recommended are sites for specific types of dictionary and thesaurus inquiries. In addition, they encourage students to explore the Web independently and bring in resources for class discussion and assessment. Advanced students learn to use collocation concordances, and they are guided to search judiciously selected authentic texts to validate or edit passages when they sense their texts do not "feel," "seem," or "sound" right.

The value of helping students work in computer-equipped classrooms cannot be understated. Students work much more successfully if teachers help them respond accurately to messages from the spelling and grammar checkers. For example, students get more effective spelling feedback if they are coached to type unfamiliar words systematically by entering letters for the "sounds" they hear.

Sometimes in lab sessions it is thought provoking to ask students to keep a running log of helpful information they gain from computer feedback. Instructors can follow up with a group discussion to report individual discoveries. Instructors also caution students that the software often cannot parse higher level grammar structures effectively.

Resources for Rhetorical Knowledge

Another part of editing is dealing with rhetorical issues of content, vocabulary, and organization for each form. The teaching of various rhetorical modes has its supporters and detractors (Foster & Russell, 2002; Fukuoka & Spyridakis, 1999; Hinkel, 2004). However, instructors in this program conferred with college professors in various fields. They validated introducing ESL students to rhetorical modes so that students could anticipate their professors' expectations. In addition, teaching common writing modes provides students with insight into how to organize their thoughts and utilize linguistic structures and lexical items associated with various modes (Foster & Russell, 2002), thereby increasing students' autonomy.

Students are introduced to rhetorical modes as types of organized thought patterns to accomplish a particular task which may be related to an academic field. For example, biology labs require students to write process analysis essays explaining how a particular lab was performed. Students briefly discuss how these thought patterns may differ from those of their L1s (Foster & Russell, 2002; Swan & Smith, 2001). Then students are provided with examples from textbooks and Web sites. To build self-confidence, students identify criteria for rating the appropriateness and effectiveness of the examples and use these criteria to rate their own writing.

Introducing rhetorical modes in ESL writing classes engenders student confidence when tackling academic writing assignments by providing templates for both content and common linguistic elements (Reid, 2006).

Assessing Editing Skills

Assessing editing skills is an ongoing task for instructors and students. Continued assessment illuminates students' abilities to detect writing errors and measures their abilities to diagnose and correct them autonomously (Flower et al., 1999; Grabe & Kaplan, 1996). The goal is to pass the responsibility of assessment from instructors to students as early as possible.

Students' personal editing logs are vehicles by which they identify recurring errors and their solutions (Ferris, 2002; Madraso, 1993). Instructors review the log notes and provide advice. In the event student progress stalls, teachers can suggest remedies from specific sources such as textbooks and Web sites. Over time, students assume ownership of mapping their own progress and seeking the kinds of assistance they find most valuable.

Students are also asked to assess various editing strategies in terms of their usefulness in identifying and correcting errors. This assessment allows students and instructors to reflect on the editing process and seek additional resources and strategies.

Throughout the term, instructors make students aware that becoming an autonomous editor is a process that requires more than a term, a year, or even a lifetime. The rewards often do not become fully apparent until students are involved in academic courses. In fact, the progression to independence can be frustrating. However, with perseverance, time, and dedication, ESL writing students can and do achieve a good measure of autonomy in editing.

REFLECTIONS

The approach for developing editing autonomy that has been discussed in this chapter has been particularly successful with students who are academically prepared. It is especially so for those who already have a metacognitive understanding of language. These students are able to produce polished, level-appropriate texts and often test out of ESL and developmental writing courses one term ahead of their peers. This result has been encouraging at a time when some educational officials are calling for accelerated course completion. In contrast, students who are used to a teacher-centered approach or are less mature struggle to assume proofreading and editing responsibilities. Many of them, nonetheless, do succeed. It is necessary to admit, however, that some students continue to resist, believing that it is the instructor's duty to proofread and "fix" their writing.

Instructors adopting the approach described need to be aware that increased attention to proofreading and editing can claim time from instruction traditionally devoted to rhetorical aspects of writing. Thus, they need to devote appropriate attention to the more global aspects of composition so that students understand the role that textual features, in general, play in determining the quality of a text. By providing balanced instruction in various aspects of textual quality, by engaging students in taking responsibility for their own texts, and by promoting effective use of meaningful resources, instructors advance the autonomy of student writers.

Donald Weasenforth holds a doctorate in applied linguistics from the University of Southern California, in the United States, and has taught languages for 30 years. His research focus is written discourse analysis, and his teaching experience is primarily in ESL writing. He currently teaches ESL and English composition at Collin County Community College in Plano, Texas, in the United States.

Margaret Redus holds a master's degree in liberal arts with specialization in bilingual education from Southern Methodist University, in the United States. She has taught language arts in primary grades as well as ESL and English for speakers of other languages courses at local colleges. Her teaching focus is writing and grammar with student autonomy extended through technology. She currently teaches at Richland College in Dallas, Texas, in the United States.

Nancy Ham Megarity holds a master's degree in English as a Second Language from the University of Arizona and has taught ESL in Japan as well as in the United States. She currently teaches at Collin County Community College in Plano, Texas, in the United States, where her foci are writing, grammar, and Test of English as a Foreign Language preparation.

APPENDIX A: EDITING LOGS

Editing Log for Individual Writing Assignments			
Directions: Identify 3–5 <u>types</u> of errors in your essay. Record the type of error and the specific examples. Then explain how you would correct these errors (all errors of the same type) and why you would correct them that way.			
Error Type	**Specific Error**	**Correction**	**Reason for Correction**
art.	The popular music is an important part of life.	The Popular music is an important part of life.	No article with a noncount noun with general meaning

Editing Log for Term Progress						
Directions: Throughout the term, record the most frequent types of errors you find in each of your essays. When you proofread your writing, check for these specific errors.						
Type of Error	**ESSAY #1**	**ESSAY #2**	**ESSAY #3**	**ESSAY #4**	**ESSAY #5**	**I need to proofread for:**
art.	✓	✓	✓			articles with noncount nouns with general meaning

APPENDIX B: ONLINE EDITING RESOURCES

Grammar Usage Web Sites

A Guide to Grammar & Writing—Capital Community College
http://grammar.ccc.commnet.edu/grammar/

- grammar topics (click "index" button on home page)
- PowerPoint presentations (click "Peripherals & PowerPoints" on home page)

Sentence Sense—Capital Community College
http://www.ccc.commnet.edu/sensen/

- grammar, usage, writing, resources

ELC Study Zone—University of Victoria
http://web2.uvcs.uvic.ca/elc/studyzone/index.htm

- instruction, practice (click "extras" for index to grammar materials)

English Works!—Gallaudet University
http://depts.gallaudet.edu/englishworks/grammar/main/index.htm

- instruction, practice

The Internet Grammar of English—University College London
http://www.ucl.ac.uk/internet-grammar/

- instruction, practice

Purdue University ESL Resources
http://owl.english.purdue.edu/handouts/esl/

- information, exercises on grammar topics

Dictionary Web Sites

Longman Dictionary of Contemporary English Online
http://www.ldoceonline.com/

- organized by parts of speech; includes collocations; provides contextualized usage examples

One Look
http://www.onelook.com

- table of quick definitions; easy to read and understand; audio pronunciation; listings of generalized and specialized definitions drawn from 1,100 dictionaries

References

Advertisement for Banner Japan K.K. (2006, March). *Metropolis Magazine, 626,* 45.

Anderson, D. G. (2004). *Sowing the seed: Wiki and student-initiated student support in distance learning.* Unpublished master's thesis, Aston University, Birmingham, England.

Arizona State University Writing Programs. (2009, July 20). *Mission statement.* Retrieved August 5, 2009, from http://english.clas.asu.edu/wp-mission

Arneil, S., & Holmes, M. (2006). Hot Potatoes (Version 6.0) [Computer software]. Victoria, BC, Canada: Half-Baked Software.

Aubry, K. (Producer), & Coppola, F. F. (Director). (1983). *The outsiders* [Motion picture]. United States: Warner Bros.

Azar, B. (2007, March 21). *Teaching amid change: Perspectives from 42 years in ESL.* Opening Plenary presented at 2007 TESOL Convention, Seattle, WA.

Badger, R., & White, G. (2000). A process genre approach to teaching writing. *ELT Journal, 54*(2), 153–160.

Bagwell, O. (Producer). (2004). *Citizen King* [Motion Picture]. Boston: PBS Home Video.

Bakhtin, M. M. (1999). The problem of speech genres. In A. Jaworski & N. Coupland (Eds.), *The discourse reader* (pp. 121–132). New York: Routledge.

Baldwin, C. A. (2006). *Big Ben exam writing.* Retrieved June 1, 2007, from http://www.seedwiki.com/wiki/big_ben_exam_writing/

Bazerman, C. (1988). *Shaping written knowledge: The genre and activity of the experimental articles in science.* Madison: University of Wisconsin Press.

Beaufort, A. (1998). Transferring writing knowledge to the workplace: Are we on track? In M. S. Garay & S. A. Bernhardt (Eds.), *Expanding literacies: English teaching and the new workplace* (pp. 179–199). New York: SUNY Press.

Belcher, D. (2006). English for specific purposes: Teaching to perceived needs and imagined futures in worlds of work, study, and everyday life. *TESOL Quarterly, 40*(1), 133–156.

Benson, P. (1997). The philosophy and politics of learner autonomy. In P. Benson & P. Voller (Eds.), *Autonomy and independence in language learning* (pp. 18–34). New York: Longman.

Benson, P. (2001). *Teaching and researching: Autonomy in language learning.* London: Longman.

Benson, P. (2003). Learner autonomy in the classroom. In D. Nunan (Ed.), *Practical English language teaching* (pp. 289–308). People's Republic of China: McGraw Hill.

Berger, J. (1990). *Ways of seeing.* London: Penguin.

Biber, D., Johansson, S., Leech, G., Conrad, S., & Finegan, E. (1999). *Longman grammar of spoken and written English.* Harlow, Essex, England: Pearson.

Blakeslee, A. (2001). Bridging the workplace and the academy: Teaching professional genres through classroom–workplace collaborations. *Technical Communication Quarterly, 10,* 169–192.

Blanton, L. L. (2002). As I was saying to Leonard Bloomfield: A personalized history of ESL/writing. In L. L. Blanton & B. Kroll (Eds.), *ESL composition tales: Reflections on teaching* (pp. 135–163). Ann Arbor: University of Michigan Press.

Blood, R. (2002). Weblogs: A history and perspective. In Editors of Perseus Publishing (Ed.), *We've got blog: How weblogs are changing culture* (pp. 7–16). Cambridge, MA: Perseus.

Breen, M. P. (1985). Authenticity in the language classroom. *Applied Linguistics, 6,* 60–70.

Brinton, D. M., Snow, M. A., & Wesche, M. B. (2003). *Content-based second language instruction.* Ann Arbor: University of Michigan Press.

Brisk, M. (1998, March 17). *The transforming power of critical autobiographies.* Paper presented at the annual meeting of TESOL, Seattle, WA.

Broner, M., & Tarone, M. (2000). Language plan in immersion classroom discourse: Some suggestions for language teaching. *Australian Review of Applied Linguistics, 16,* 121–133.

Brown, A. (2005). Self-assessment of writing in independent language learning programs: The value of annotated samples. *Assessing Writing, 10*(3), 174–191.

Brown, H. (2000). *Principles of language learning.* White Plains, NY: Longman.

Brown, J. D. (2000). University entrance examinations: Strategies for creating positive washback on English language teaching in Japan. *Shiken: JALT Testing & Evaluation SIG Newsletter, 3*(2), 4–8. Retrieved December 15, 2007, from http://www.jalt.org/test/bro_5.htm

Buckley, C. (2007, January 3). A man down, a train arriving, and a stranger makes a choice. *The New York Times*, p. A1.

Burden, P. (2005). The castor oil effect: Learner beliefs about the enjoyment and usefulness of classroom activities and the effects of student motivation. *The Language Teacher, 29*(10), 3–9.

Butin, D. (2005). *Service learning in higher education*. New York: Palgrave-Macmillan.

Campbell, A. P. (2004). Using LiveJournal for authentic communication in EFL classes. *The Internet TESL Journal, 10*(9). Retrieved November 13, 2007, from http://iteslj.org/Techniques/Campbell-LiveJournal

Campbell, C. (1990). Writing with others' words: Using background reading text in academic compositions. In B. Kroll (Ed.), *Second language writing*. Cambridge, MA: Cambridge University Press.

Canagarajah, S. (2002). *Critical academic writing and multilingual students*. Ann Arbor: University of Michigan.

Caplan, N. A., McCullough, A. S., & Stokes, L. R. (2006). Beyond the writing textbook. In C. M. Pearson, N. A. Caplan, & C. Wilson-Duffy (Eds.), *State of the art: Selected proceedings of the 2005 Michigan Teachers of English to Speakers of Other Languages (MITESOL) Conference* (pp. 92–101). East Lansing: Michigan State University Press.

Carey, M., & Afanasieff, W. (1993). Hero [Recorded by M. Carey]. On *Mariah Carey: Music Box* [CD]. Nashville, TN: Sony Songs Inc./Rhye Songs (BMI)/WB Music Corp./Wallingworld Music, Columbia (USA).

Carter, R. (2004). *Language and creativity: The art of common talk*. London: Routledge.

Carter, R., & McCarthy, M. (2006). *Cambridge grammar of English*. Cambridge: Cambridge University Press.

Casanave, C. (2002). *Writing games: Multicultural case studies of academic literacy practices in higher education*. Mahwah, NJ: Lawrence Erlbaum.

Casanave, C. P. (2003). Multiple uses of applied linguistics in a multi-disciplinary graduate EAP class. *ELT Journal, 57*, 43–50.

Chamot, A. U. (2001). The role of learning strategies in second language acquisition. In M. P. Breen (Ed.), *Learner contributions to language learning: New directions in research* (pp. 25–43). New York: Longman.

Chandler, J. (2003). The efficacy of various kinds of error feedback for improvement in the accuracy and fluency of L2 student writing. *Journal of Second Language Writing, 12*, 267–296.

Chao, C. (2004). CALL opens language learning windows in Taiwan. *Essential Teacher, 1*(3), 22–25.

Charles, M. (1990). Responding to problems in written English using a student self-monitoring technique. *ELT Journal, 44,* 286–293.

China Higher Education English Teaching Committee for English Majors. (2000, March). *National College English curriculum for English majors in China.* Retrieved October 10, 2007, from http://www.bfsu.edu.cn/chinese/site/gxyyzyxxw/zywj/yyjxdg.htm

Cobb, T. (2007). *The compleat lexical tutor.* Retrieved October 9, 2007, from http://www.lextutor.ca

Conrad, S. (2002). Corpus linguistic approaches for discourse analysis. *Annual Review of Applied Linguistics, 22,* 75–95.

Cook, D. (2001). Revising editing. *Teaching English in the Two-Year College, 29,* 154–161.

Cook, G. (1989). *Discourse.* Oxford: Oxford University Press.

Cook, G. (2000). *Language play, language learning.* Oxford: Oxford University Press.

Coulthard, M. (1994). On analyzing and evaluating written text. In M. Coulthard (Ed.), *Advances in written text analysis* (pp. 1–11). New York: Routledge.

Coxhead, A. (2000). The new academic word list. *TESOL Quarterly, 34*(2), 213–238.

Crandall, J., & Kaufman, D. (Eds.). (2002). *Content-based instruction in higher education settings.* Alexandria, VA: TESOL.

Cresswell, A. (2000). Self-monitoring in student writing: Developing learner responsibility. *ELT Journal, 54,* 235–244.

Daniels, H. (2002). *Literature circles: Voice and choice in book clubs and reading groups* (2nd ed.). Portland, ME: Stenhouse.

Davidson, C., & Tomic, A. (1994). Removing computer phobia from the writing classroom. *ELT Journal, 48*(3), 205–213.

Day, R. (2004). A critical look at authentic materials. *The Journal of Asia TEFL, 1*(1), 101–114.

Dias, P., Freedman, A., Medway, P., & Pare, A. (1999). *Worlds apart: Acting and writing in academic and workplace contexts.* Mahwah, NJ: Lawrence Erlbaum.

Dieu, B. (2004, Fall). Blogs for language learning. *Essential Teacher, 1*(4), 26–30.

Donley, K. M., & Reppen, R. (2001). Using corpus tools to highlight academic vocabulary in SCLT. *TESOL Journal, 10*(2/3), 7–12.

Dougiamas, M. (2008). Moodle (version 1.9.3) [Computer software]. Perth, Australia: Moodle Pty. Ltd.

Dyke Ford, J. (2004). Knowledge transfer across disciplines: Tracking rhetorical strategies from a technical communication classroom to an engineering classroom. *IEEE Transactions on Professional Communication, 47,* 301–315.

Edge, J. (1989). *Mistakes and correction.* London: Longman.

Eisenberg, N. (2000). *From the frozen sky.* Retrieved November 1, 2007, from the City University of New York Web site: http://writesite.cuny.edu/grammar/hotspots/sentence/basic/index.html

Elbow, P. (1991). Reflection on academic discourse: How it relates to freshmen and colleagues. *College English, 53*(2), 135–155.

Equipped for the future. (2004) Knoxville, TN: Equipped for the Future at the Center for Literacy. Retrieved October 31, 2008, from the Equipped for the Future Web site: http://eff.cls.utk.edu/

Erdrich, L. (2005). *The game of silence.* New York: HarperCollins.

Espinosa, D. (1998). English education in the Philippines. In J. Kahny & M. James (Eds.), *Perspectives on secondary school EFL education* (pp. 127–128). Odawara, Japan: Language Institute of Japan.

Ferris, D. (2002). *Treatment of error.* Ann Arbor: The University of Michigan Press.

Ferris, D. (2003). Responding to writing. In B. Kroll (Ed.), *Exploring the dynamics of second language writing* (pp. 119–140). New York: Cambridge University Press.

Ferris, D. (2004). The "Grammar Correction" debate in L2 writing: Where are we, and where do we go from here? (and what do we do in the meantime . . . ?). *Journal of Second Language Writing, 13*(1), 49–62.

Ferris, D., & Hedgcock, J. (2004). *Teaching ESL composition: Purpose, process, and practice.* Mahwah, NJ: Lawrence Erlbaum.

Ferris, D. R. (1999). The case for grammar correction in L2 writing classes: A response to Truscott (1996). *Journal of Second Language Writing, 8*(1), 1–10.

Ferris, D., & Roberts, B. (2001). Error feedback in L2 writing classes: How explicit does it need to be? *Journal of Second Language Writing, 10*(3), 161–184.

Fertoli, A. (2007, December 13). The changing face of community colleges. *Queens Chronicle, Western Queens Edition,* p. 12.

Flaitz, J. (2003). *Understanding your international students: An educational, cultural, and linguistic guide.* Ann Arbor: The University of Michigan Press.

Flaitz, J. (2006). *Understanding your refugee and immigrant students: An educational, cultural, and linguistic guide.* Ann Arbor: The University of Michigan Press.

Florio-Ruane, S. (2001). *Teacher education and the cultural imagination: Autobiography, conversation, and narrative.* Mahwah, NJ: Lawrence Erlbaum.

Flower, L., Hayes, J., Carey, L., Schriver, K., & Stratman, J. (1999). Detection, diagnosis, and the strategies of revision. In L. Ede (Ed.), *On writing research: The Braddock essays 1975–1998* (pp. 191–228). New York: Bedford/St. Martin's.

Flowerdew, J. (1993). An educational, or process, approach to the teaching of professional genres. *ELT Journal, 47*(4), 305–316.

Folse, K. (2004). *Vocabulary myths: Applying second language research to classroom teaching.* Ann Arbor: The University of Michigan Press.

Foster, D., & Russell, D. (Eds.). (2002). Introduction: Rearticulating articulation. In *Writing and learning in cross-national perspective, transitions from secondary to higher education* (pp. 1–47) [Introduction]. Mahwah, NJ: Lawrence Erlbaum.

Freire, P. (1998). *Pedagogy of freedom: Ethics, democracy, and civic courage.* New York: Rowman & Littlefield.

Fukuoka, W., & Spyridakis, J. H. (1999). The organization of Japanese expository passages. *Institute of Electrical and Electronics Engineers Transactions on Professional Communication, 42*(3), 166–174.

Funk, W., & Lewis, N. (1942). *30 days to a more powerful vocabulary.* New York: Pocket Books.

Gentleman, A. (2006, August 2). In India, a maid becomes an unlikely literary star. *The New York Times,* pp. E1, E3.

Gianelli, M. (1997). Thematic units: Creating an environment for learning. In M. Snow & D. Brinton (Eds.), *The content based classroom* (pp. 142–148). New York: Addison Wesley Longman. (Reprinted from *TESOL Journal,* 1991, *1,* pp. 13–15.)

Godwin-Jones, R. (2003). Blogs and wikis: Environments for on-line collaboration. *Language Learning & Technology, 7*(2), 12–16. Retrieved from http://llt.msu.edu/vol7num2/emerging/

Goldman, S., & Rakestraw, J. (2000). Structural aspects of constructing meaning from text. In M. Kamil, P. Mosenthal, P. D. Pearson, & R. Barr (Eds.), *Handbook of reading research, III* (pp. 311–335). Mahwah, NJ: Lawrence Erlbaum.

Google Docs. (2006). (BETA) [Computer software]. Mountain View, CA: Google.

Grabe, W. (2001). Reading–writing relations: Theoretical perspectives and instructional practices. In D. Belcher & A. Hirvela (Eds.), *Linking literacies: Perspectives on L2 reading–writing connections* (pp. 15–47). Ann Arbor: University of Michigan Press.

Grabe, W., & Kaplan, R. B. (1996). *Theory and practice of writing.* London: Longman.

Grandin, T. (1995). *Thinking in pictures and other reports from my life with autism.* New York: Random House.

Granger, S., & Tribble, C. (1998). Learner corpus data in the foreign language classroom: Form-focused instruction and data-driven learning. In S. Granger (Ed.), *Learner English on computer* (pp. 199–209). London: Longman.

Gross, A. (1990). *The rhetoric of science.* Cambridge, MA: Harvard University Press.

Grundy, P. (1994). *Beginners: Resource books for teachers.* Oxford: Oxford University Press.

Guerrero, M. C. M. D., & Villamil, O. S. (2000). Activating the ZPD: Mutual scaffolding in L2 peer revision. *The Modern Language Journal, 84*(1), 51–68.

Haar, C., & Horning, A. (2006). Introduction and overview. In A. Horning & A. Becker (Eds.), *Revision: History, theory and practice* (pp. 3–9). West Lafayette, IN: Parlor Press.

Halder, B. (2005). *A life less ordinary* (U. Butalia, Trans.). New Delhi, India: Zubaan Books.

Hale, G., Taylor, C., Bridgeman, B., Carson, J., Kroll, B., & Kantor, R. (1996). *A study of writing tasks assigned in academic degree programs.* Princeton, NJ: Educational Testing Service.

Halliday, M. A. K., & Hasan, R. (1976). *Cohesion in English.* New York: Longman.

Halliday, M. A. K., & Matthiessen, C. M. I. M. (2004). *An introduction to functional grammar.* London: Hodder Arnold.

Hedgcock, J., & Lefkowitz, N. (1996). Some input on input: Two analyses of student response to expert feedback in L2 writing. *Modern Language Journal, 80*(3), 287–308.

Hertz-Lazarowitz, R., & Bar-Natan, I. (2001). Writing development of Arab and Jewish students using cooperative learning (CL) and computer-mediated communication (CMC). *Computers & Education, 3,* 19–36.

Hinkel, E. (2004). *Teaching academic writing: Practical techniques in vocabulary and grammar.* Mahwah, NJ: Lawrence Erlbaum.

Hinkel, E. (2005). Hedging, inflating, and persuading in L2 academic writing. *Applied Language Writing, 15,* 29–53.

Hinton, S. E. (1967). *The outsiders.* New York: Penguin.

Hoey, M. (2001). *Textual interaction.* New York: Routledge.

Holliday, A. (1997). Six lessons: Cultural continuity in CLT. *Language Teaching Research, 1*(3), 212–238.

Horowitz, D. (1986). Process, not product: Less than meets the eye. *TESOL Quarterly, 20*(1), 141–144.

Huntley, H. (2006). *Essential academic vocabulary: Mastering the academic word list.* Boston: Heinle.

Hyde, L. (2007). *The gift: Creativity and the artist in the modern world* (2nd ed.). New York: Vintage Books.

Hyland, K. (1994). Hedging in academic writing and EAP textbooks. *English for Specific Purposes, 13,* 239–256.

Hyland, K. (2000). Hedges, boosters, and lexical invisibility: Noticing modifiers in academic texts. *Language Awareness, 9,* 179–197.

Hyland, K. (2002). *Teaching and researching writing.* London: Pearson ESL.

Hyland, K. (2003a). Genre-based pedagogies: A social response to process. *Journal of Second Language Writing, 12*(1), 17–29.

Hyland, K. (2003b). *Second language writing.* New York: Cambridge University Press.

Hyland, K. (2005). *Metadiscourse: Exploring interaction in writing.* London: Continuum International.

Hyland, K., & Milton, J. (1997). Hedging in L1 and L2 student writing. *Journal of Second Language Writing, 6,* 183–206.

James, M. A. (2006). Transfer of learning from a university content-based EAP course. *TESOL Quarterly, 40*(4), 783–806.

Janzen, J. (2002). Teaching strategic reading. In J. C. Richards & W. A. Renandya (Eds.), *Methodology in language teaching: An anthology of current practice* (pp. 287–294). New York: Cambridge University Press.

Jaworski, A., & Coupland, N. (1999). Perspectives on discourse analysis. In A. Jaworski & N. Coupland (Eds.), *The discourse reader* (pp. 1–44). New York: Routledge.

Johns, A. (1999). Opening our doors: Applying socioliterate approaches (SA) to language minority classrooms. In L. Harklau, K. Losey, & M. Siegel (Eds.), *Generation 1.5 meets college composition* (pp. 159–174). Mahwah, NJ: Lawrence Erlbaum.

Johns, T. (1994). The text and its message. In M. Coulthard (Ed.), *Advances in written text analysis* (pp. 102–117). New York: Routledge.

Johnson, A. (2004). Creating a writing course utilizing class and student blogs. *The Internet TESL Journal, 10*(8). Retrieved November 13, 2007, from http://iteslj .org/Techniques/Johnson-Blogs

Jordan, R. R. (1997). *English for academic purposes: A guide and resourcs book for teachers.* Cambridge: Cambridge University Press.

Kachru, B. (2005). *Asian Englishes: Beyond the canon.* Hong Kong: Hong Kong University Press.

Kaufman, D., & Crandall, J. (Eds.). (2005). *Content-based instruction in primary and secondary school settings.* Alexandria, VA: TESOL.

Kawabata, T. (2006, July). Ask not what computers can do for language teaching; instead, ask what you can do for language teaching using computers. In *The use of computer-assisted language learning*. Retrieved August 15, 2006, from http://www .eltnews.com/features/special/

Keh, C. L. (1990). Feedback in the writing process: A model and methods for implementation. *ELT Journal, 44*(4), 294–304.

King, M. L., Jr. (1963, April 16). Letter from a Birmingham jail. In *African studies center: University of Pennsylvania*. Retrieved January 15, 2008, from http://www .africa.upenn.edu/Articles_Gen/Letter_Birmingham.html

King, M. L., Jr. (1963, August 28). I have a dream. In *The U.S. Constitution online*. Retrieved January 15, 2008, from http://www.usconstitution.net/dream.html

Koch, R. (2007). Beyond handbooks and textbooks—Teaching about writing. *National Writing Project*. Retrieved November 2, 2007, from http://www.nwp.org/ cs/public/print/resource/2468

Krajka, J. (2000). Using the Internet in ESL writing instruction. *The Internet TESL Journal, 6*(11). Retrieved from http://iteslj.org/Techniques/Krajka-WritingUsingNet.html

Kubota, R. (2004). Critical multiculturalism and second language education. In B. Norton & K. Toohey (Eds.), *Critical pedagogies and language learning* (pp. 30–52). Cambridge: The Cambridge University Applied Linguistic Series.

Kubota, R., & Lin, A. (2006). Race and TESOL: Introduction to concepts and theories. *TESOL Quarterly, 40*(3), 471–493.

Labov, W. (1999). The transformation of experience in narrative. In A. Jaworski & N. Coupland (Eds.), *The discourse reader* (pp. 221–235). New York: Routledge.

Langer, J. A. (1990). The process of understanding: Reading for literacy and information purposes. *Research in the Teaching of English, 24*(3), 229–260.

Leki, I. (1991). Building expertise through sequenced writing assignments. *TESOL Journal, 1*, 19–23.

Leki, I. (1995). *Academic writing: Exploring processes and strategies* (2nd ed.). New York: St. Martin's Press.

Leki, I., & Carson, J. G. (1994). Students' perceptions of EAP writing instruction and writing needs across the disciplines. *TESOL Quarterly, 28*(1), 81–101.

Leki, I., & Carson, J. G. (1997). "Completely different worlds": EAP and the writing experiences of ESL students in university courses. *TESOL Quarterly, 31*(1), 39–69.

LeLoup, J. W., & Ponterio, R. (2006). Wikipedia: A multilingual treasure trove. *Language Learning & Technology, 10*(2), 4–7. Retrieved from http://llt.msu .edu/vol10num2/pdf/net.pdf

Leno, J. (n.d.). *The Tonight Show with Jay Leno* "Headlines" [Television series ongoing segment]. New York: NBC Universal.

Letterman, D. (n.d.). *Late Show with David Letterman* "Small Town News" [Television series ongoing segment]. New York: CBS Broadcasting.

Linville, C. (2004). Editing line by line. In S. Bruce & B. Rafoth (Eds.), *ESL writers: A guide for writing center tutors* (pp. 84–93). Portsmouth, NH: Heinemann.

Madraso, J. (1993). Proofreading: The skill we've neglected to teach. *The English Journal, 82*(2), 32–41.

Main Page. (2008, September 6). In *Wikipedia, The Free Encyclopedia*. Retrieved 12:51, September 16, 2008, from http://en.wikipedia.org/w/index.php?title=Main_Page&oldid=236740618

Massey, D. (2007, January 5). Catch of their lives: Seconds after falling from 4th floor fire escape in Bronx, boy, 3, is caught by two good Samaritans. *Newsday,* p. A03.

Matsuda, P. K. (2003). Process and postprocess: A discursive history. *Journal of Second Language Writing, 12,* 65–83.

Matsuda, P. K., Canagarajah, A. S., Harklau, L., Hyland, K., & Warschauer, M. (2003, May). Changing currents in second language writing research: A colloquium. *Journal of Second Language Writing, 12*(2), 151–179. Retrieved May 6, 2009, from http://matsuda.jslw.org/abstracts/pdf/jslw2003b.pdf

Matsumura, S., & Hann, G. (2004). Computer anxiety and students' preferred feedback methods in EFL writing. *The Modern Language Journal, 88*(3), 403–415.

McCarter, S. (1997). *A book on writing.* Midlothian, Scotland: Intelligene.

McCarthy, M. (1991). *Discourse analysis for language teachers.* Cambridge, MA: Cambridge University Press.

McEachern, R. (2001). Problems in service learning and technical/professional writing: Incorporating the perspective of nonprofit management. *Technical Communication Quarterly, 10*(2), 211–224.

McEnery, T., Xiao, R., & Tono, Y. (2006). *Corpus-based language studies: An advanced resource book.* London: Routledge.

McVeigh, B. (2002). *Japanese higher education as myth.* Armonk, NY: M.E. Sharpe.

Megheirbi, A., Quirke, A., Kennedy, A., Mougharbel, H., Bampton, M., & Yates-Knepp, T. (2003–2004). *English for scientific studies.* Al-Ain, UAE: Publication Department, UAE University.

Meyers, L. (2000). Barriers to meaningful instructions for English learners. *Theory into Practice, 39*(4), 228–236.

Mezey, P. (Producer), & Marston, J. (Writer/Director). (2004). *Maria full of grace* [Motion picture]. United States: HBO Home Video.

Miceli, T. (2006, December). Foreign language students' perceptions of a reflective approach to text correction. *Directory of Open Access Journals, 3*(1). Retrieved July 14, 2009, from http://ehlt.flinders.edu.au/deptlang/fulgor/back_issues.htm

Miller, A. (1947). *All my sons.* New York: Penguin.

Milton, J. (1998). Exploiting L1 and interlanguage corpora in the design of an electronic language learning and production environment. In S. Granger (Ed.), *Learner English on computer* (pp. 187–198). London: Longman.

Milton, J. (2006). Resource-rich web-based feedback: Helping learners become independent writers. In K. Hyland & F. Hyland (Eds.), *Feedback in second language writing: Contexts and issues* (pp. 123–139). New York: Cambridge University Press.

Min, H. T. (2006). The effects of trained peer review on EFL students' revision types and writing quality. *Journal of Second Language Writing, 15*(2), 118–141.

Morrison, B. (1989). Using news broadcasts for authentic listening comprehension. *ELT Journal, 43*(1), 14–18.

Murphey, T. (1998). *Language hungry! An introduction to language learning fun and self esteem.* Tokyo: Macmillan Language House.

Murphy, J. M., & Stoller, F. L. (2001). Sustained-content language teaching: An emerging definition. *TESOL Journal, 10*(2/3), 3–5.

Murray, D. M. (2004). *A writer teaches writing* (Rev. 2nd ed.). Boston: Heinle.

NASA Earth Observatory. (2007). Tropical deforestation. In *NASA Earth Observatory.* Retrieved October 12, 2007, from http://earthobservatory.nasa.gov/Features/Deforestation/

Nation, I. S. P. (2001). *Learning vocabulary in another language.* New York: Cambridge University Press.

National Commission on Writing. (2004, September). Writing: A ticket to work . . . or a ticket out, a survey of business leaders. In *College Board.* Retrieved July 11, 2005, from http://www.writingcommission.org/prod_downloads/writingcom/writing-ticket-to-work.pdf

National Commission on Writing. (2005, July). Writing: A Powerful message from state government. In *College Board.* Retrieved July 11, 2005, from http://www.writingcommission.org/prod_downloads/writingcom/powerful-message-from-state.pdf

National Council of Teachers of English. (2004). NCTE beliefs about the teaching of writing. NCTE guideline. Retrieved August 2, 2009, from http://www.ncte.org/positions/statements/writingbeliefs

Newell, G., Garriga, M. C., & Peterson, S. S. (2001). Learning to assume the role of author: A study of reading-to-write one's own ideas in an undergraduate ESL composition course. In D. Belcher & A. Hirvela (Eds.), *Linking literacies: Perspectives on L2 reading–writing connections* (pp. 164–185). Ann Arbor: University of Michigan Press.

Nieto, S. (1999). *The light in their eyes: Creating multicultural learning communities.* New York: Teachers College Press.

Nieto, S. (2002). *Language, culture, and teaching: Critical perspectives for a new century.* Mahwah, NJ: Lawrence Erlbaum.

Nunan, D. (1999). *Second language teaching and learning.* Boston: Heinle and Heinle.

O'Keeffe, A., McCarthy, M., & Carter, R. (2007). *From corpus to classroom: Language use and language teaching.* Cambridge: Cambridge University Press.

Oliveira, L. P. de (2002). Explicitação do context em textos de alunos brasileiros e americanos [Context explicitation in texts by Brazilian and American students]. *Palavra, 8,* 112–126.

Ortega, L. (1997). Processes and outcomes in networked classroom interaction: Define the research agenda for L2 computer-assisted classroom discussion. *Language Learning and Technology, 1*(1), 82–93. Retrieved from http://llt.msu.edu/vol1num1/ortega/default.html

Ovando, C., Combs, M., & Collier, V. (2006). *Bilingual and ESL classrooms: Teaching in multicultural contexts.* Boston: McGraw-Hill.

Oxford, R. (2003). Toward a more systematic model of L2 learner autonomy. In D. Palfreyman & R. Smith (Eds.), *Learner autonomy across culture: Language education perspective* (pp. 75–91). Basingstoke, Hampshire, England: Palgrave Macmillan.

Pally, M. (2000a). "Film and society": A course for analyzing readings, writing, and critical thinking. In M. Pally (Ed.), *Sustained content teaching in academic ESL/EFL* (pp. 1–18). Boston: Houghton Mifflin.

Pally, M. (2000b). Sustaining interest/advancing learning: Sustained content-based instruction in ESL/EFL. In M. Pally (Ed.), *Sustained content teaching in academic ESL/EFL* (pp. 1–18). Boston: Houghton Mifflin.

Park, G. (2004, March). The cultural and linguistic autobiography writing project: My journey in bridging culture, bridging language in adult ESL classrooms. In *Colloquium bridging culture and bridging language.* Colloquium panel presented at the 38th Annual TESOL Convention, Long Beach, CA.

Park, G. (2006). *Unsilencing the silenced: The journeys of five East Asian women with implications for TESOL teacher education programs.* Unpublished doctoral dissertation, University of Maryland, College Park.

Park, G. (2007, October). *Critical narrative research in adult ESL classrooms: Learning about our ESL students.* Paper presented at Penn-TESOL East 2007 Conference at the University of Pennsylvania, Philadelphia, PA.

Park, G. (2008). Lived pedagogies: Becoming a multi-competent ESL teacher. In J. A. Carmona (Ed.), *Perspectives on community college ESL: Volume 3: Faculty, administration, and the working environment* (pp. 17–29). Alexandria, VA: TESOL.

Park, G., & Suarez, D. (2007, April). *Critical action research: Power of engaging in cultural and linguistic autobiographical narratives.* Paper presented at the Narrative and Methodology SIG at the American Educational Research Association, Chicago.

Parsons, M. H. (1996). *Promoting community renewal through civic literacy and service learning.* San Francisco: Jossey-Bass.

Pavlenko, A. (2003). "I never knew I was a bilingual": Reimagining teacher identities in TESOL. *Journal of Language, Identity, and Education, 2*(4), 251–268.

Peacock, M. (1997). The effect of authentic materials on the motivation of EFL learners. *ELT Journal, 51*(2), 144–154.

Pearson, P. D., & Gallagher, G. (1983). The gradual release of responsibility model of instruction. *Contemporary Educational Psychology, 8,* 112–123.

Perkins, D. N., & Salomon, G. (1994). Transfer of learning. In T. Husen & T. N. Postle (Eds.), *The international encyclopedia of education* (2nd ed., Vol. 11, pp. 6452–6457). Oxford, England: Pergamon.

Perl, S. (1979). The composing processes of unskilled college writers. In V. Villaneuva (Ed.) *Cross-talk in comp theory: A reader* (pp. 17–42). Urbana, IL: National Council of Teachers of English.

Perpignan, H. (2003). Exploring the written feedback dialogue: A research, learning and teaching practice. *Language Teaching Research, 7*(2), 259–278.

Petit, A. (2003). The stylish semicolon: Teaching punctuation as rhetorical choice. *English Journal, 92,* 66–72.

Pibulchol, C. (1998). English education in Thailand. In J. Kahny & M. James (Eds.), *Perspectives on secondary school EFL education* (pp. 137–138). Odwara, Japan: Language Institute of Japan.

Pope, J. (2005, July 4). Poor writing costs taxpayers millions. *Tampa Tribune.* Retrieved May 14, 2009, from http://www.freerepublic.com/focus/f-news/ 1436110/posts

Porter, J., Sullivan, P., & Johnson-Ellis, J. (2009). *Professional writing online, Version 3.0.* Upper Saddle River, NJ: Pearson Education, 2009. Retrieved January 30, 2009, from http://www.pearsonhighered.com/educator/academic/product/ 0,3110,0205652123,00.html

Postman, N., & Weingartner, C. (1969). *Teaching as a subversive activity*. New York: Dell.

Powell, B., & Ponder, R. (2001). Sourcebooks in a sustained-content curriculum. *TESOL Journal, 10*(2/3), 18–22.

Price, J., & Osborne, M. (2000). Challenges of forging a humanizing pedagogy in teacher education. *Curriculum and Teaching, 15*(1), 27–51.

Prodromou, L. (1995). The washback effect: From testing to teaching. *ELT Journal, 49*(1), 13–25.

Purpura, J. (2004). *Assessing grammar*. Cambridge: Cambridge University Press.

Qin, J. (2007, April 25). Activities on the use of hedging in academic writing. Message posted to http://pine.ucc.nau.edu/jq5/activities_and_exercises_on_the_ use_of%20hedging.htm

Raimes, A. (1991). Out of the woods: Emerging traditions in the teaching of writing. *TESOL Quarterly, 25*(3), 407–430.

Raimes, A. (2002a). Ten steps in planning a writing course and training teachers of writing. In J. C. Richards & W. A. Renandya (Eds.), *Methodology in language teaching: An anthology of current practice* (pp. 306–314). New York: Cambridge University Press.

Raimes, A. (2002b). *Keys for writers: A brief handbook* (3rd ed.). Boston: Houghton Mifflin.

Ramanathan, V., & Atkinson, D. (2006). Individualism, academic writing, and ESL writers. In P. Matsuda, M. Cox, J. Jordan, & C. Ortmeier-Hooper (Eds.), *Second language writing in the composition classroom: A critical sourcebook* (pp. 159–185). Boston: Bedford/St. Martin's. (Reprinted from *Journal of Second Language Writing, 8*[1], 45–75.)

Reid, J. (2000). *The process of composition* (3rd ed.). New York: Addison Wesley Longman.

Reid, J. (2006). *Essentials of teaching academic writing*. Boston: Houghton Mifflin.

Reppen, R. (2002). A genre-based approach to content writing instructions. In J. C. Richards & W. A. Renandya (Eds.), *Methodology in language teaching: An anthology of current practice* (pp. 321–327). New York: Cambridge University Press.

Richards, J. C., and Lockhart, C. (1996). *Reflective teaching in second language classrooms*. Cambridge: Cambridge University Press.

Rorschach, E. (2004). The five-paragraph theme redux. *The Quarterly, 26*(1), 16–19, 25.

Rot, S. (2007). The effect of frequency of input-enhancements on word learning and text comprehension. *Language Learning, 57*, 165–199.

Rutherford, W. E. (1987). *Second language grammar and teaching*. Harlow, England: Pearson Education.

Ryder, R. J., & Graves, M. F. (2003). *Reading and learning in content areas*. New York: John Wiley & Sons.

Salager-Meyer, F. (1997). I think that perhaps you should: A study of hedges in written scientific discourse. In T. Miller (Ed.), *Functional approaches to written texts: Classroom applications* (pp. 105–118). Washington, DC: United States Information Agency English Language Programs.

Sanderson, P. (1999). *Using newspapers in the classroom*. Cambridge: Cambridge University Press.

Schmidt, R. (1990). The role of consciousness in second language learning. *Applied Linguistics*, 11, 129–158.

Scriven, M., & Paul, R. (2001). Defining critical thinking: A statement by Michael Scriven & Richard Paul for the National Council for Excellence in Critical Thinking Instruction. In *The critical thinking community*. Retrieved February 20, 2008, from http://www.criticalthinking.org/aboutCT/definingCT.cfm

Seow, A. (2002). The writing process and process writing. In J. C. Richards & W. A. Renandya (Eds.), *Methodology in language teaching: An anthology of current practice* (pp. 315–320). New York: Cambridge University Press.

Service-learning program faculty manual. (2004). Seattle, WA: Seattle Central Community College Service-Learning Program.

Silva, T. (1990). Second language composition instruction: Developments, issues, and direction in ESL. In B. Kroll (Ed.), *Second language writing: Research insights for the classroom* (pp. 11–23). Cambridge: Cambridge University Press.

Silva, T. (1993a). Toward an understanding of the distinct nature of L2 writing: The ESL research and its implications. *TESOL Quarterly, 27*(4), 657–677.

Silva, T. (1993b). Toward an understanding of the distinct nature of L2 writing: The ESL research and its implications. In T. Silva & P. K. Matsuda (Eds.) *Landmark essays on ESL writing* (pp. 191–208). Mahwah, NJ: Lawrence Erlbaum.

Silva, T., & Matsuda, P. (Eds.). (2001). *Landmark essays on ESL writing*. Mahwah, NJ: Running Press.

Sinclair, J. (2005). Corpus and text: Basic principles. In M. Wynne (Ed.), *Developing linguistic corpora: A guide to good practice* (pp. 1–16). Oxford: Oxbow Books. Retrieved September 7, 2007, from http://www.ahds.ac.uk/creating/guides/linguistic-corpora/chapter1.htm

Spatt, B. (2003). *Writing from sources* (6th ed.). Boston: Bedford/St. Martin's.

Stoller, F. L. (2002). Project work: A means to promote language and content. In J. C. Richards & W. A. Renandya (Eds.), *Methodology in language teaching: An anthology of current practice* (pp. 107–119). New York: Cambridge University Press.

Sugita, Y. (2006). The impact of teachers' comment types on students' revision. *ELT Journal, 60*(1), 34–41.

Swales, J. M. (1990). *Genre analysis.* Cambridge: Cambridge University Press.

Swan, M., & Smith, B. (2001). *Learner English: A teacher's guide to interference and other problems.* New York: Cambridge University Press.

Tarone, E. (2000). Getting serious about language play: Language play, interlanguage variation, and second language acquisition. In B. Swierzbin, F. Morris, M. Anderson, C. Klee, & E. Tarone (Eds.), *Social and cognitive factors in SLA: Proceedings of the 1999 Second Language Research Forum* (pp. 31–54). Somerville, MA: Cascadilla Press.

Tarone, E. (2005). Speaking in a second language. In E. Hinkel (Ed.), *Handbook of research in second language teaching and learning* (pp. 485–502). Mahwah, NJ: Lawrence Erlbaum.

Teaching/learning toolkit: Purposeful learning. (n.d.) Knoxville, TN: Equipped for the Future at the Center for Literacy. Retrieved January 21, 2008, from http://eff.cls.utk.edu/toolkit/support_purposeful_learning.htm

The Washington state adult learning standards. (2006). Olympia, WA: State Board of Community and Technical Colleges. Retrieved January 21, 2008, from http://www.sbctc.edu/College/_e-abe_learningstandards.aspx

Tobón, O. (2006). *Jackson Heights chronicles: When crossing the border isn't enough* (K. Cordero, Trans.). New York: Atria Books.

Tognini-Bonelli, E. (2001). *Corpus linguistics at work.* Amsterdam/Philadelphia: John Benjamins.

Tribble, C. (1996). *Writing.* Oxford: Oxford University Press.

Tribble, C., & Jones, G. (1990). *Concordances in the classroom: A resource book for teachers.* London: Longman.

Truscott, J. (1996). The case against grammar correction in L2 writing classes. *Language Learning, 46,* 327–369.

Tsui, A. B. M. (2004). What teachers have always wanted to know—and how corpora can help. In J. Sinclair (Ed.), *How to use corpora in language teaching* (pp. 39–61). Amsterdam/Philadelphia: John Benjamins.

Tudor, I. (2001). *The dynamics of the language classroom.* Cambridge: Cambridge University Press.

Tyler, K. A. (2001). *Seed wiki.* Retrieved 1 June 2006 from http://www.seedwiki.com

University of Cambridge ESOL Examinations. (2005). *PET handbook for teachers.* Cambridge: University of Cambridge Local Examinations Syndicate.

University of Cambridge ESOL Examinations. (2007a). *CAE handbook for teachers.* Cambridge: University of Cambridge Local Examinations Syndicate.

University of Cambridge ESOL Examinations. (2007b). *FCE handbook for teachers.* Cambridge: University of Cambridge Local Examinations Syndicate.

van Patten, B. (2003). *From input to output: A teacher's guide to second language acquisition.* Boston: McGraw Hill.

van Slyck, P. (2006). Learning communities and the future of the humanities. *Profession 2006, 14,* 163–176.

Viana, V., & Zyngier, S. (2008). EFL through the digital glass of corpus linguistics. In R. de C.V. Marriott & P. L. Torres (Eds.), *Handbook of research on e-learning methodologies for language acquisition* (pp. 219–236). Hershey, PA: IGI Global.

Vygotsky, L. S. (1978). *Mind and society: The development of higher psychological processes.* Cambridge, MA: Harvard University Press.

Weidauer, M. H. (2002). *Tapestry writing 3.* Beijing: Tsinghua University Press.

Weigle, S. (2002). Assessing writing. New York: Cambridge University Press.

West, M. (1953). *A general service list of English words.* London: Longman.

White, R. V. (1988). *The ELT curriculum.* Oxford: Blackwell.

Wickliff, G. (1997). Assessing the value of client-based group projects in an introductory technical communication course. *Journal of Business and Technical Communication, 11,* 170–191.

Widdowson, H. G. (1995). Discourse analysis: A critical view. *Language and Literature, 4*(3), 157–172.

Williams, J. (Producer). (1987). *Eyes on the prize: Part I (1954–56), Awakening* [Motion Picture]. Boston: PBS Adult Learning Service/Blackside.

Williams, J. M. (2003). *Style: Ten lessons in clarity and grace* (7th ed.). Chicago: University of Chicago Press.

Williams, J., & Evans, J. R. (2000). *Getting there: Tasks for academic writing.* Fort Worth, TX: Harcourt.

Willingham, D. (2007, Summer). Critical thinking: Why is it so hard to teach? *American Educator: The Professional Journal of the American Federation of Teachers, 30*(2), 8–19.

Winokur, J. (Ed.). (1986). *Writers on writing.* Philadelphia: Running Press.

Wolfersberger, M. (2003). L1 to L2 writing process and strategy transfer: A look at lower proficiency writers. *TESL-EJ, 7*(2), A-6. Retrieved August 15, 2006, from http://www-writing.berkeley.edu/TESL-EJ/archives.html

Woods, N. (2006). *Describing discourse.* London: Hodder and Arnold.

Wu, R. (1994, May). *ESL students writing autobiographies: Are there any connections?* Paper presented at Annual Meeting of the Rhetoric Society of America, Louisville, KY.

Xiang, W. (2004). Encouraging self-monitoring in writing by Chinese students. *ELT Journal, 58,* 238–246.

Yang, M. (2005). Exploring writing approaches in Chinese EFL class. *Academic Exchange Quarterly, 9*(3), 95–99.

Yang, M., Badger, B., & Yu, Z. (2006). A comparative study of peer and teacher feedback in a Chinese EFL writing class. *Journal of Second Language Writing, 15*(3), 179–200.

Young, R. F. (2004). Learning as changing participation: Discourse roles in ESL writing conferences. *The Modern Language Journal, 88*(4), 519–535.

Zemach, D. E., & Rumisek, L. A. (2003). *Success with college writing: From paragraph to essay.* Tokyo: Macmillan Language House.

Zhu, W., & Flaitz, J. (2005). Using focus group methodology to understand international students' academic language needs: A comparison of perspectives. *TESL-EJ, 8*(4), A-3. Retrieved August 15, 2006, from http://www-writing.berkeley .edu/TESL-EJ/archives.html

Zwier, L. J. (2002). *Building academic vocabulary.* Ann Arbor, MI: University of Michigan Press.

Index

Page numbers followed by an *f* or *t* indicate footnotes or tables.

Also Available From TESOL

TESOL Classroom Practice Series
Maria Dantas-Whitney, Sarah Rilling, and Lilia Savova, Series Editors

Language Games: Innovative Activities for Teaching English
Maureen Snow Adrade, Editor

Authenticity in the Classroom and Beyond: Adult Learners
Sarah Rilling and Maria Dantas-Whitney, Editors

Adult Language Learners: Context and Innovation
Ann F. V. Smith and Gregory Strong, Editors

Insights on Teaching Speaking in TESOL
Tim Stewart, Editor

Explorations in Second Language Reading
Roger Cohen, Editor

Using Textbooks Effectively
Lilia Savova, Editor

Classroom Management
Thomas S. C. Farrell, Editor

❋ ❋ ❋ ❋ ❋

Language Teacher Research Series
Thomas S. C. Farrell, Series Editor

Language Teacher Research in Africa
Leketi Makalela, Editor

Language Teacher Research in Asia
Thomas S. C. Farrell, Editor

Language Teacher Research in Europe
Simon Borg, Editor

Language Teacher Research in the Americas
Hedy McGarrell, Editor

Language Teacher Research in the Middle East
Christine Coombe and Lisa Barlow, Editors

Language Teacher Research in Australia and New Zealand
Jill Burton and Anne Burns, Editors

✳ ✳ ✳ ✳ ✳

Collaborative Partnerships Between ESL and Classroom Teachers Series
Debra Suarez, Series Editor

Helping English Language Learners Succeed in Pre-K–Elementary Schools
Jan Lacina, Linda New Levine, and Patience Sowa

Helping English Language Learners Succeed in Middle and High Schools
Faridah Pawan and Ginger Sietman, Editors

✳ ✳ ✳ ✳ ✳

TESOL Language Curriculum Development Series
Kathleen Gr   eries Editor

Planning and Teaching Creatively Within a Required Curriculum for Adult Learners
Anne Burns and Helen de Silva Joyce, Editors

Revitalizing an Established Program for Adult Learners
Alison Rice, Editors

Developing a New Curriculum for Adult Learners
Michael Carroll, Editor

Developing a New Course for Adult Learners
Lía Kamhi-Stein and Marguerite Ann Snow, Editors

✳ ✳ ✳ ✳ ✳

CALL Environments: Research, Practice, and Critical Issues, 2nd ed.
Joy Egbert and Elizabeth Hanson-Smith, Editors

Learning Languages through Technology
Elizabeth Hanson-Smith and Sarah Rilling, Editors

Global English Teaching and Teacher Education: Praxis and Possibility
Seran Dogancay-Aktuna and Joel Hardman, Editors

Local phone: (240)646-7037
Fax: (301)206-9789
E-Mail: tesolpubs@brightkey.net
Toll-free: 1-888-891-0041
Mail Orders to TESOL, P.O. Box 79283, Baltimore, MD 21279-0283
ORDER ONLINE at www.tesol.org and click on "Bookstore"